FADE

FADE

My Journeys in Multiracial America

ELLIOTT LEWIS

CARROLL & GRAF PUBLISHERS
NEW YORK

FADE
My Journeys in Multiracial America

Carroll & Graf Publishers
An Imprint of Avalon Publishing Group Inc.
245 West 17th Street
11th Floor
New York, NY 10011

AVALON
publishing group incorporated

Library of Congress Cataloging-in-Publication Data is available.

ISBN-10: 0-7867-1668-1
ISBN-13: 978-0-78671-668-5

Printed in the United States of America
Interior design by Maria E. Torres
Distributed by Publishers Group West

To my mother and father,
Betty Dent Lewis McNeal and Coleman Alderson Lewis, Jr.

Contents

Acknowledgments

This project would not have been possible without the help of many people. I am especially appreciative of all of those I interviewed for this book for their willingness to share their stories and expertise. I would also like to extend my thanks to my literary agent, Audra Barrett, and my editor at Avalon Publishing, Don Weise, for believing in this project.

PART 1

WHO AM I?

Don't Adjust Your Television, I'm Biracial

"CAN I ASK YOU SOMETHING?" THE MAN SAID.

"Sure," I said.

"What is your racial background?"

Here we go again, I thought.

It was Thanksgiving Day, 1996. I was working as a reporter at WKMG-TV, the CBS affiliate in Orlando, Florida. I had just arrived at the local homeless shelter to prepare a report on a holiday tradition. Volunteers from throughout the community had gathered to serve up hundreds of free turkey dinners to those in need.

That's the story I was covering. But at that moment, a black man at the homeless shelter was the one asking the questions.

"What is your racial background?" he wanted to know.

That question has dogged me for as long as I can remember. As a child, I wasn't quite sure what to say. Now, after years of practice, I've developed a standard answer.

"I'm biracial," I told him.

"So that means what?" he asked, his face contorting as if he'd never heard the term before.

"I'm a mixture of black and white," I continued.

"Oh . . . just curious," he said. Then he changed the subject.

No more than five minutes later, another black man at the shelter called me over to his table. I thought he was going to ask not to have his picture taken, or ask me what time he might be on the news, or try to give me a tip on a possible story. That's usually what happened whenever I visited homeless shelters before. But he had something else on his mind.

"Hey, are you black?" he blurted out.

Before I could even answer, the man spoke up again.

"You're sort of black. Aren't you? Sort of?"

"I'm biracial," I said, trying to act casual. "I'm both black and white."

At this point, I was beginning to wonder how many times I would have to go through this little interrogation before the day was over. That's when the third black man approached me.

"I was just wondering," he began. "What race are you?"

Maybe I should just wear a sign around my neck. "I'm biracial. Get over it." Or, "Stop staring. I'm mixed race." Or, better yet, "It's a multiracial thing. You wouldn't understand."

But that was before the U.S. Census Bureau took a significant step toward reshaping how many Americans think about race and racial labeling. The 2000 census marked the first time in U.S. history that Americans had the option to check more than one racial category in the official government head count. Whereas previous census forms had instructed respondents to "check only one" racial category, the directions on the form used in 2000 read, "Mark one or more races to indicate what this person considers himself/herself to be." Nearly seven million Americans checked more than one box on their questionnaire. News organizations around the country took notice, sparking numerous articles examining this "new" population and delving into why we chose to identify ourselves the way we did.

The media exposure has brought more attention to the existence of interracial families in the United States and created more awareness of the dynamics of multiracial identity issues. But even in a post–Census 2000 world, old attitudes, misunderstandings, and outdated models of thinking about our identity choices persist. We've also had our share of disagreements within Interracial Family Circles over many of these issues and the public policy implications of formally recognizing those who identify with more than one race.

Nevertheless, if there is one universal experience commonly cited among those who have embraced a multiracial identity, it is the frequency with which we are asked the "What are you?" question. We are constantly called upon to either explain what others perceive as our ambiguous racial appearance, or to choose sides and declare an allegiance to one ethnic group over another. Meanwhile, those biracial people whose looks are more easily aligned with traditional, single-race categories do not face such interrogation to nearly the same degree. "I can't racially classify you, and it's bothering me," the questioners seem to be saying, "so tell me what you are so I can figure out which box to put you in and determine how to relate to you."

The easy thing for me to do would be to say that I am black. Period. End of story. And leave it at that. That's what many people would still prefer that I do. Their argument goes something like this: even if you're only part-black, our race-conscious society will judge you to be all-black and treat you accordingly. So you might as well just say you're black, get used to it, and move on with your life.

I've been called the N-word enough times to know that argument has some validity. I also know that while being biracial doesn't grant anyone immunity from racial discrimination, it doesn't necessarily make someone "all-black, all the time" in society's eyes, either. If it did, then those black men at the homeless shelter wouldn't have spent so much time wondering out loud, "Hey, what are you?" The fact that the question even arises tells me there is a considerable degree of uncertainty over just how "black" I am.

Thanksgiving Day at the homeless shelter was certainly not the first time in my television career that I'd faced questions about my racial identity. It started years earlier in Reno, Nevada, the twenty-four-hour gambling town in the shadow of the Sierra Nevada that the local tourism industry has branded "The Biggest Little City in the World." I had worked at KTVN-TV, Reno's CBS affiliate, as an unpaid intern while in college. Six months later, in January 1988, I joined the staff as an on-air reporter. I worked the night shift, appearing on the station's 11 P.M. newscast, and covered everything from homicides to house fires, from sex scandals to school board meetings.

The white news director who hired me (at a whopping salary of $14,000 a year) predicted that one day I might have a prosperous television career in a city such as New Orleans. With its large Creole population, he reasoned, a newscaster with my skin color would appeal to black viewers while being light enough to not drive away racist white viewers. So far, my television career has taken me to six different cities: Reno, San Diego, Portland (Oregon), Cincinnati, Orlando, and Washington, D.C. I have never been offered a job in New Orleans.

I was still learning my way around northern Nevada when a news photographer I was working with brought up the race issue. We had just finished shooting our last story of the night and were on our way back to the station. Scotty, a nervous, blond-haired, middle-aged white guy who often paced the newsroom holding a portable police scanner up to his ear, mentioned that a friend of his had seen me on the air the night before.

"Funny thing," Scotty began. "This guy was telling me how he ended up adjusting the color on his television set while you were on, because he couldn't figure out what you were. . . . Didn't know whether you were white, black, Hispanic, or what!"

I rolled my eyes. "He doesn't need to adjust his TV," I said as our white Jeep Cherokee pulled up to the station. "Hasn't he ever seen a biracial person before?"

Multiracial people certainly aren't anything new. Miscegenation— a word once commonly used to refer to "race-mixing"—has been going on for some time. As University of California sociologist Reginald Daniel told *The New Yorker*, "In my family, like many families with African American ancestry, there is a history of multiracial offspring associated with rape and concubinage."

"The legacy of this intermingling," concluded the magazine, "is that Americans who are descendants of early settlers, of slaves, or of Indians often have ancestors of different races in their family tree."[1]

That being the case, it would seem just about anyone nowadays could claim with some legitimacy to be multiracial or to come from an interracial family. But what I'm talking about here goes beyond having an intellectual understanding about being racially mixed. And it goes beyond the scientific arguments put forth recently that, biologically speaking, "race" does not exist.

This book is about those of us for whom being multiracial is part of our self-identity. We simply don't think of ourselves as belonging to only one "race," as contemporary American society—for better or worse—has come to use that term today. Our blended heritage is a part of our lives in a way that cannot be easily dismissed. The effect on our upbringing has been too profound for us to ignore. We come from families where the racial fault lines are exposed. Our ideas about who we are have been shaped by this peculiar racial dilemma and the various ways it plays itself out in our daily lives.

Racial blending has been going on in my family for generations. My mother, born Betty Jean Dent, is one of ten children, the products of a dark-skinned African-American father and a light-complexioned mother whom some neighbors mistook for Italian. In reality, my grandmother was a mix of black and white with perhaps some Native American thrown in. My mother's nine siblings—two brothers and seven sisters—display every shade of brown on the spectrum. My mom is one of the lightest in her family, and she married a light-skinned man.

My father, Coleman Alderson Lewis Jr., grew up as an only child, the son of a white woman and a self-identified black man. I say "self-identified" because in looking at old photos of my grandfather, I see a man with honey brown skin and straight black hair, which in my mind only raises more questions about when the racial lines in the family tree first got crossed.

In some respects, my parents are representative of the vast majority of African-Americans who are "multiracial by birth, but black through life experience." Their multiracial heritage is apparent. But their upbringing, social interactions, physical features, and other factors have led them to identify racially as "black." While estimates on the number of people who fall into that category vary, some researchers suggest up to 80 percent or more of America's "black" population have known white or Native American ancestry. But ancestry and identity are not necessarily the same thing.

"Under the law, we were black," my mother would say when describing the racial classification system she's known for most of her life. Having grown up at a time when public accommodations remained segregated and opportunities for people of color were severely limited, that "legal" identity was all that mattered. Although my mother attended a small, integrated high school in western Pennsylvania, what little integration there was in the late 1940s only went so far. When she tried out for the cheerleading squad, she didn't make the cut, "because black girls never got picked for cheerleader," she often told me. When my father decided to go to college in the 1930s, he enrolled in what is now Virginia State University. But his diploma from that institution bears its former name: Virginia State College for Negroes.

My parents' legal status as black people defined their lives in ways that are unimaginable to me. They identified as black in accordance with the rigid social customs in place in their communities and throughout the nation at the time. They would tell you there was no point in identifying otherwise, even if it had occurred to them—which I gather it never did. The idea that their racial identities might also serve as a personal statement expressing the fullness of their heritage was a foreign concept. The law was the law, and that was their reality.

For me, it has never been quite that simple. I am not only "multiracial by birth," but "multiracial through life experience," too. Taken together, the defining moments in my life have led me to think of myself as biracial. Born in 1966 and raised in a post–civil rights culture that championed integration, "color blindness," and later, "multiculturalism," any legal definition of blackness that may have existed carried less weight for me than for my parents. In my world, ideas about who is black and who isn't haven't been as clear-cut. Is pop singer Mariah Carey black? What about golfer Tiger Woods? Or actor Vin Diesel? What about me? The answers vary depending on whom you ask.

In the United States, we often think of race as something permanent, unbending, and indisputable. But the older I got, the more I traveled, and the more social encounters I had, the more I came to realize how societal views of race can fluctuate. Those views change across time, cultures, countries, geographic regions, generations, and even academic disciplines. Racial definitions—particularly for people with my shade of skin—are not set in stone; they're shifty, fluid, and evolving.

This fuzziness surrounding racial labels is a difficult thing for some people to grasp. But it's key to understanding the range of experiences multiracial people go through and the effect on our self-concept. To fully describe how I've come to terms with my racial identity and where I see myself in society today requires a longer, deeper, and more thoughtful discussion than most people have time for in everyday conversation. It's complex, and it took me more than twenty years to make sense of it all myself.

To understand that journey requires killing off some preconceived notions many people have about how identity is formed. First among these misconceptions is that my racial identity should be the same as that of my parents, since both of them also have interracial backgrounds. Well, it doesn't work that way. A mixed-race person born in the 1930s is bound to have different racial experiences than a biracial person born in the 1960s, who will in turn likely have different racial experiences than a biracial person growing up today. Those experiences are pivotal in shaping our racial identity choices—and the degree to which we feel we even have a choice in the first place.

Perhaps the most offensive misconception to me is that in saying "I'm biracial" I am in some way attempting to avoid being "stigmatized," that I somehow view being black as negative, bad, or distasteful, and that I'm trying to distance myself from a part of my heritage I don't like. I identify as biracial because, if I must choose a single racial label, then "biracial" is the one that fits me best given the totality of my life experience.

But no matter which racial label we select, trying to explain the dynamics of identity formation to someone unfamiliar with these issues can be a frustrating exercise—unless that person is willing to let go of their assumptions about multiracial people and approach the subject with an open mind. In the words of Roosevelt University sociologist Heather Dalmage, "We need to 'flip the script' and analyze why racial categories have been created in particular ways," and why certain people who identity themselves with only one race feel they have the right to pass judgment on multiracial people and their families.[2] Friends, strangers, co-workers, even some of our own relatives claim they "can't figure us out," when in reality their own biases have clouded their interpretation of the defining moments in our lives and why we identify the way we do.

Understanding the multiracial experience requires a shift in perspective. It requires making an effort to walk in our shoes, to see the racial encounters in our lives as we have experienced them. Otherwise, biracial people will continue to be misunderstood.

Long before my professional life in front of a television camera began, I knew I was different. Certainly different from white folks, but also different from black folks. I learned this from various people I now refer to as "the Messengers of Miscegenation"—individuals who in one way or another served to remind me of my blended background and the resulting ambiguity of my racial appearance.

The messenger who had the most profound impact on me was my uncle Eugene. Of my mother's nine brothers and sisters, Eugene is one of the darker-skinned. One night at a family gathering, when I was somewhere between ten and twelve years old, my mother took me over to meet him. I was too young to remember the last time I'd seen Uncle Eugene, so when Mom introduced us, I expected him to say something like, "Man, how you've grown!" Or "Gosh, the last time I saw you, you were still sucking on a bottle"—one of those tired, cliché responses children typically hear from older relatives they haven't seen in a long time.

But when Uncle Eugene's eyes met mine, he didn't say a word to me. Instead, he turned to my mother and asked in a booming voice, "Betty, where did you get this white boy from?"

Little did I know the Messengers of Miscegenation were just getting warmed up.

A Mixed and Matched Family

I LOOK LIKE MY PARENTS. BOTH OF THEM.

Right there, that sets me apart from the mental picture many people have when they visualize an interracial family. They picture a mother with clearly visible physical features representing one race, a father with easily identifiable features associated with another race, and a child whose appearance reflects some middle ground in between the two. In my nuclear family, however, our olive skin tones all matched one another, leading some people to question not only my ethnic background, but that of my parents as well.

"Is your mother Filipino?"

"Is your father from Belize?"

"I would have guessed you were Cuban."

The first comments that I can remember started coming my way in the first and second grade. We were living in Mayfield Heights, Ohio, a virtually all-white suburb of Cleveland. I had one black friend—the only other black student in my elementary school—and his family moved away at about the same time the racial questions started.

"You almost look like you're black," some of my white playmates would say to me every now and again. At which point, I'd set about reassuring them that I was just like them.

"Look," I'd say while flipping my wrist to reveal the underside of my forearm. "I'm white," I told them, casually pointing to that part of my skin, so rarely exposed to the sun.

It wasn't a lie. Before the age of nine, I really did think of myself as white. Many of the white families in our neighborhood were Italian, Greek, and Jewish. They had physical features that included olive skin and dark hair. I was no darker than some of them. And if they were white, well, surely I was white, too.

But my ideas about racial labeling were about to be turned upside down. My mixed and matched family wouldn't stay intact, and its dissolution would set into motion a series of events causing me to reexamine my place on America's racial stage.

In the spring of 1975, my mother began a shopping spree of sorts, buying a series of small appliances. One day it was a new clock radio. The next week it might be a new blender. One afternoon, while my mother and I were sitting on the small grassy hill outside our home, she let me in on what was happening.

"The reason I'm buying all these things," she said, "is because we're moving." Long pause. "I'm going to Michigan, and I want you to come with me."

The message was clear. My parents were calling off their marriage. I wasn't all that shocked, given how distant they seemed to be with one another compared to other families I knew. They no longer shared a bedroom, and the three of us rarely did anything together as a family. Any social functions that included children typically involved my mom and me, while my dad played chauffeur. So the fact that they were now headed for divorce wasn't a big surprise. Besides, several of my friends had parents who were divorced, and they all seemed pretty cool with it.

Still, I cried. Oddly enough, it wasn't their breakup that bothered me. I just didn't want to move, leaving the only school I'd known and the friends I'd made there.

"I don't want to go to Michigan," I sobbed.

"It's a beautiful state," my mother reassured me. "Come with me."

As if I had a choice in the matter.

In the days that followed, Mom talked about the move with increasing optimism and even more certainty. She showed me several tourism brochures from Michigan and described various places we could visit once we got there.

We moved out soon after the school year came to an end. Early one morning, Mom and I boarded a plane taking us from Cleveland, Ohio, to Kalamazoo, Michigan. She was on her way to begin a graduate program at Western Michigan University, where she would earn her master's degree in library science. We moved into university housing, and my mother started classes a few days later. But my mother's transition to her new school went more smoothly than my transition to mine.

Located a few blocks from downtown Kalamazoo, Lincoln Upper Elementary School was much more integrated than the school I'd left in Ohio. It was called an "upper elementary school" because the only grades it offered were kindergarten, fourth, fifth, and sixth. The neighborhood was overwhelmingly black, and the white students were bused in from other parts of the city. If there were any objections to that arrangement, the adults kept it well hidden from us. As children, most of us didn't think anything of it.

I was just tall enough to see over the counter in the school office as my mother filled out my enrollment form. I looked on as my mother wrote in my name, age, and birth date. Then she came to the section of the form that asked for my race. I watched as my mother checked the box marked "Negro."

I froze.

From that moment on, my eyes fixated on that spot and never left the paper. I was in shock.

How could I possibly be black? When I looked in the mirror, I didn't see someone I considered to be black. I didn't see someone I thought anyone else would consider black, either. I knew many of my aunts, uncles, and cousins were black. But me? I simply didn't fit the definition of what I thought a black person was supposed to look like. Neither one of my parents met the definition, either, as far as I was concerned.

Silly me, I had made the mistake of thinking "race" was synonymous with skin color. But in the United States, that's not always how it works.

I didn't know it at the time, but standing there in the school office I had just run smack into America's "one-drop rule." This is the idea that "one drop" of black blood is enough to legally classify someone as black. The rule has its roots in slavery. By using the broadest definition possible to define who is black, slave owners could then maximize the number of people they could enslave. Generations later, the rule came to be embraced by black people to maximize political leverage in the fight for civil rights. It is still ingrained in American culture to some degree, so that even today, anyone with black ancestry who says "I'm multiracial" better be prepared to have the one-drop rule thrown in his face.

"If you're mixed, you're black!"

"One drop, that's all it takes!"

The people who make such statements are correct if they are talking about the history of racial classification in the United States in a legal or political context. They have a lot to learn, however, if they are talking about present-day issues surrounding racial identification from a social or psychological perspective. It just isn't as simple anymore.

The adults in the Kalamazoo public school system may have looked at me as black. But my fourth-grade classmates, both black and white, never quite bought it. Like me, they had never heard of any "one-drop rule" to determine a person's race.

That became apparent on the first day of school. All the fourth graders had to report to the auditorium to find out who our homeroom teacher would be. As our names were called, we moved to the front of the stage, where we'd stand until the names of everyone in our class had been read. When the roll call was complete, the teacher would escort the group to homeroom. As I stood in line waiting for the rest of my class to assemble, a black student next to me began counting heads.

"Let's see, how many blacks we got in our class? One, two, three, four. . . ."

When he got to me, he stopped cold.

"Hey, are you black?" he asked.

I didn't know what to say. Being checked off as "Negro" on the school form just a few days earlier had thrown me for a loop. So I did the only thing I felt I could do at that moment. I stalled for time, a talent that would later serve my broadcasting career well.

"Well, what do you mean?" I asked him.

"Are you, you know, black? Are you a black person?"

"Umm . . . I'm not real sure," I said.

He skipped over me and resumed counting. "Five, six, seven. . . ."
Then he came to another kid who looked very similar to me but was a shade or two darker. His name was Ronnie Wilson.

"Hey, are you black?" he asked Ronnie.

"Yeah, I'm black," he said, like it was nothing.

Wow, I thought, after seeing the way Ronnie responded. He just came right out and said it, no hesitation at all. He wasn't wishy-washy about it, either, like I was. When asked, he had an answer. He knew who he was. Why couldn't I do that?

I realized back then that being black, or at least proclaiming myself to be black, was something I was going to have to work on. The "one-drop" mentality of racial categorization was new to me. But I wanted to be like Ronnie, to have an answer when someone asked, "What are you?" And like Ronnie, I wanted to be able to say with confidence, "I'm black."

It felt awkward and contradictory given the way I looked. But back then, the terms "biracial" and "multiracial" weren't exactly in the national vocabulary the way they are today. If I was going to be a "Negro" on my official school enrollment form, then "black" is what I would be if the question ever came up again. My new environment had somehow changed everything. Suddenly, saying "I'm white" no longer seemed like an option. Saying "I'm black" was better than having no racial identity at all.

In fact, that seemed to be the prevailing conventional wisdom at the time, that black-white biracial children are best served by adopting an all-black identity starting at an early age. If society at large will judge these children to be black, isn't it in their best interest to learn to go with the flow and align themselves with the black community?

But the conventional wisdom was flawed. The underlying assumption that biracial children will automatically be accepted as full-fledged members of their minority race with no questions asked simply doesn't hold up. Psychologist Maria Root, a former University of Washington professor and one of America's leading experts on interracial family issues, examined racial identity theories that emerged in the 1970s and 1980s. "All describe a stage in which one seeks immersion in [his or her] socially assigned racial group as refuge from the oppression and racial assaults dealt by society," she writes in *Cultural Diversity and Mental Health*. But Root found that such refuge, while virtually assured for most, "is not guaranteed for multiracial individuals."[1]

In other words, the strategy may work for some biracial people, some of the time. But it doesn't work for all of us all of the time. And as my fellow fourth graders were quick to illustrate, our racial group membership is not always easily defined.

"You're a half-breed," one of my black classmates told me one day.

"What does that mean?" I asked her.

"It's someone who is half-black and half-white," she said.

"Oh."

Judging from her tone, I don't think she meant it as an insult, and at the time I didn't take it that way. She said it as a statement of fact in her role as one of the early Messengers of Miscegenation in my life. Although "half-breed" sounded to me like a term she'd just made up, to her it explained everything about me—my appearance, my family background, and my racial identity. I was a half-breed, simple as that, and it was perfectly fine with her.

Still, the internal tug-of-war I was going through didn't end there. My back-and-forth, push-me-pull-me struggle to figure out what to call myself continued for some time, which, it turns out, is not at all unusual for children in interracial families. In fact, it is quite normal.

In a study of biracial children of black-white heritage in the United States published in *Racially Mixed People in America*, psychologist James Jacobs found that children typically pass through three stages with respect to their racial identity. In the first stage, which occurs from birth to age four, children are in the process of learning to distinguish between colors and learning the names of different colors. But the idea of "race" has not yet taken hold. In the second stage, which occurs between ages four and eight, Jacobs writes, "The [biracial] child becomes ambivalent about his or her racial status. . . . The child's concept of social grouping by race is still confounded with skin color." 2

That certainly described me. At that age, I thought race and skin color were the same thing. And it didn't strike me as at all odd that members of my extended family could be black while my parents and I were white. At the same time, ambivalence about my racial identity had also set in.

Such ambivalence can manifest itself in a number of ways. Jacobs found that biracial children may go through periods in which they show signs of rejecting their blackness, followed by similar indications of rejecting their whiteness. For example, the parents of one child in his study reported that at age five their son wanted his hair to be straighter, but by age seven he complained that he could not grow a more "natural" Afro.

In the third stage, ages eight to twelve, the concept of race becomes more nuanced. As Jacobs puts it, "The [biracial] child discovers that racial group membership is correlated with, but not determined by, skin color." 3

Bingo! That's exactly the revelation that came to me at age nine, though I certainly couldn't have expressed it in such language at the time. Yes, race and skin color are connected. But something else is at work, too. Our ideas about race have to do with history, culture, and the makeup of one's family, in addition to outward appearance. But I had yet to put all the pieces of the puzzle together.

Jacobs suggests this is all very natural and that the mixed emotions biracial children feel about race must be allowed to play themselves out. "This stage of ambivalence is necessary," he writes; eventually, the biracial child will progress to a level "where discordant elements can be reconciled in a unified identity." 4 So according to this study, my momentary confusion was normal, and my development was right on schedule.

That's important to note, because it would be easy to misinterpret a child's responses to certain racial events or discussions. Adults who are not familiar with the developmental issues unique to biracial youth may overreact to what they view as maladaptive or disturbing behavior. In fact, such periodic shifts in racial awareness and self-concept may just be part of the natural development process. My life to this point represented a textbook case of the identity stages common among biracial children.

By the end of the fourth grade, Ronnie Wilson had become one of my best friends. I'm sure the fact that we were both visibly racially mixed had, on some unconscious level, something to do with why we hit it off so well.

The last time I saw Ronnie was on my tenth birthday. That's when I told him I wouldn't be back at school in the fall. My mother had completed her master's degree, and we were moving to Washington.

"Washington, D.C.?" Ronnie asked.

"No, Washington State," I told him.

We were moving to a small college town called Pullman, where my mother had just accepted a job as a librarian at Washington State University. I'd never heard of either the town or the college. But before we left Kalamazoo my mother was introduced to someone who once lived there. He was a black man named LeRoi (which he pronounced "Le-WAH") who had at one time been a student there. Whatever LeRoi had to say about what life in Pullman would be like, only one thing stuck in my mind.

"There are no black people there," he told us.

That didn't sound good.

Going West, Growing Up

THE GREYHOUND BUS MADE ITS WAY DOWN A TWO-LANE ROAD THE locals called a "highway." To a kid who'd spent most of his life living near a large city, the stretch of pavement cutting a path through the golden wheat fields of eastern Washington hardly seemed to qualify as an interstate. But I knew the road would lead to Pullman, and even though I still knew next to nothing about our destination, I was anxious to get there just the same.

Life in academia seemed to agree with my mother. During the year we'd spent living on the Western Michigan University campus in Kalamazoo, she made sure we took advantage of all the cultural events the university had to offer, dragging me to concerts, plays, and campus festivals of one sort or another. We were season ticket holders to the college's football and basketball games, and I had begun to follow sports more closely than I ever had back in Ohio.

With our move to the West Coast, we would be living in the shadow of another college campus. As isolated as Washington State University seemed to be from the rest of civilization as I knew it, the campus community did offer similar sorts of cultural events, and as small a town as it was, it had a well-deserved reputation as a good, safe place to raise children.

On an August afternoon in 1976, our bus pulled up to the diner that also served as Pullman's Greyhound bus terminal. The city's public library, a one-story building attached to a gas station, was across the street. My mother—who would be working at the much larger, four-story social science library on the university campus— had told me our new town would be smaller than any place we'd ever lived before. But I didn't realize it would be this small.

My new surroundings looked nothing like the suburbs of Cleveland or the city of Kalamazoo. No trees, no buildings, no six-lane freeways as you looked out toward the horizon. Only farmland.

The university and surrounding community just sort of sprouts up out of the wheat fields in a part of the state known as the Palouse, some eighty miles south of Spokane. Twenty-five thousand people live in Pullman during the school year. Most of them are college students, leaving less than ten thousand people who are considered permanent residents.

We'd only been in town a few days when we discovered what LeRoi had told us about our new home wasn't true at all. There *were* black people in Pullman. Not many, mind you. But my mother and I certainly weren't the only people of color in town. The community was not as diverse as Kalamazoo's, but having spent most of my early school years in an almost all-white suburb in Ohio, I didn't see any racial adjustment as that big of a hurdle. It was the rural setting that took some getting used to.

A few weeks after we settled in, we met Don and Judy Lee, an elderly Chinese couple who owned the mom-and-pop convenience store my mother would pass on her way to and from work. Don's Midway Grocery had been around for as long as anyone could remember. Inside, the place looked like a miniature version of the old-fashioned candy store in the movie *Willy Wonka and the Chocolate Factory*, with items stacked from floor to ceiling. The Lees, who lived in the basement apartment directly underneath their store, would add up their customers' purchases on a rickety old cash register they kept at the main counter. My mother and I quickly became regular customers, since it was the only shop of its kind near our home.

I was in the store by myself one day after school weaving my way through the store's narrow, cluttered aisles, when Don Lee called me over to the counter. "Can you come here for a minute? I want to ask you something," he said in his accented English. He leaned forward on the countertop and appeared to be quite serious. "Your father . . ." he began. "Is he white?"

After all I'd experienced in Kalamazoo, you'd think I'd have had an answer already in mind. But this time, the question wasn't about *my* race. It was about my father's. So I was stuck again. And I reverted to the same response I'd given standing in that school auditorium.

"Umm . . . I don't know," I said.

"You've never seen your father?" asked Mr. Lee.

"Oh no, I've seen my father. I know my father," I assured him.

"Well, is he a white man?" he repeated.

Why was this tripping me up? I knew by now that my parents thought of themselves as black. Why couldn't I just say, "No, my dad is a black man," and be done with it? I suppose my hesitation had to do with what I figured was the intent of Mr. Lee's question. Describing my father as a black man doesn't convey the right mental picture in terms of a physical description. Mr. Lee knew what my mother looked like. Now he was fishing for some genealogical explanation of why I turned out looking the way I do, an outcome that in his mind was more likely if my father were white. What I really wanted to communicate to him was that my dad, like my mother, looked like me. There was no mystery here; we all had similar complexions. But at that moment, I didn't have the words.

"I don't really know," I finally said.

Once again, the intertwining of race, color, and ancestry had rendered me speechless. I had no vocabulary to respond confidently or effectively to questions about my mixed and matched family. I left Don Lee's store that afternoon mulling things over in my mind and decided I'd ask my mother about Dad's race when she got home from work. But as it turned out, she was the one who brought up the subject.

"You know, I stopped at Don Lee's on the way home," she said. "And Judy asked me if your father was a white man."

"They asked me the same thing, too," I said. "So what did you say?"

"Well, I told them that on your father's birth certificate it says he's mulatto."

"Mulatto? What on earth is that?" I wondered.

"It's a term for someone who is half-black and half-white," my mom explained.

Finally, I felt like I was getting a better picture of the family's racial history. I had clearly reached the developmental stage where biracial children begin to learn that American ideas about racial group membership are not as simple as mere skin color. So at some point, the racial identities I had previously assigned to various relatives had to be reevaluated. Hearing that my father had been labeled "mulatto" somehow seemed to reconcile the conflict between his light appearance and my parents' sense of being legally black. It was just the kind of vocabulary I could use to handle such racial questions in the future.

But while "mulatto" sounded much more sophisticated to my young ears than "half-breed," both terms have since fallen out of favor. Many biracial people find "mulatto" to be particularly offensive based on popular beliefs about its origin. It is widely thought that "mulatto" comes from the word "mule"—a mule being the offspring of a horse and a donkey. A mule is also sterile, therefore implying there is something genetically defective about a person of mixed race. The true origin of the word, however, may be more complicated than that. Professor Reginald Daniel has reported that there is linguistic evidence to suggest that "mulatto" is actually derived from "muwallad," an Arabic word for people of mixed African and Arab descent.[1]

As the conversation unfolded that afternoon, my mother began to reveal other details about my father's background. He was the oldest of three children. But his two younger brothers died before they reached the age of five. At some point his parents divorced, and my father went to live with his dad. From what I could tell, he was estranged from his mother from that point on, rarely seeing her even though they lived in the same city.

I sometimes wonder how my dad's relationship with his parents affected his views of his racial identity and of racial matters in general. There he was, virtually white in appearance, but being raised by his black father. What would his life have been like if his white mother had raised him instead? Would he have adopted a white identity? Would he have married a white woman? Would his children never have known about their black grandfather?

We never talked about it. That silence, I would later discover, was not unusual among interracial families of that era, particularly a multigenerational interracial family such as mine. Before I was old enough to even think about asking either of my parents about any of this myself, my father and I became even more distant. Less than a month before my twelfth birthday, my dad's life took a sudden and unexpected turn, and he would never be the same again.

The Sunday before Memorial Day passed without the phone

ringing even once. "Did Dad call?" I asked my mom before I went to bed.

"Nope," she said casually.

That was strange. Ever since my parents' separation, he'd always called on Sunday. Every week. Usually in the early afternoon. Without fail. Until this weekend.

So when the phone rang the following morning, I was sure it was him. But when I picked up the receiver, I heard an odd sound on the other end of the line. Beeping noises. Muffled voices. Lots of static.

"Hello?" I said.

"Hello. This is the Pullman police," said a woman. The noises I was hearing were coming from the police radio blaring in the background. "Is this the home of Betty D. Lewis?"

"Yes, but she's not in right now."

The university kept the library open on Memorial Day. So while I had the day off from school, my mother still had to work.

"I'm calling on behalf of a relative in Ohio who's been trying to get ahold of her," the policewoman continued. "Could you have her call the Pullman Police Department as soon as possible."

"Yes, I'll give her the message." I hung up the phone and dialed Mom's work number without fully comprehending the urgency of the situation.

"OK," said my mother, quite calmly. "I'll call them and see what they want."

Twenty minutes later, my mother came running up the steps to our apartment. By then, I'd put it all together. The phone call that never came from my dad the day before . . . the Pullman police trying to put us in touch with someone in Ohio . . . something terrible had happened. Before my mother reached our apartment, I opened the front door and shouted:

"What's wrong with Dad?"

"I don't know," she said, almost out of breath. "I have to make some phone calls and find out." She came inside, took off her coat, and began dialing.

My dad had been a diabetic for most of his adult life. Our home in Cleveland had been filled with artificial sweeteners, diabetic candies, and the syringes he would use for his daily insulin shots. Had something gone wrong with his medicine? Had he been in some sort of accident? Was he OK? After several anxious minutes, my mother hung up the phone and calmly tried to explain to me what she had just learned.

"Your dad is in the hospital. He's suffered what they call a localized stroke," she began. "He was taken in after his aunt Nina spoke to him on the telephone and he was talking out of his head."

"What do you mean?" I asked.

"Well, he was disoriented, like he didn't know where he was," she explained. "The stroke has apparently affected a part of his brain that controls his speech and his ability to think clearly all the time. But I have a number for his hospital room. I'm going to call and see how he's doing."

I began to tear up. "I'm scared."

She gave me a hug. "I'm scared, too."

I sat on the living room couch while my mother went back into the kitchen and got on the phone once more.

"Hi, Coleman? This is Betty."

OK, she'd gotten through.

"Betty Lewis."

Long pause.

"My name is Betty Lewis."

Another long pause.

"This is Betty. I'm your wife."

Legally they were still married.

"Betty . . . Betty Lewis, your wife," my mother kept repeating. Then finally, "I'm trying to reach Coleman Lewis." Now she was overenunciating her words. "Are you Coleman Lewis?"

Oh, dear God. He didn't even recognize his own name.

My father didn't know who he was, didn't know who my mother was, and wouldn't have known who I was had I been on the phone at the time.

Several weeks would pass before I spoke to my father again. Then one Sunday afternoon, the telephone rang. After exchanging their usual pleasantries, Mom was ready to pass the phone to me. But before doing so, she cupped her hand over the receiver.

"It's your father," she whispered. "But he's having trouble remembering your name. Sometimes he's calling you 'Vernie.' Just go along."

"Hello?" I said, my heart pounding.

"Hello! It's so good to hear you!" Dad replied. "I would have called before calling, but I didn't know to talk or call or how to call to call you before."

He was talking in gibberish, but I understood what he meant. My mother and I took it as a sign of progress that he at least recognized our voices.

In time, my father became well enough to leave the hospital, but he was never well enough to live entirely on his own again. Some longtime friends of the family took him in until he was ready to move to an assisted living center. His speech improved, and he regained some limited reading ability. But he frequently had to ask me to spell or repeat words when we spoke on the phone. We had never been close, and his impairment increased the distance between us over the years. In some ways it was like trying to carry on a conversation with a child. I often found myself having to speak more slowly and taking great care to properly enunciate key words.

His ability to articulate his thoughts on an adult level—man to man, or father to son—was lost forever.

By the time my father passed away in the spring of 1989, our communication had become infrequent at best. He died from complications arising from his diabetes, or, as it was phrased on his death certificate, "Renal failure as a consequence of diabetic cardiomyopathy."

Until his passing, I had never seen an official death certificate before. At first glance, it looks much like any other government form, with various boxes to type in a name, age, and address. And then comes box number fifteen, which asks for the decedent's race. In my father's case, it read "black."

So there it was. Dad was born mulatto. He died black. And he would by no means be the last in the family whose identity would change between cradle and grave.

The Wonder Years

"SO WHAT DO YOU WANT TO TALK ABOUT?" ASKED THE PSYCHOLOGIST. He looked like a therapist right out of central casting—white male, about forty years old, balding, glasses, with a mustache and goatee.

"I guess I'm here to talk about relationships, mainly," I told him.

I was seventeen years old and on the verge of an emotional breakdown. I'd confessed to a friend that if I could take my own life without causing anyone else emotional pain I would find a way to kill myself. I was at an age when peer acceptance and approval mean everything, and I was starting my senior year of high school and still hadn't found a place where I belonged.

Of course, that was a long time ago, and I can't say I've ever felt that way since. Maybe I was suffering from some sort of chemical imbalance. Or maybe I just grew up and managed to develop the social network I'd been aching for back then.

Whatever the reality, the details of this story tend to freak out those I'm closest to today and anyone who knew me back in high school. No one has ever seen me in such a desperate state. And even

I have trouble visualizing how I ended up on such a dark path and how close to the edge I came.

In the year before I landed on that shrink's couch, two teenagers in our town committed suicide. What people did not know is that I once contemplated a similar fate, and had not entirely ruled it out in the future. Clinically speaking, I now know I was suffering from mild depression, which of course is by no means "mild" to the person who has it, especially when that person is a hormonally volatile teenager.

I simply didn't want to live anymore, and my sense of despair went far beyond typical teenage blues. My mind had entered a cold, dark, lonely place, and I couldn't pinpoint why. On the outside, I was carrying on as if I had my whole life ahead of me. On the inside, I had fallen into an emotional black hole and saw no way out. In secret, private moments, tears would run down my face as feelings of loss, betrayal, unhappiness, and rejection overwhelmed me for no apparent reason, at least none that I could see. If anyone had caught me in one of those moments and asked what was wrong, I would have said to them in all honesty, "I don't know."

It was as if some deep-seated emotional pain kept replaying itself in my head week after week—an endless loop on a mental soundtrack that kept getting louder, though I could never quite make out the words. I was not somebody *with* a problem; I *was* the problem. And the only way to put an end to the misery was to end my very existence.

The closest I ever came was when I was home alone one Saturday afternoon. I'd cried myself to sleep the night before and woke up feeling even worse. I made my way to the bathroom, rummaged through the medicine cabinet, and grabbed all the bottles of pills I could find until both my hands were full. I set them down on the desk in my bedroom, then frantically started to open each one, dumping the over-the-counter drugs on the desktop. I wanted so much to down them all and end the pain right there.

But that would leave my mother to find the body, and I wasn't sure I wanted to do that to her. I considered writing a one-line suicide note: "Dear Mom, It's not your fault." As if that would provide some comfort. For hours, I paced the house crying, wandering from room to room, asking myself what was wrong with me, waffling over what to do.

When I couldn't cry anymore, I looked in the mirror and decided I couldn't bring myself to do it. Those pills wouldn't have done the job anyway. Nothing there in that rainbow of tablets on my desk was lethal. Might give me an upset stomach, or cause me to pass out, or give me diarrhea, or make me blind for life, or produce one of a dozen other side effects that flashed through my crazed head that day. But it wouldn't kill me.

Damn.

I knew I wasn't well. And now I felt stuck. The schoolmate I'd confided in expressed to me how much my loss would hurt her and urged me to talk to someone who could get me help. Within a couple of days, I had an appointment at the local mental health center.

"Do you have many friends?" the psychologist asked.

"Lots of acquaintances, I would say. Not many people I'd consider really close friends anymore," I answered.

"Do you feel like you're part of any particular group or clique at school?"

"No, I'm pretty much a loner in that regard."

"Do you go to parties, school dances, that kind of thing?"

"Occasionally."

"When you're at a party or some other event, how do you spend your time? Are you off in a corner by yourself? Do you find yourself talking with one person or one group of people the entire time? Would you say you move around the room, floating from group to group but never really settling in anywhere?"

"Oh, I'm definitely a floater," I said without hesitation. "I don't stay in a conversation with any one group for very long."

"Now, you're obviously racially mixed," he said, taking our conversation down a road I hadn't expected. "Tell me about your family background."

I was surprised he brought up the race issue, but also impressed by the way he brought it up. The way the words just rolled out of his mouth. No awkward stare. No search for the politically appropriate phrase to broach the subject. And he didn't say, "What are you?" He was very matter-of-fact about it—the grass is green, the sky is blue, and, oh yeah, "You're obviously racially mixed." He said it just like that.

"It's kind of complicated," I began. "On my birth certificate, it says both my parents are black"—I then paused to make quotation marks with my fingers—"or 'Negro' as they called it back then. But on my father's birth certificate, because his mother was white, it says he's mulatto."

"I'm just going to make some notes here as we talk," the therapist interjected. He opened a manila folder and began writing. His timing suggested to me that he now needed a scorecard to keep things straight.

"And my mother is also light-skinned and she's sometimes mistaken for Filipino," I continued. "And even though she says she's legally black, she has some white ancestors. Like I'm pretty sure my great-grandmother on her side was white, and for the longest time I thought my grandmother was white, also."

"So how do you see yourself racially?" he asked.

"Well, if someone asks me, I'll generally just keep it simple and say I'm black," I answered. "I go with what's on the birth certificate. Sometimes I don't think it totally fits, but it's just easier to say I'm black and move on."

My counselor took a deep breath. "You know, I guess I bring this up because we live in a pretty homogeneous, pretty white community here," he said.

Pullman, Washington, was definitely that.

"So," the psychologist continued, "if you're not clear about your racial background, or there's some uncertainty around it and which racial group you belong to, do you think maybe you don't know where you're supposed to fit in?" He paused to allow me to think about his words. "It could be part of the reason you're a floater, trying to find where you'll be most comfortable," he added.

We peeled back other layers of my life as well, focusing on the trials of adolescence. In the process, I began to put together the pieces of the puzzle that had led to my downward spiral. It wasn't any one thing. It was a lot of little things left unresolved, adding up over time: My mother had now remarried, and the adjustment for me had been difficult. I hadn't had a relationship all through high school, and it bothered me. My closest friend had moved away after our sophomore year, contributing to my sense of loneliness. A white, freckle-faced, redneck jock called me a "white nigger," and it stung.

I left the psychologist's office an hour or so later, feeling like a huge burden had been lifted from my shoulders. The counseling session was the first time I'd had the chance to seriously reflect on the complexities of my racial background, my outward appearance, my family circumstances, and how they may have affected my social interactions. I wasn't sure about his theory concerning my tendency to drift from group to group as being tied to my racial history. But on some level, it also seemed to ring true. Could my feelings of depression really be the result of some repressed racial baggage I'd been carrying?

Well, yes and no. There were many factors involved. But being biracial likely played a part.

"When multiracial adolescents encounter adjustment difficulties, it may or may not be related to being multiracial," write psychologists Karen Suyemoto and Juanita Dimas in *The Multiracial Child Resource Book*. "On the other hand, the experience of being multiracial and multiethnic may affect or shape the ways in which other challenges are met or addressed."[1]

One study on multiracial youth published in November 2003 did find that adolescents who identified with more than one race showed higher rates of depression than their monoracial peers. The findings appeared in the *American Journal of Public Health* and were based on surveys of ninety thousand middle and high school students. Researchers found multiracial teens were also more likely to skip school, have trouble sleeping, smoke, and drink alcohol.[2]

"It did not matter what races the students identified with, the risks were higher for all of them if they did not identify with a single race," Professor J. Richard Udry, principal author of the study, told the Associated Press. "The most common explanation for the high-risk status is the struggle with identity formation, leading to lack of self-esteem, social isolation, and problems of family dynamics in biracial households."[3]

On the surface, the study appears to reinforce all the negative stereotypes about mixed-race people—that we're a bunch of mixed nuts doomed to a life of racial confusion and associated mental health problems if we do not identify with a single race. When put in the proper perspective, however, the numbers do make some sense. The survey did not find depression among multiracial teens to be the norm; rather, it found that they have *higher rates* of depression and other social ills than their peers.

Considering how turbulent those middle school and high school years can be for all young people, it doesn't surprise me that statistically the multiracial student population is more adversely affected. Clearly, the adolescents in this group see themselves as fitting into multiple racial categories. I would argue that the very pressure imposed by others to choose only one race contributes significantly to the higher stress levels and associated problems this particular study recorded.

It's also important to note that the data used in the survey was actually collected in 1994–1995, well before the 2000 census, in which families could check more than one category to define their children's race. So the study captured attitudes at a time when the concept of embracing a multiracial identity had not yet exploded in the national media, and federal recognition of the multiracial population had not yet been achieved. As public awareness increases and teachers, counselors, and peers become more attuned to the cross-cultural issues involved, I would hope that a more supportive environment for multiracial teens would emerge, whatever their identity choices might be.

My choice at that point still wasn't 100 percent clear. As I told my shrink: when asked, I'd say that I was black. Maybe I thought if I said it often enough, it would solidify in my mind. But it seemed that I also wanted to leave the door open for further explanation in some way. Racial ambivalence revisited.

But again, none of this is unusual for multiracial teens. In her book *Why Are All the Black Kids Sitting Together in the Cafeteria*, Spelman College president and professor of psychology Beverly Daniel Tatum describes the process of identity development as "circular" rather than linear. "It's like moving up a spiral staircase: as you proceed up each level, you have a sense that you have passed this way before, but you are not exactly in the same spot."[4]

Sociologist Kathleen Odell Korgen, author of *From Black to Biracial*, adds, "There is never a perfect correlation between one's self-identity and one's perceived identity. Identities can ebb and flow depending upon the response they receive."[5]

For members of interracial families, the gap between self-identity and perceived identity can be especially wide. Societal responses to multiracial people vary greatly. As a result, we're bound to do more ebbing and flowing as we move up the staircase of development. Researchers Jewelle Taylor Gibbs and Alice Hines have run across various studies concluding that biracial children develop racial attitudes and self-concepts in ways that are different from black or white children.[6] The outcome can still be positive, but the process is not as straightforward. Picking a racial identity may not sound terribly complicated to most young people, or to most adults for that matter. But for multiracial teenagers, it can be a different story.

Like all teens, I had reached that stage in life when young people are in the process of becoming more independent, from getting a driver's license to preparing for life away from their parents. That involves solidifying a sense of personal identity on a number of fronts—race, religion, gender, sexual orientation, aptitude, interests, potential career paths, and so on. Some struggle more than others. In my case, I was confronting issues surrounding friendships, dating, changes in family structure, and questions about what to do after high school. Nothing unusual about that, but being biracial introduced another variable into the mix.

For multiracial people, there is an additional layer in the identity development process. It involves creating a sense of self by assembling pieces of their heritage that others view as incompatible or mutually exclusive. No two people will assemble the pieces in exactly the same way. Some will end up emphasizing one part of their background over another. Others will end up balancing them all with equal weight. For some, the process unfolds quite naturally. For others, it is a struggle. But the additional introspection required can be a source of stress, particularly in those young people who may already be having difficulty in other areas.

Psychologists Suyemoto and Dimas offer a number of recommendations for parents and teachers to help multiracial teenagers through this period. None of their suggestions involve trying to force a particular identity down a young person's throat. Instead, adults should understand that identity development is a process and should see identity as a changing, evolving thing. They write, "The ways in which multiracial adolescents feel about their own race and ethnicity and about family, peers, and particular ethnic groups or heritages rarely remain the same over time . . . feelings of difference and exclusion are based in rigid ideas about race and racial purity and not related to any shortcoming of who they are as people."[7]

I stopped going to see the psychologist a couple of months after my first session. The therapy had been helpful, but I didn't feel I needed it anymore. And before graduation day came, I finally did find a social group I was comfortable with, where I no longer played the role of the floater to the extent that I had. I became a member of my high school's international club. The group was made up of students who had recently immigrated to the United States, foreign-exchange students spending the academic year living with American host families, and a cross section of U.S.-born students interested in expanding our cultural horizons.

The international club was the one place where individual racial and cultural differences were the norm. In fact, such differences were welcomed, accepted, and celebrated. It was my kind of club. At dances, parties, and social get-togethers the club sponsored, I fit right in. It was effortless. For all I knew, I might have been mistaken for a new American immigrant myself. I didn't care. At last, I seemed to have discovered a level of group acceptance that I hadn't achieved anywhere else in the previous four years.

Thoughts about taking my own life became a thing of the past. Instead, I was looking to the future, growing confident with the progress I was making in finding my way in the world. Yet when it came to matters of race, I still had a lot of things left to figure out.

The Science and Folly of Race

"RACE DOES NOT EXIST."

"Aren't we all multiracial?"

"You're confusing race with ethnicity."

Walk in to any diversity conference, multicultural lecture, or panel discussion on race relations, and I can almost guarantee that before the event is over, someone will attempt to make one or all of these points.

They are not necessarily wrong. But I don't think they are seeing the whole picture, either.

Frankly, it is difficult, if not impossible, to have a conversation about race without incorporating verbiage that some people will find problematic. I'm not talking about language that is offensive. I'm talking about terminology that is bound to be challenged given the imprecise nature of the notion of race itself. What I hope to offer here is a way out of that semantic forest.

When I was in elementary school, our reading teacher told the class that when we encountered a word we didn't know, sometimes it was possible to learn its meaning from the "context"—which, at that time, was a word we didn't know. She later explained "context" as the surrounding words, the other words in the sentence or in the paragraph. We had to look at the whole picture.

Context is often what's needed to make sense of discussions surrounding racial identity. Take the phrase, "She's Hispanic but looks Jewish, and she grew up white." In one sentence, I've combined terms of race (white), ethnicity (Hispanic), and religion (Jewish) while also trying to communicate something about culture, or how this person "grew up."

Have I "confused" the labels? Not at all. I am simply using them in a way that requires more interpretation. Some might argue that this is wrong and that I should stick to more narrow, dictionary definitions. Yet when I've used this example in some of those same diversity workshops in which participants complain about racial terminology, I've had people tell me, "You know, I actually understood what you meant."

On one level, "being Hispanic but looking Jewish and growing up white" makes absolutely no sense. But when viewed in the right context, it makes perfect sense. Finding the right meaning involves finding our way through the linguistic fog of race, ethnicity, culture, and identity.

Consider the position put forth by Ellis Cose in his book *Color-Blind.* "We can theoretically create races at will," Cose writes. "If Americans agreed, for instance, that people with red hair constitute a separate race, these people would be one. And if we proceeded to treat all people with red hair differently from everyone else, they would soon take on all the attributes we associate with 'real' races. If, for instance, they were allowed only to do menial labor, refused an education, compelled to intermarry, forced to live in predominantly redhead communities, and told that their only real gifts were drinking and song, they would eventually develop a culture that embodied the new redhead stereotype. But all we would have proved is that human beings have the power to define (and thereby create) races—not that the classification has any value or makes any sense."[1]

In other words, races exist because once upon a time, we said they did. And we put in place a massive social, political, and economic structure to back up what we said. That structure has not been fully dismantled. But many attitudes have changed over time, and so too has our language about race.

As the American Anthropological Association noted in a position paper on racial categorization, "Today's ethnicities are yesterday's races. In the early twentieth century in the U.S., Italians, the Irish, and Jews were all thought to be racial (not ethnic) groups whose members were inherently and irredeemably distinct from the majority white population. Today, of course, the situation has changed considerably. Italians, Irish, and Jews are now seen as ethnic groups that are included in the majority white population. The notion that they are racially distinct from whites seems far-fetched, possibly 'racist.'"[2]

So the labels we use at any point in history to identify certain population groups are suspect. They could refer to physical appearance, or cultural traits, or family heritage, or social and economic status, or any stereotypes associated with all of the above. Sometimes we'll use the same racial term to refer to different things at the same time. We'll change the meaning in midsentence and not bother to tell anyone we're doing so. As in, "He doesn't look black, but he is black," or, "She's Asian, but I don't think of her as Asian."

It's twisted, I know. Still, we manage to communicate.

This contextual nature of race seems to cause the most consternation in the field of science. As biologist Armand Marie Leroi wrote in a 2005 article for the *New York Times*, "If modern anthropologists mention the concept of race, it is invariably only to warn against and dismiss it." He goes on to quote Dr. J. Craig Venter, who described race as a social concept, not a scientific one. "He should know," writes Leroi, "since he was the first to sequence the human genome."[3]

Like many Americans, my understanding of DNA, the human genome, and scientific phenomena in general is rather fuzzy. Even as advancements in the field of forensics have made headlines and been the focus of any number of TV cop shows, I wouldn't dare to pretend I understand the intricacies of how all that stuff works.

But the vast majority of scientists with expertise in this area seem to be in agreement. How our society has generally thought of race does not align with the facts. If, for example, we were capable of lining up every person on the planet from the darkest-skinned to the lightest-skinned, most of us would have a hard time trying to pinpoint where along that spectrum one "race" of people ended and another "race" of people began.

"These facts render any attempt to establish lines of division among biological populations both arbitrary and subjective," says the the anthropological association's statement. "Evidence from the analysis of genetics (e.g., DNA) indicates that most physical variation, about 94 percent, lies *within* so-called racial groups."[4]

In other words, if we took a roomful of people of various "races" and asked them to cluster into groups according to commonly held racial definitions, with "black" people in one corner, "Asian" people in another, and so on around the room, and we stopped to analyze everyone's DNA, something interesting would happen. We would likely find more genetic variation within each racial group than between the different groups.

As an article by Sally Lehrman in *Scientific American* pointed out, "The genetic difference between two individuals of the same race can be greater than those between individuals of different races—table sugar may look like salt, but it has more similarities with corn syrup."[5]

As a nonscientist, the salt versus sugar versus corn syrup analogy actually makes sense to me. Based on appearance alone, we would assume that salt and sugar have more in common than sugar and corn syrup. But chemically speaking, that's not the case. The similarities are merely visual ones, and they can be misleading. Researchers make the same point about race.

"Physical variations in the human species have no meaning except the social ones that humans put on them," the American Anthropological Association concluded.[6]

But I'm afraid those "social meanings" are huge. As some folks like to say, race is fiction, but racism is real. As much as scientists like to talk about race as a social construct, the construct is no trivial matter. There are social consequences that flow out of it, and those consequences have to be dealt with.

I can't tell you how many times I've referred to myself or someone else as "multiracial" only to hear the response, "But isn't everybody multiracial? Who is pure anything?" For some reason, people accept that "black" and "white" are socially defined terms but assume that when I use the word "multiracial," I must be talking strictly about biology. I am not. Although certain biological factors may be involved, I am essentially talking about an identity that results from a lived experience. If race itself is a social construct, then by definition, to be biracial or multiracial must be a social construct, too.

In his *New York Times* essay, Armand Marie Leroi touched off a controversy of sorts when he warned that we may be overlooking something significant in our rush to declare race an obsolete notion, scientific or otherwise. "Race is merely a shorthand that enables us to speak sensibly, though with no great precision, about genetic rather than cultural or political differences," he writes.

"The shapes of our eyes, noses, and skulls; the color of our eyes and our hair; the heaviness, height, and hairiness of our bodies are all, individually, poor guides to ancestry. But this is not true when the features are taken together," he contends. "Certain skin colors tend to go with certain kinds of eyes, noses, skulls, and bodies. When we glance at a stranger's face, we use those associations to infer what continent, or even what country, he or his ancestors came from—and we usually get it right. To put it more abstractly, human physical variation is correlated; and correlations contain information."[7]

Of course, there are many other things people tend to infer based on racial appearances that are flat-out wrong. Nevertheless, there does seem to be some merit in examining the interplay between socially defined racial categories and biological science.

Health care is one area in which racial considerations become important. The National Marrow Donor Program, for example, has issued a call specifically for more African-Americans to register as bone marrow donors, citing a "pressing need" to diversify the registry's genetic pool. "While patients of any racial or ethnic heritage may have difficulty finding a donor for their transplant, black and African American patients face the greatest challenge," says the organization's Web site. "Marrow and cord blood transplants require matching certain tissue traits of the donor and patient. Because these traits are inherited, a patient's most likely match is someone of the same racial or ethnic group."[8]

In 1995, baseball Hall of Famer Rod Carew made a public appeal to recruit more minority donors into the registry in hopes of saving the life of his daughter, Michelle, who was dying of leukemia and needed a bone marrow transplant. She was considered a particularly difficult match because she was biracial. "Her father is of West Indian descent and was born in Panama," reported United Press International, "and her mother is a Caucasian of Jewish descent." Michelle's two sisters were suitable matches for each other, but not for Michelle.[9]

Although no suitable donor was found before she died, Michelle Carew's story circulated among interracial families and made the rounds on multiracial Web sites. According to UPI, the family's plea generated seventy thousand calls to the National Marrow Donor Program.[10]

I guess I was one of them. As soon as I heard about her plight, I made an appointment to have my blood drawn to see if I might be a match. I am still in the marrow registry today. The fact that Michelle was biracial probably had something to do with why I acted with such urgency.

But many scientists still caution against overemphasizing any connection between race and genetics. In an online discussion of the groundbreaking PBS series *Race: The Power of an Illusion*, experts who participated in the broadcast would only go so far in acknowledging the relevancy of race in making sound medical determinations.[11]

"It's true that people who are closely genetically related are more likely to have a good genetic match on organs. For example, siblings can often donate organs to each other or will be well matched for each other. It doesn't always happen, but it's more likely to happen," says Pilar Ossorio, a University of Wisconsin professor and an associate of the Center for the Study of Cultural Diversity in Health Care. "So if you're studying a group of people who are actually related because they all live in the same city and their ancestors all came to the U.S. from the same village or community, then it would make some sense that within that group they would be more likely to have matched organs."

"I think there is a crude assumption out there that race is a metaphor for family. That the family is a small related group and a race is a big related group," offers Alan Goodman, a founding member of the American Anthropological Association's commission on race. "People take that metaphor too literally."

For example, sickle-cell anemia, an inherited condition that results in misshapen blood cells, is often thought of as "a black person's disease," while Tay-Sachs, a fatal disease that causes a buildup of fat in the brain, is found among Ashkenazi Jews.

"But in any study, you're looking at a subpopulation within that race," cautions Ossorio. "It may mean that this particular subpopulation experienced some interesting historical event which shaped it in a certain way. People of northern European Jewish ancestry may be at higher risk because of something that happened to an ancestral population. So if you're descended from this ancestral population, you'll have that higher risk. If you include those people in the overall 'white' population, it might look like there's a slightly elevated risk for white people to pass on Tay-Sachs, but it only appears that way because of an elevated risk within this one little subpopulation."

As for sickle-cell anemia, although statistically blacks are at higher risk in the United States, Ossorio notes that the disease is also found in people in Greece. "The island of Orchomenos, in particular, has very high carrier rates for sickle-cell. There are also high carrier rates among people on the Arabian peninsula and people in India. There are parts of India where the sickle cell carrier rate is as high as it is anywhere in Africa," she says.

"I also think it's worth pointing out," she continues, "while we make claims about the sickle cell carrier rate in black people and white people in the U.S., if you were to go to a period of our history where we defined black and white differently, then those numbers would be different. Or if we were to go to the Bahamas or maybe to Brazil, where currently the perceptions of black and white are different than they are here in the U.S., then the carrier rate numbers would be different. There would probably be a higher carrier rate for sickle cell gene variants in the white population in the Bahamas or Brazil than there is here. That's because in the U.S. we draw the line so that anybody who looks like they have the slightest bit of African ancestry gets put in the black category. But that's not true everywhere, and it's not even necessarily true at all times in the United States."

I get that. Believe me, I do. As Leroi admits, race is a form of shorthand, a way of "rounding off," if you will. It may be imprecise, but I don't think we can afford to discount it altogether. It seems this shorthand can lead to information that is quite useful, perhaps even life-saving.

Not so fast, argues R. C. Lewontin, professor emeritus at Harvard University. In an article published by the Social Science Research Council, Lewontin states, "Racial identification simply does not do the work needed. What we ought to ask on medical questionnaires is not racial identification, but ancestry. 'Do you know of any ancestors who were Ashkenazi Jews, or from West Africa, from certain regions of the Mediterranean . . . ?' Once again, racial categorization is a bad predictor of biology." [12]

So does this thing called "race" exist, or doesn't it?

There is, I believe, a practical way out of this madness. Again, I go back to context. Race, in my mind, is something of a catch-all term referring to a loosely defined population group. Beyond that, biologists, sociologists, anthropologists, historians, and the layperson will all define it differently and then argue over the definitions they've come up with. I have no desire to join them in that endless, circular debate. So when racial labels present themselves—whether in this book or in life in general—I suggest it's most practical to accept the label at face value and then consider its context to glean the true meaning.

I happen to view racial categories as similar to the borders that exist between counties, states, and nations. They exist, though their visibility and importance fluctuates.

For instance, whenever I'm flying cross-country, I look down from thirty-five thousand feet and frequently don't know what state I'm traveling over at any given moment. Even when I have to change planes at Chicago's O'Hare International Airport and the flight plan takes us over Lake Michigan, I still can't tell where the state of Illinois ends and the state of Wisconsin begins. One sort of blends in to the other.

Astronauts who have gone into space have reported experiencing a similar revelation when they look back at planet Earth. There are no lines separating the countries. The land masses appear seamless.

We've grown so accustomed to looking at satellite photographs and atlas pages with the boundaries drawn in, we're almost taken by surprise when we see the planet as it truly is. We're reminded that the borders are created. They're political borders, socially constructed borders, made-up borders.

But do they exist? You bet they do.

The last time I drove from Madison, Wisconsin to Chicago, when I reached the Illinois state line, there was a toll to pay. When I travel outside the country, I need a passport, and sometimes a visa, and I must clear customs and immigration upon my arrival.

At the risk of overextending the analogy, multiracial people are like travelers who carry two passports or who have dual citizenship. That status can either ease the process or complicate it, depending on the immigration official.

Such borders, while not naturally occurring, are nonetheless real. Biologists, looking down from on high through the lens of science, may not see them. But down here on the ground, we know they exist. And when crossing those racial borders, there may be a toll we will have to pay. Many interracial families know that all too well.

PART 2
BEIGE LIKE ME

The Bahá'í in Me

I CALL IT "MULTIRACIAL RADAR."

It's some sort of sixth sense that members of interracial families learn to develop over the years. It allows us to spot other multiracial people who share similar experiences of living between two worlds.

Of course, like all such facilities, multiracial radar is often suspect. As with "gay-dar"—that intuition that's supposed to detect whether someone is gay or lesbian—multiracial radar isn't always accurate. It can register false positives, misreading certain traits or outward appearances as proof of a person's identity. It can also overlook those who have embraced their mixed-race heritage but whose physical features wouldn't necessarily lead others to conclude they come from an interracial family.

My multiracial radar is what told me that Sundee Tucker Frazier was biracial. Sundee and I were mere acquaintances in high school. Since then, we've become confidants in matters relating to growing up biracial. I don't remember when the fact that she had a multiracial background dawned on me. Maybe I always knew from the moment I first saw her. We'd crossed paths any number of times in the hallways of Pullman High School—the only high school in our small college town.

What I do remember is that when Sundee invited me to meet her family for the first time, I wasn't the least bit surprised by their racial makeup. They were just how I'd pictured them.

Winter had just set in as I made my way up to their modest home located near the edge of the university campus. Sundee's mother opened the door and welcomed me in from the cold night air, greeting me with a wide, pleasant smile. She was a white woman with tightly curled, shoulder-length light brown hair. Sundee's father was a tall black man with an athletic build, sporting a closely cropped Afro and a neatly trimmed mustache. Both Sundee and her younger brother, Isaac, seemed to embody equal blends of both heritages in their physical appearance with their light tan complexions and wavy brown hair.

Somebody phone Hallmark, I thought. The Tuckers belong on a greeting card. In my mind, they were exactly what an interracial family was supposed to look like. Unraveling all the racial blending in my family required going back at least two generations to my paternal grandparents and even further back on my mother's side. With Sundee and Isaac, if anyone were ever in doubt about their racial heritage, meeting their mom and dad would instantly end the speculation.

But at that time, Sundee and I never talked about our racial backgrounds, or what it meant to be biracial, or which racial label we attached to ourselves. Deep down, we sensed we had much in common along those lines, but it was an unspoken understanding. We weren't ready yet to openly discuss it. That dialogue would unfold gradually over the next two decades as we drifted in and out of each other's lives, reconnecting for one reason or another every couple of years.

"I can't remember when the word 'biracial' came into my lexicon, but I don't think it was there in high school. I don't think people used that term much in the 1980s," Sundee told me one evening from her home in the Los Angeles area. "I knew my family was interracial, and I loved who my family was. But I think I kind of kept it a little bit guarded, like it was too sacred to put it out there because I knew no one in Pullman would understand if I tried to talk to them about it. I don't know why I never thought to talk to you about it. I guess because I didn't know you identified as biracial, and I don't know if you did at that point, or if you identified more as black."

"Could we have talked about it then?" I asked.

"I don't think I could have. I don't think I had the language, I don't think I had the consciousness," Sundee replied. "There's much more of a sense of a movement of multiracial people who want to be recognized for having a mixed racial background, and we didn't have that in the late '80s."

Before moving to Pullman at the end of her sixth-grade year, in 1980, Sundee had attended several different schools in suburban Seattle. By the time we finally ran into each other, she was a high school freshman; I was a junior. Like many people who eventually come to embrace a biracial identity, Sundee and I both had difficulty finding the right vocabulary to describe our shifting sense of where we fit on the racial spectrum, which probably had something to do with why we never discussed the issue during our teenage years.

"In elementary school, as far back as I can remember having to choose a race, I chose black," she said. "It was probably one of those things where I had a form to fill out and I didn't know what to check, and an adult informed me of what I should choose. I guess I took on that label and it was fine with me, but I didn't think that much about race."

But that would soon change. As our conversation progressed, Sundee recounted another incident in elementary school when she accidentally cut herself on the playground. Her white classmates expressed surprise when they saw that her blood was the same color as theirs. "When you start to realize you're being singled out as being different, that certainly influences your identity and how you identify with the minority group," she said, taking stock of the emotional impact it had on her.

To others, however, Sundee is perceived as white, and that impression helped ease the transition when her family moved from the Seattle area to rural eastern Washington. She suspects her light complexion made it easier for her to blend in with white classmates as she navigated her junior and senior high school years.

"Publicly, I was 'Sundee.' I was an individual person, and I just strove to be my best at everything I did," she said. "I got involved in things schoolwise. But socially, I pretty much kept my distance. I was sort of an island unto myself. Not that I didn't have any friends, but they were more acquaintances. And I think the reason I was more of a loner is because inside I knew I was different. I didn't feel totally comfortable with people."

That feeling, however, didn't stop her from building an impressive record of accomplishments as a teenager. A self-described overachiever—which is exactly how I remember her during those years—Sundee excelled academically and became involved in extracurricular activities. I was in the audience the night she was crowned Pullman's Junior Miss, and only her family cheered louder than I did when she went on to become first runner-up in the Washington State Junior Miss competition.

Still, there were issues. White students who were unaware of her family background would occasionally make racist remarks in her presence. "It was like, does this person know I'm black and not care?

It's probably that they just don't know. They think I'm one of them. Those kinds of incidents would smack me in the face . . . because I'm the person they're ridiculing or that they're mocking," she said.

"I've always lived with that tension of knowing that I'm like an undercover black person. I'm incognito, never feeling completely recognized for who I am, but still identifying myself as African American," she continued. "I think that's been one of the biggest challenges for me in accepting myself and liking who I am, and coming to a place where I can say, 'I'm biracial; I'm African American, I'm white, I'm both.'"

Ultimately, Sundee found the way to come to terms with the racial issues in her life through her faith. A devout Christian, she says her parents laid the foundation for her religious beliefs but never forced the issue directly. "My parents were only involved in organized religion as kids under their parents' roofs," she said. "My impression is they gave up church attendance as soon as they were out on their own. I was not raised with any sense of the value of church, although my mom did make sure I had a copy of the Children's Living Bible. She said she wanted me to have the opportunity to make my own choice about God."

Although her parents turned away from organized religion as adults, Sundee turned toward it. Decisively so. While in college at the University of Southern California, she became active in Inter-Varsity Christian Fellowship, a campus ministry organization, and later joined its staff.

"There was this consciousness of there being a creator, a larger force that's responsible for my life from a very early age," said Sundee. "There's a passage of scripture that says, 'It was You who formed my inward parts. You knit me together in my mother's womb. I praise You for I am fearfully and wonderfully made. Wonderful are Your works. And my soul knows it very well.' (Psalm 139:13–14).

"I think knowing that I was intentionally created the way I am, as a person of mixed race or multiracial heritage, helps me to embrace it, to accept it, and to want to know what role I have to play in this world."

She elaborates on the path she took toward reconciling her dual heritage in her book, *Check All That Apply*, which offers a faith-based approach to issues confronting multiracial people. She writes, "I believe God couldn't help but create diversity—he's too grand for his image to be reflected in just one ethnicity. In fact, he's so vast and multifaceted that his creativity expands beyond the racial categories humans have established."[1]

But Sundee's journey has at times been deeply painful. One incident described in her book stands out. While participating in a diversity-training exercise during college, the workshop's facilitator called on attendees to separate themselves into groups by race. The idea was to create a smaller environment of one's "own people" where participants would feel free to openly discuss their thoughts and feelings.

"Ironically, the activity that everyone else perceived as the easiest and most comfortable undid me," Sundee writes. As the group divided and separated into the four corners of the room, Sundee stood in the center until the facilitator prodded her to choose a racial group. "All my body heat relocated to my face and armpits. Don't cry, don't cry, I pleaded with myself," she writes.[2]

Black participants were also divided as to where Sundee belonged. Some encouraged her to join them. Others felt that if she had been raised around white people and felt more comfortable with them, then she should go with the white group.

"My mind spun in confusion and fear of making the wrong choice. I had grown up in mostly white settings, but I had also always been around both the white and black sides of my family. With them I never had to choose a side—we were all on the same side," Sundee writes. "I wanted my choice to state clearly, 'I'm proud to be black,' but more than anything I wanted to scream, 'Why are you making me choose? Why?'"[3]

Sundee eventually chose to sit with the black students but wasn't entirely comfortable. "I laughed when others laughed, even if I didn't totally get it. I mostly understood what everyone was talking about, though I hadn't always had the same experiences. I was accepted as part of the group, but I also had to face the lonely truth that this 'racial awareness and sensitivity training' had completely overlooked my racial reality," she writes.[4]

"I'm glad that it happened, because it confronted me with the reality that in this world, black and white don't get along," said Sundee, reflecting on the incident. "Where do I belong in this discussion about race? What do I have to say about it, and what do I have to offer? What will I choose in terms of my identity? Obviously at that time, I didn't have the tools to say, 'I'm biracial, and I'll form my own group.' I'll go with the black students, but I'm fully conscious of the fact that I'm coming from a different point of view.

"At that time, I felt like I needed to fit in, I needed to be accepted, I needed to belong. And so I sat there with the black students, just hoping and praying that they would accept me as one of them. And of course, I still have that. I still want to be affirmed and accepted by my African American brothers and sisters as belonging. But I don't think I have that same sense of desperation, because I'm more confident in the fact that I am meant to be the way I am."

If there is a spiritual component to resolving the race-related questions facing members of interracial families, Sundee has obviously found it in Christianity. My parents, on the other hand, found it in the Bahá'í faith—a lesser-known religion in the United States but one with an estimated six million followers around the world. In the Bahá'í faith, advancing the cause of racial harmony is a central theme.

Compared to other religions, the Bahá'í (pronounced "Bah-HI") faith is relatively new. Its history, according to several official Bahá'í publications, goes like this: the founder of the Bahá'í faith, named Bahá'u'lláh, was born in 1817 in Persia, or what is now Iran. In 1844, at the age of twenty-seven, Bahá'u'lláh became a follower of a spiritual leader known as The Báb. The Báb had announced the coming of a prophet who would lay out a blueprint for the spiritual regeneration of the human race. Bahá'u'lláh and other followers of The Báb were soon denounced as heretics and persecuted for their beliefs. While imprisoned, Bahá'u'lláh is said to have received a revelation that he was the Promised One foretold by The Báb who would fulfill the prophesies of earlier religions and guide humanity to its spiritual maturity.[5]

"Bahá'í" means "follower of Bahá'u'lláh," and his writings are seen as the sacred scripture of the faith. Central to Bahá'í teachings is "the oneness of humanity" and a recognition of the universal principles found in virtually all religions. Bahá'ís believe that throughout history God has sent a series of divine messengers to Earth. Jesus was one such messenger, but not the only one. Abraham, Muhammad, Moses, Buddha, and others were all divine messengers sent to reveal God's heavenly plan. The latest in this string of messengers was Bahá'u'lláh himself.

Followers of the Bahá'í faith believe religious truth is in harmony with science and reason and that religion should be a force for unity in the world. Specifically, Bahá'í principles include equality between men and women, the elimination of all forms of prejudice, universal education, world peace, an international tribunal, and a universal auxiliary language. Said Bahá'u'lláh, "The diversity in the human family should be the cause of love and harmony, as it is in music where many different notes blend together in the making of a perfect chord."

Not only are interracial dating, marriage, and families accepted in the Bahá'í faith, but some would say they are even encouraged. Various passages in Bahá'í writings attributed to Bahá'u'lláh speak to the benefits of interracial unions:

"In the world of being, the meeting is blessed when the white and colored races meet together with infinite spiritual love and heavenly harmony. When such meetings are established, and the participants associate with each other with perfect love, unity, and kindness, the angels of the Kingdom praise them, and the Beauty of Bahá'u'lláh addresseth them, 'Blessed are ye! Blessed are ye!' . . . Strive earnestly and put forth your greatest endeavor toward the accomplishment of this fellowship and the cementing of this bond of brotherhood between you. . . . For the accomplishment of unity between the colored and white will be an assurance of the world's peace."

There are no clergy in the Bahá'í faith. Instead of a professional priesthood, affairs are coordinated through local and national "spiritual assemblies" whose members are elected by followers of the faith. Internationally, a nine-member body known as the Universal House of Justice acts as the legislative authority directing spiritual and administrative affairs worldwide.

Prior to his death in 1892, Bahá'u'lláh appointed his eldest son, 'Abdu'l-Bahá, as the head of the faith and interpreter of Bahá'í teachings upon his passing. In further advancing the ideals of racial diversity, 'Abdu'l-Bahá wrote:

"Consider the flowers of a garden: though differing in kind, color, form and in shape, yet, inasmuch as they are refreshed by the waters of one spring, revived by the breath of one wind, invigorated by the rays of one sun, this diversity increaseth their charm, and addeth unto their beauty. Thus when that unifying force, the penetrating influence of the Word of God, taketh effect, the difference of customs, manners, habits, ideas, opinions and dispositions embellisheth the world of humanity. . . . How unpleasing to the eye if all the flowers and plants, the leaves and blossoms, the fruits, the branches and the trees of that garden were all of the same shape and color! Diversity of hues, form and shape, enricheth and adorneth the garden, and heighteneth the effect thereof. In like manner, when diverse shades of thought, temperament, and character, are brought together under the power and influence of one central agency, the beauty and glory of human perfection will be revealed and made manifest."

I can understand why the Bahá'í faith was attractive to my parents. "That old saying about eleven o'clock Sunday morning being the most segregated hour in America, that never made sense to me," my mother would say. In the Bahá'í faith, both my parents found a religion that championed integration and suggested that racial mixing is not an abomination or something to shy away from, but part of a larger, master plan.

Although my mother essentially left the Bahá'í faith when we left my dad, my father remained an active member of the Cleveland Spiritual Assembly. Upon his death, I relied heavily on the Bahá'í community to plan the funeral program and handle burial arrangements, as cremation is not allowed in the Bahá'í faith.

If there is such a thing as a "cultural Bahá'í," then the term would surely apply to me. Many Bahá'í teachings and principles rubbed off on me, and I find many Bahá'í writings inspirational. But I cannot consider myself a follower of the Bahá'í faith—or of any faith. My journey of coming to terms with being biracial followed a more secular path.

Having said that, I sometimes wonder if we are now entering a time in which the racial identity development process, at least among biracial people, will more closely resemble the process that leads to the formation of one's religious identity: We are certainly influenced by the beliefs of our parents, by the examples they set, by family tradition and community customs. But we are not bound by them. Ultimately it's up to each of us to find our own way and make our own choices.

Although Sundee Tucker Frazier and I had different religious upbringings and hold altogether different views on spirituality today, we do have one thing in common when it comes to religion and race: neither one of us was raised in a black church. In Pullman, Washington, there was none.

Both of us visited black churches at one time or another, usually when staying with relatives out of town. But we did not grow up in the cultural institution that is so central to the lives of so many African-Americans.

"My black grandma took me to her AME church whenever I visited," said Sundee, AME standing for African Methodist Episcopal. "It gave me a shiver of pride to know that my grandma went to a church with 'Africa' in its name, and that when I went there I was accepted as Willa Tucker's granddaughter, one of the clan."

But then, Sundee is a believer. I am not. Whenever I've accompanied relatives to church, I've been there to observe, not to worship.

My lack of religious conviction today represents one less connection I have to mainstream African-American culture. And at times, it serves as one more reminder of my outsider status.

The Chameleon Effect

MADISON AVENUE NOW HAS A TERM FOR PEOPLE LIKE ME. WE'RE the "ethnically ambiguous." That's how advertising executives are apparently referring to individuals whose skin color, hairstyle, and other physical features make their racial backgrounds hard to pin down. Professional models who meet that criteria have turned up in ad campaigns for everything from blue jeans to video games.

As Marie Anderson of the Ford modeling agency told the *Chicago Tribune*, "Clients like to hire somebody who looks like they have an interracial composition because their face speaks to many different cultures—not just one."[1]

It's easy to see why the ability to connect with consumers of different racial backgrounds would be attractive to advertisers looking to reach an increasingly diverse customer base. "Oh, that model looks like me," people will say, if only subconsciously. "Hey, she's one of us."

But it's one thing to make that kind of psychological connection while flipping through the pages of a magazine or watching a television commercial. It's another thing to be on the receiving end of these racial mind games people play with themselves on a daily basis. While we may appear ethnically ambiguous to modeling agencies and casting directors, their target audiences like to think they know exactly how to peg us and may attempt to do so directly to our faces. It results in something I call "the Chameleon Effect," and it happens to multiracial people all the time.

"We are inkblots," psychologist Maria Root told author Pearl Gaskins. "People see us and they project what they need onto us to make themselves feel comfortable."2

How people classify me varies from place to place, from circumstance to circumstance, from individual to individual. Where I am, who I'm with, and how I speak can shape the racial labels people choose to attach to me. Whenever someone asks, "Don't most people see you as black when you're walking down the street?" my reply is always the same.

"Depends on which street you're talking about," I'll say. "The streets of Washington, D.C., or the streets of south Florida? The streets of Jakarta, Indonesia, or the streets of Johannesburg, South Africa?" In each place—and I've been to all of those places—racial perceptions vary. Some people see only the black in me. Others don't see any black in me. The most significant factor in this process is the frame of mind of the person doing the labeling.

I got my first real taste of how the Chameleon Effect works the summer after I graduated from high school. Having finally found my social niche in my high school's international club, I applied to become an exchange student myself. Word of my initial acceptance arrived in the mail first, followed by a letter a few weeks later telling me that I'd been placed in Panama.

Next came a picture and a description of my host family. They appeared to be interracial. My host mother had light skin and straight black hair. My host father had chocolate skin and curly black hair. Their two sons had tan complexions. Their daughter favored the father in skin color. Was it just a coincidence that I'd been placed with them? I have no idea.

I would spend eight weeks in their home in Panama City, attending a private Catholic school with my host siblings, who ranged in age from ten to fifteen. My host father, a business executive with a U.S.-based company, spoke fluent English. The rest of the family spoke almost none.

Why I'd been selected for the Panama program was something of a mystery to me. I hadn't exactly been on the honor roll when it came to Spanish class. Back then, I'd thought of Spanish as just another course I was supposed to take to get into college. But my perspective changed as my departure date came nearer. Now, Spanish was no longer just a class but a language I would need to survive in my new surroundings. And since it was the only foreign language I'd ever studied, I guess placing me in Panama made as much sense as any other country under consideration.

I was excited about the experience that awaited me. Being an exchange student, I thought, it would be OK to be different. After all, I would be seen as a foreigner. It was *expected* that I would be different.

I was one of several hundred teenagers spending the summer of 1984 in Latin America through AFS Intercultural Programs, an international youth exchange organization. Before departing for our host countries, we gathered at the University of Miami in Coral Gables, Florida, for an intensive orientation. Two days were set aside for former exchange students, host parents, and AFS staff members to prepare us for the upcoming experience. We attended workshops on dealing with culture shock, adjusting to our host families, and overcoming the language barrier.

There were twenty-two of us in the group headed for Panama—

eighteen white, three black, and me. At least that's how I remember it. If there were others in our group who thought of themselves as multiracial, it remained a secret to me.

"Are most Panamanians black or white?" one student asked during our first session together.

Our group leader, who was Panamanian herself, looked at me. "Most are about your color," she said, pointing in my direction.

I didn't share it with the rest of the group, but deep down I felt relieved. My days of being "ethnically ambiguous" were about to be put on hold. I was going to spend the summer in a country where I would be surrounded by people whose skin color was just like mine. Even though I could barely speak the language, physically at least I would blend in rather than stand out.

If race ever became an issue during my interactions with the Panamanians that summer, I was too busy struggling with the language barrier to notice. It was a different story, however, when interacting with some of my fellow American exchange students.

From time to time during our stay, the local AFS staff arranged various activities for our group to get together and check in with one another on how we were handling our experience. One session included an afternoon trip to the beach.

"Let's have a tanning contest!" one of the white students yelled.

"I'm going to win!" shouted the darkest-skinned black girl in our group.

"And I'll never win!" said another student with porcelain white skin.

I don't remember what I was wearing, or if I even took off my shirt that day. But before the afternoon was over, someone saw my tan lines. My neck and arms were clearly a darker shade of bronze than my chest and shoulders, a startling color contrast between the patches of skin my clothes normally covered and the darker parts of me that had the benefit of sunlight.

A black girl in our group gasped. "Oh, my god!" she exclaimed. "You're white!"

The look of shock I saw on her face took me aback. It was as if she had just seen a ghost. Then she broke into a smile and gave me one of those I-know-something-nobody-else-knows kind of looks.

"Is that a perm in your hair or what?" she asked jokingly.

I nervously laughed off the entire episode, pretending to find her comments more humorous than I actually did. Literally, in a matter of seconds, her perception of me had changed. Suddenly, I'd gone from "light-skinned black guy" to "white guy with a tan" to what I suspect was a return to my "ethnically ambiguous" status.

As I got older, I learned it wasn't necessary to travel a few thousand miles away from home, cross an international border or two, and immerse myself in a new culture to feel the Chameleon Effect. Life in the United States is rich with opportunities.

While working as a reporter at WKMG-TV in Orlando, I found myself the subject of a news story on multiracial identity. It was the spring of 1997, and Tiger Woods had just won the Masters golf tournament for the first time. With his victory, the public debate over mixed-race people and what we ought to call ourselves soared to new levels. It was at that same time that Woods appeared on *The Oprah Winfrey Show* and told Winfrey that as a child, he had invented the term "Cablinasian" to describe himself, referring to his particular mixture of Caucasian, black, Indian, and Asian heritage.

Reporter Maria Padilla of the *Orlando Sentinel* got wind of both my background and my passion for the subject and gave me a call. It would be a rare opportunity to talk openly in such a public forum about being biracial.

"I'm too dark one minute, too light the next," I said in describing the varied reactions to my appearance. Up until then, I'd seldom tried to explain coming to terms with racial identity in a sound bite.

After our telephone interview, we made arrangements for one of the paper's photographers to pay a visit to the television station and snap some pictures to accompany the article. The *Sentinel's* Red Huber was waiting for me when I arrived at work on the day of our scheduled shoot. We had run into one another several times on the street while covering stories, and he was a familiar face to many other newsroom staffers as well. It didn't take long for my co-workers to wonder why he was following me around at work with his still camera.

"It's for a story the paper's doing on multiracial identity," I explained.

"Oh, and you're part Hispanic, right?" remarked one producer.

"Um . . . well . . . no."

"But you speak Spanish. I've heard you," she continued.

"Well . . . yeah . . . some."

I speak English, too, I wanted to say sarcastically, yet no one has ever mistaken me for being British.

I turned to Red, the newspaper photographer. "You see what we have to deal with?" I said to him.

My being mistaken for Latino is hardly unusual. It happens with increasing frequency the more my Spanish improves. As a result of my experience as an exchange student, I decided to continue studying the language when I returned to the United States and started college. Subsequent trips to Spain and Latin America have further enhanced my speaking skills. I'm still not fluent in the language, but my ability to read a Spanish newspaper or carry on even the most basic conversation in a foreign tongue tends to confuse anyone attempting to categorize me. One native Spanish speaker even told me that, based on my accent, he thought I was someone who'd been born and raised in the United States but learned Spanish from my parents to communicate with relatives still residing in Latin America, specifically Cuba. Go figure.

Picture day at the television station wasn't the only time I left my co-workers scratching their heads about my ethnic background. Election day provided another example of the Chameleon Effect at work.

I'd received my voter registration card in the mail months before and put it in a special place where I wouldn't lose it. But with election day fast approaching, I couldn't remember where that special place was. I had no clue what precinct I lived in or where I was supposed to vote. When I finally found the voter card, I scanned it, looking for the information I needed. There was a box for my name, address, precinct number, party affiliation, and, to my surprise, race. It read "W"—as in "white."

I just about fell over.

I took the voter registration card to work and passed it around the newsroom, first showing it to some of my black co-workers. Mouths dropped.

"Who wrote this on there?" asked one.

"The woman who registered me to vote," I answered.

"Was she blind?" As if to say that anyone with two good eyes should automatically know to classify me as black.

"And you didn't say anything?" questioned another.

"No one asked me," I explained. "I registered to vote when I got my new driver's license. I couldn't see what the woman was typing into the computer. The registration card just arrived in the mail one day."

"Well, are you going to get it changed to black?" asked someone else.

"I don't know."

Then I showed the card to another co-worker, who happens to be Jewish.

"See if you can find something there that looks a little out of place," I told her.

She stared at it for quite a while, her eyes scanning the paper. Finally, she gave up. "I'm not getting it," she said.

"See, right there," I said, pointing out the section indicating my race. "It's marked 'W' for white."

She glanced up at me, looked me in the eye, and said, in all seriousness, "So what's wrong with it?"

The Chameleon Effect was happening in my own newsroom. Again.

I mentioned the voter card incident to Bill Cowles, the Orange County elections supervisor whom I'd gotten to know during the course of my work covering local politics. When I told him what had happened, his mouth nearly dropped, too. First, he explained, the woman who registered me to vote had no business typing in my race without asking me, even if my race may have seemed obvious to her. That's against policy. Second, Cowles said, it was not necessary to answer the race question for the voter registration to be processed. So had I been given the opportunity, I could have chosen to leave it blank, which is exactly what I would have elected to do absent the opportunity to check multiple categories or identify as biracial.

I used to think that being viewed as white was extraordinarily rare. But I'm beginning to wonder how many times others have formed that impression of me without my knowing it—and what sort of advantages I might be enjoying as a result.

Such incidents stand in sharp contrast to those moments in my life when others have seen only my blackness and gone to great lengths to point it out, sometimes in a most offensive way. That's what happened as I was walking home from a shopping mall one afternoon, and a car full of white teenagers pulled up beside me. One of them stuck his head out the window.

"Hey, nigger!" he yelled at the top of his lungs.

As quickly as the words spewed from his mouth, the car sped up and drove away. An epithet out of nowhere. I could feel my blood starting to boil, and I imagined what I would have done to that carload of Caucasians had I been armed. It wasn't the first time the racial slur had been hurled in my direction, but never before had it come and gone in such a random fashion. All I could do was continue walking home with the N-word echoing in my head the whole way.

The Chameleon Effect works in strange ways, I keep telling myself. One day, the world sees me as black. The next day, I'm Hispanic. The day after that, I'm white. And then there are days when I'm a nigger walking down the street.

Madison Avenue might think I'm ethnically ambiguous. But to others, my race is perfectly clear. It is whatever they want it to be.

The Clorox Complex

SOMETIMES I FEEL LIKE SMACKING CERTAIN WHITE PEOPLE UPSIDE the head. And sometimes, life does it for me.

Like the white high school classmate who, upon learning my family was interracial, asked, "So which of your relatives are black, and which ones are normal?" I later learned that he went on to major in sociology in college.

Or the white people who don't think race is an issue in the United States anymore. Then they marry interracially, have children, and are shocked—*shocked*, mind you—to discover the extent to which racism still exists.

Or the white people who are just plain ignorant about light-skin versus dark-skin discrimination within black communities. "I never knew it was an issue," said a white co-worker after seeing the Spike Lee movie *School Daze* about life on a black college campus.

Where have these folks been?

I suspect Ashley Edelhart Hall knows where I'm coming from. She is the biracial daughter of a white man and a black woman who openly acknowledges her blended heritage. In fact, she made a point of asking that I include her maiden name—Edelhart—in honor of her father. Yet she considers herself black and says she cannot remember a time when she identified otherwise, despite her outward appearance.

She spoke with me over the phone from her home in Southern California. "I look like whoever I'm standing next to," said Ashley. "If I'm standing in a group of Italian girls, people will think I'm a white Italian. If I'm standing next to Latina girls, they'll think I'm Latina. If I'm standing next to Middle Eastern girls, they'll think I'm Middle Eastern. No one ever thinks I'm black, though. I have to be with New Orleans Creole girls for them to think that I'm black," she explained, providing further evidence that the Chameleon Effect isn't just something I made up.

"People would always say stupid stuff to me when they'd find out that I was black," she said. "I've had people say, 'Oh, but you're so beautiful. Why would you say that you're black? Just don't say anything.' And I'm thinking, do you even know how ignorant you sound saying something like that? You are talking to a black person."

Born in 1967, Ashley has a twin sister, Courtenay Edelhart, a newspaper reporter whom I met at a National Association of Black Journalists' convention in 2001. We had both attended a panel discussion on negotiating multiple identities expecting to hear from Rebecca Walker, author of *Black, White, and Jewish*. Walker, however, was called away on a family emergency at the last minute. On the final day of the convention, I spotted Courtenay in the hotel lobby and struck up a conversation. What started out as a casual chat about our multiracial experiences led to a series of discussions over the years, which eventually led me to contact Ashley.

The two sisters are fraternal, not identical, twins. Courtenay has a medium brown complexion and jet black curly hair. Ashley has a lighter complexion and straight brown hair that is not as thick as her sister's.

At a young age, Ashley began to notice both subtle and not-so-subtle differences in the way people interacted with her and Courtenay—including members of their own family. According to Ashley, there was a time when she was considered "the favored twin." She remembers her black grandmother telling Courtenay, "'Why can't you have hair like your sister? Why can't you be like your sister?' Always putting my sister down, always making her feel bad," Ashley recalled. "And me, out of protection for my sister, I wanted to kill this woman. I hated every person who made comments like that about my sister. I did not like people comparing us. How could that possibly make her feel for people to constantly say that?

"And I knew that what people were seeing was that I looked more white," she continued. "It wasn't that I was prettier, 'cause I'm not. It was that I looked more white. And that's what angered me. That's probably what set everything off. I knew that from early on—I look whiter, so everybody's more accepting of me. So what I did was I acted out so bad that my grandmother began to hate me because I was a behavior problem, and then my sister became the favored twin. And I was comfortable with that. I preferred that because my sister would be wounded by the comment, and I knew my skin was thicker. When the tide changed and the comments were being negative about me—and they're still not being negative about how I looked, now they were just negative about how I was acting—now I was hyper, I was too sassy, always needed to be spanked, that sort of thing. And I was OK with that. Just don't say anything bad about my sister."

The color consciousness within black communities that Ashley alludes to has been well documented. One book that tackles the subject is *The Color Complex*, written by three coauthors, Kathy Russell, Midge Wilson, and Ronald Hall. Two of the three, Wilson and Hall, were called to testify as expert witnesses in a lawsuit on intraracial color discrimination in the 1990s. The authors suggest that if white folks today aren't aware of such color discrimination, there may be a legitimate reason for it. Many blacks, they contend, do not want to discuss the issue in the company of whites, preferring not to air what they view as a "dirty little secret" in public.[1]

"The color complex may reveal itself in a variety of ways wherever blacks come together—in families, at work, in social situations," write the authors. "An uncensored comment may slip unexpectedly into a conversation, wreaking emotional havoc. An insensitive relative may criticize a black child for having a 'nappy head.' A black supervisor may create tension in the office by harping on a subordinate's lighter skin color, saying he or she has had it 'too easy.' The revelation of a hidden bias may even bring a promising relationship to an end."[2]

The tension, the authors note, dates all the way back to slavery, when lighter-skinned slaves received preferential treatment. Slave masters awarded less-demanding indoor assignments to light-skinned slaves while their darker-skinned counterparts handled the more physically taxing work in the fields. "As color increasingly divided the slave community, frictions developed in the cabins. Light-skinned slaves returning home from their days in the 'big house' imitated the genteel ways of upper-class white families," they write. "Many field hands both envied and resented the house servants. Yet working in daily close proximity to a white master had its own risks, especially if one was female. Rape was a fact of life on the plantations."[3] Which of course led to the births of more light-skinned slaves.

A social hierarchy based on skin tone became ingrained in subsequent generations of both blacks and whites. A well-known rhyme among black folks spells it out clearly: "If you're white, you're all right; if you're brown, stick around; if you're black, get back."

Lawrence Otis Graham, who explored his life growing up as a member of America's black upper class in his book *Our Kind of People*, writes, "This is not to say that affluent blacks want to be white, but it certainly suggests that they have seen the benefits accorded to lighter-skinned blacks with 'whiter features'—who are hired more often, given better jobs, and perceived as less threatening."[4] Graham himself admits to having a nose job after graduating from Harvard Law School, "so that I could further buy into the aesthetic biases that many among the black elite hold so dear."[5]

Yes, colorism among black people has sometimes gone to outlandish extremes. Historians have written of the "brown paper bag test," a ritual in which those whose skin was darker than a brown paper bag were denied admission to various black social institutions, including churches. In some places of worship, a comb was hung on a rope near the entrance. Supposedly, if someone's hair got stuck in the comb, they were turned away, while those whose fine hair could pass through the comb were admitted.[6]

But no matter how widespread such colorism may have been within the black community as a whole, I never got the impression growing up that such color conflicts existed within my own family. After all, my parents were Bahá'í who embraced their faith's teachings about the oneness of humanity. Besides, racial mixing had been going on for who knows how many generations before them. It was all water under the bridge. Surely, I thought, none of that color superiority crap was part of our recent history.

But my impression was wrong.

Soon after my mother's father passed away, at the age of ninety-three, I got a glimpse into his courtship of my light-skinned, mixed-race grandmother, the one I thought was white throughout most of my childhood. Grandma Dent died in 1986. Grandpa Dent was buried next to her in the fall of 2000 in the side-by-side plots he had picked out in the hillside cemetery not far from their home in western Pennsylvania.

"He once said he married your grandma to improve the Negro race," several of my aunts told me.

"Huh?" It was the first time I'd heard the story.

"Oh, yeah," they said. "He used to say that he didn't want to have any 'black beetles' running around." They described a man who was filled with self-hate about being black in general and about the dark shade of his skin in particular. So much so that he made a conscious effort to marry a light-skinned woman.

If any of his ten children bought into his particular methodology for "improving the Negro race," there are no obvious signs of it. Nine of the ten married brown-skinned partners, most of them darker in complexion than they were. The exception was my mother, whose light-skinned husband—my father—was a virtual match to her skin tone. Her second husband, a former high school sweetheart, is brown-skinned.

The more Ashley revealed about her own family history, the more it appeared that both her black mother and black grandmother were carrying much of the same psychological baggage that my grandfather had when it came to race and skin color.

"She was just really wounded by her experience," Ashley said of her mother, who grew up in Arkansas before the dawn of the civil rights movement. "I think she married white to 'cleanse' herself of that flaw that she internalized. She internalized her blackness as a flaw. Part of that was because my grandparents are more caramel-complexioned, and she came out dark. My grandmother was horrified because she thought she would have a light child. Her husband was light and she was light. She treated my mother horribly about her color. So my mom internalized that it was a negative thing to be brown and made sure by marrying white that her children would not be. And I think it was her dream and desire to just cleanse the bloodline of that black blood. Just cleanse it out. And that would have done it. If my sister and I had gone with white husbands, that would be it. The kids would only be a quarter black."

"Your mom specifically wanted you to marry a white man?" I asked.

"Absolutely," she said, without missing a beat. "She thought for sure I could pull a white husband."

"And this was communicated to you?"

"Oh, yeah," she answered, again without hesitation.

Ashley went on to describe how her mother would react after meeting any dark-skinned young men she and her sister were dating. "[With] a few of them, she would even say, 'He looks like a monkey. I don't want to have ugly monkey grandchildren running behind me at the store. You better not have children with him.' She would actually say that. The blacker you looked, the more African your features, the more disturbed she was."

As chilling as such comments are, there is another side to the color consciousness that exists within black circles that both whites and blacks too often fail to recognize, which in turn makes me want to smack certain black people upside the head. The notion that such colorism negatively impacts only darker-skinned African-Americans is false. In fact, the issue cuts both ways.

"While many Blacks can sympathize with those who are 'too' dark-skinned, few are willing to acknowledge the pain of those who are very light-skinned," write the authors of *The Color Complex*.[7] "Traditionally, the color complex involved light-skinned Blacks' rejection of Blacks who were darker. Increasingly, however, the color complex shows up in the form of dark-skinned African Americans spurning their lighter-skinned brothers and sisters for not being Black enough."[8]

Ashley has experience with that latter form of discrimination, too. While in college at the University of Nevada, Las Vegas in the late 1980s, a group of black students made up a rap song about her. She never heard the lyrics firsthand, but says her white roommate at the time did. "It was something about me being very snobby, thinking I'm all that, thinking I'm cute 'cause I had long hair," Ashley said. "I made it a point to prove that I wasn't, quote, 'whitewashed,' and they didn't have to be concerned with that. But a lot of them just wanted to party and I wasn't interested in that. I really wanted to know if I could make it in college. I was there to prove something to myself." As a result, she spent more of her free time in her dorm room, convinced she needed to hit the books.

Another part of the problem, she explains, was that she was one of the few students on campus who had a car—albeit a 1969 Volkswagen Bug—which she refused to let anyone else drive. "Do I have 'stupid' written on my head?" Ashley said, recalling an encounter with her college classmates. "No, you're not going to borrow my car. I'll take you, but you're not going to take my car," she told them. "One girl in particular, that just pissed her off. Now, all of a sudden I'm not black, all of a sudden I'm not down for the cause, all of a sudden everything's all flip-flopped."

The taunting ultimately reached a point where Ashley and her roommate decided to move out of the university residence hall and into an apartment. Later, she left UNLV altogether and ultimately completed her degree at California State University, Northridge.

She also refused to listen to her mother when it came to choosing a husband. She is now married "to a nice chocolate man," she says, and works as an occupational therapist. They live in the Los Angeles area and have two daughters, both brown-skinned, who were ages two and eleven at the time we spoke.

As for her mother's color preferences, "she's getting over it now,"

Ashley said. But there have still been instances when it's become an issue, such as when Ashley would sit her older daughter down to do her hair in her mother's presence. "She would say, 'Oh, you got that nappy hair, and I feel sorry for you, and I used to have to sit like that.' She would say it like that, like she's trying to identify with her, but it was always in a negative way. And I had to tell her, you're not allowed to comment on her hair like that. I'm not raising her to think that it's bad hair. I'm raising her to think that it's a beautiful thing."

While maintaining a black identity for herself, Ashley also wants her daughters to appreciate their multiracial background, something she says she's having difficulty communicating to them now that her father has died. "My father looked and sounded like Orson Welles. You know, 'We will sell no wine before its time.' He talked in those kinds of phrases. For me, he always talked over my head 'cause he was kind of a brainiac," she said. With her father gone, the relatives her daughters have the most contact with are black.

"In the public school system, they're teaching about the civil rights movement, and I've got my daughter in the backseat saying, 'I hate white people because they wanted black people to be slaves.' Really painful for me to hear her saying that. And I understand why she's saying that, because of what she's learning in school. But if she had the family members and the kind of upbringing and saw the role model that I had with my father who did not see race in people"—she stopped in midsentence and recalled the values her father instilled in her—"if she knew him, she would never say that," Ashley continued. "He really took people for who they were. He really judged you by your character, honestly."

She added, "I miss him so much because my daughter now can't relate to the fact that she's a quarter white. I make it a point to let her know, you're a quarter white. You are in no position to hate white people, because you are one-fourth white."

As for Ashley's own sense of her rightful place in the world, she admits it took time for that to crystallize. "When I was younger, I would have always been working to fit in with certain groups. I would spot certain people out and need to make friends with that girl over there because she's the black one, or the cool girl, or whatever, and I just don't need those things," she said.

"I feel black, I identify with black causes, I vote politically in accordance with what would be good for the black community, but I'm no longer interested in proving that I'm black. I no longer need that. I feel the same inside. It's all about the energy I'm willing to commit for other people. To me, that's what changes," she explained. "My friends are my friends since college and it has nothing to do with race. The young ladies I work with, they're just all different colors and races and religions, and it just doesn't matter. It doesn't matter to them, and it doesn't matter to me. In my opinion, it's a more grown-up way of being alive."

Two of a Kind

ARCHIE EDELHART WAS DYING. HIS TRANSPLANTED HEART—THE second one he had received—was failing. He knew it. And so did his twin daughters, Courtenay and Ashley. As his health deteriorated, he made what family members describe as a deathbed request: find Dave Edelhart—the son he had fathered with his first wife, who is white.

At the time their father made his request, twenty-five years had passed since his first marriage ended in divorce. Armed with the address her father last had for his ex-wife, Courtenay, an experienced newspaper reporter, tracked down a telephone number and called the home. Her father's former wife had since moved, the new homeowner told her, and was living in Portland, Oregon. She called directory assistance and dialed the number the operator gave her. A young male voice answered the phone. Her half-brother, it turned out, was living with his mother at the time.

"I said, 'Is this David?' He said, 'Yes.' And I just hung up," said Courtenay, not knowing what to say after locating him so quickly. She called back, this time with her dad on the line.

"He said, 'I'm Archie Edelhart, your father.' There was a pause, and then Dave said, 'Hi, Dad.' He was fine with it," said Courtenay. "It was like, 'Hi, guess what? You have a couple of black sisters, and your father would like to meet you.' He actually took it pretty well."

"It was a bit of a shocker," Dave told me, recalling that moment from his current home in Palo Alto, California. "It's almost as much of a shock to me that I knew what the hell was going on," he laughed. "It was like instant family. I had no idea that they existed until they reached out to me."

Archie Edelhart's estrangement from his son had been triggered by his 1960s-era divorce settlement. Courtenay and Ashley were born before their dad's divorce from his first wife became final. In fact, the twin sisters are only a few months younger than Dave. The divorce decree, which Courtenay has kept a copy of, reads, "The defendant shall have the right of reasonable visitation with the minor child of the parties, but the defendant is hereby prohibited from taking the said child into the presence of any other spouse or offspring of the defendant."

That last phrase was the operative one. Archie Edelhart could visit his son as long as he didn't bring the boy into the presence of his soon-to-be second wife and his new twin daughters.

"It was the only way she would grant him a divorce," Courtenay explained. "It was Chicago in 1967, and you don't leave a white woman for a black woman in 1967." Her father chose to stand by his new family. "He told her, 'Look, I'll pay child support. But I'm not going to see my son as long as this prohibition exists, because I'm not going to lie about having a black wife and black children. I'm not willing to do that. I think it's immoral.' And she said, 'Fine, you'll never see your son.' I think from Dave's point of view, her defense was, it wasn't a race thing. It was more of an 'other woman' thing. She was just angry. Basically, Dave wasn't ever to know that my father had a second wife who was African American. And he didn't," she said.

Understandably, Dave's perspective on what transpired is somewhat different. "My dad walked completely away. So we didn't really have a line on what was going on," he said. "When you have a dad that's taken off from day one, you have no real relationship with your father other than speculation and conjecture and fantasy."

"To find out about the racial aspect, what was that like?" I asked him.

"I grew up on Indian reservations and [in] mixed neighborhoods. I've never had any huge issues in race," he said, explaining that for two years in the mid-1970s, he and his mother lived on the Warm Springs Indian Reservation in central Oregon, where she had taken a job.

"You seem pretty cool with it," I told him, referring to the discovery of his biracial siblings.

"Yeah. I really admire my sisters," he added. "I feel bad that I haven't had as much time to spend with them as I could have."

But most importantly, Dave did get to spend time with his father. Though they only met in person twice, Archie Edelhart's deathbed wish was fulfilled. "I met him briefly over a Christmas and once when he was in the nursing home. And that was pretty much it," Dave said. His father died in 1993.

By that time, Courtenay's identity as a biracial woman had gone through a number of stages. In separate interviews, both Courtenay and her sister at first indicated that they hold identical views on racial issues. But in my extended conversations with them, it became apparent the two have notable differences.

Said Courtenay, "Up until adolescence, I thought of myself as white. In my teenage years and twenties, I thought of myself as black. And as thirtysomething and on, I thought of myself as biracial."

Ashley, on the other hand, says she has always considered herself black. That was the case as early as age seven, whereas Courtenay at that time had a very different impression of her identity. One childhood encounter in a public park looms especially large in illustrating how their views split. Both women remember it vividly.

"My father was a social worker, and I think he had something he had to do, pick up some paperwork somewhere in some office building. There was a park next door, and rather than have us sitting in the lobby bored, he just let us play in the park while he ran upstairs to get whatever it was and come back down. We were playing on the playground and these white kids start running up and shouting, 'Nigger, nigger, get out, nigger, get out, nigger!' It was the first time I had been called a nigger," Courtenay said. "I had obviously heard the word, and I knew what it meant. But it was the first time it had been directed at me. I remember smiling to myself and thinking, oh, they don't know. And I said that out loud to my sister, 'They don't know.' And she's like, 'What are you talking about?' 'Well, they don't know Daddy is white.' She gave me this look like, you stupid idiot, and she said, 'It doesn't matter.' I was like, 'What do you mean it doesn't matter?' She said, 'It doesn't matter. They still think we're niggers.'"

"Oh, I was so mad at her," said Ashley, who still gets agitated recalling the incident and her sister's reaction more than thirty years later. "She's just, 'Oh, we're really not niggers.' What do you mean we're not niggers? As if somebody *is* a nigger? What are you saying when you say that? You cannot separate yourself from what they hate."

"I just didn't get it. I really, truly didn't get it," said Courtenay, picking up the story. "I remember thinking at the time, this doesn't apply to me. Why are they calling me that? They're confused. These poor misguided people, they've got it wrong. They can't call me a nigger."

"I was really upset with her," Ashley reiterated. "I think that's probably the single most important thing that defines my identity is knowing that it isn't about what you look like. It's about another group's ability to hate you. I just never was confused about that. And I think it was because I knew I didn't look black, but people still hated me. So why was that? It's not about how I look. It's about who I am."

Ashley had the urge to give the white children a taste of their own medicine. But even at that age, she was also worried about how her white father might interpret what she was about to do.

"I didn't want to hurt my father's feelings . . . but I really wanted to wound these boys. So I had to ask my father's permission if I could yell a racial slur back," she said. "He giggled. I didn't know it at the time, but he liked that I was feisty. He said absolutely, by all means. So as we were walking to the car—my father thought it would be best if we just left—I turned and I yelled back, 'Honkies!' My father just laughed, and they yelled back, 'Niggers!' And I said, 'Honkies!' It was just a yell-off until we got away."

Even in the aftermath of that incident, Courtenay's interpretation of her own racial identity remained largely the same. "I think I was just in denial," she said. "I wasn't a biracial child who could pass. I clearly was a child of some kind of color." But at seven years old, unlike her sister, Courtenay still did not see herself as black.

At the time, the family was living in Chicago Heights, Illinois, in a racially integrated neighborhood. Yet it wasn't until they moved to Albuquerque, New Mexico, when the twins entered sixth grade that Courtenay adopted a black identity, or, as she put it, "I started to refer to the black community as 'we' instead of 'they.' When I would talk about black people before, I would say, 'Well, they have this, or they do that.' Because I just really didn't think of myself as black."

"Did you identify as white as more of a cultural thing?" I asked her. "I was listening to black music. But my social circle was primarily white kids," she said. "It's not that I had no black friends. I had a few. But the black friends I had were people who lived on my street. They couldn't make all the assumptions about, 'Oh, she's lighter, she thinks she's better than me.' They knew my parents, they knew my sister, they knew me. And they'd get to know me and say, 'You know, she really isn't stuck up.' I tokenized my black neighbors, who I liked. But I thought that for the most part, the black community in general was full of bullies who wanted to come beat me up and cut my hair off.

"So my friends were white because they didn't want to beat me up. They didn't really recognize any degrees of blackness. If you were black, you were black. And if you were the kind of person who cared about that, then you didn't associate with me. But if you *didn't* care about that, then you didn't pay much attention to the fact that I was light. I mean, it just wasn't something white people thought about."

In contrast, Ashley—who has the lighter complexion of the two—says most of her close friends during those elementary school years were black. "I think sometimes it's the activities and the games that you are attracted to," Ashley explained. "If you're attracted to the dancing and the double Dutch and all the things the black girls do, your identity kind of gets a little wrapped up into that." As Ashley remembers it, Courtenay, the future journalist, preferred the arts, writing poetry, and reading books. "I was the athletic twin; she was the smart twin," Ashley added.

But the roles shifted with the family's move to the Southwest during their middle school years. "There were so few black people in Albuquerque that you really don't have the luxury of saying, 'Well, I'm not going to talk to this one.' There were just not enough of us," said Courtenay. "The black girls in Albuquerque—after they got through a few petty encounters where they were calling me names and rolling their eyes—eventually kind of came around and wanted to be my friend. So I had black people reaching out to me, going out of their way to get to know me, for the first time in my life. Being the new kid in town, and not knowing anybody, I was really grateful for anybody who wanted to be my friend. So very quickly, everyone I knew became black. It was just the total reverse of Chicago, ironically, of all places. In Albuquerque, for the first time, most of my social circle was people who were African American, and I pretty much stuck with that until college."

Courtenay's college years would serve as another turning point in the evolution of her identity, on a number of levels. After graduating from high school in 1985, she returned to the Chicago area to attend Northwestern University.

"I ran into a group of black people who were really, really anti-Semitic," she said. That didn't sit well with Courtenay, because her dad was Jewish. Well, sort of.

Under Jewish law, a child's mother must be Jewish for the child to be Jewish. Archie Edelhart's father was Jewish. His mother was not. Although he later converted to Judaism, according to Courtenay, he did so largely to appease his first wife, who was Jewish.

"He embraced the culture, but not the religion," said Courtenay. "In fact, he was kind of an atheist." But in much the same way that something about the Bahá'í faith seemed to rub off on me, something about Courtenay's Jewish heritage seemed to awaken in her. Like her father, she did not have a Jewish mother and as such was not considered Jewish. Not yet, that is.

"While I wasn't a practicing Jew, I had at least been raised with an awareness that I had Jewish ancestors and was taught that that was nothing to be ashamed of. So when I was hearing these horrific anti-Semitic comments from many, many black students at Northwestern, that really made me angry. And I started to question my identity again. Because if this is what it means to be black, then I don't really want anything to do with that. That's when I started thinking of myself as biracial.

"So that's what ironically sparked my whole exploration into Judaism," she continued, "because I felt like these people are saying these terrible things about Jews and I'm not really in a position to defend myself. I didn't go to Hebrew school or synagogue, so I didn't know anything about Jewish thought or theology or the religion or the institutions. Anybody can tell me anything, and I'm not in a position to say, 'No, that's not true.' And I thought, that's not acceptable to either one of my cultures, because I don't ever want anybody to know more about who I am than I do."

Already a journalism major, Courtenay added a second major in African-American studies and says she would have added Jewish studies as well had it been a major offering. She enrolled in several of the Jewish studies courses the university had available and found herself attracted to the religion.

"It felt very familiar and very comfortable," she said. "I thought, well, since I'm already acting like a Jew and didn't know it, I might as well be a Jew. So then I formally converted."

"What all is involved in converting to Judaism?" I asked.

"There is a period of study which, depending on which movement you convert under, is various lengths of time. I'm a Reform Jew," Courtenay explained. "You take a written test and an oral test, and then, it's the Jewish equivalent of being baptized. You go into what's called a *mikveh*, which is a ritual bath. Under Jewish law, it has to have so many drops of water from a natural body of water. You say some prayers and you basically dunk three times. Then you come up, and you're a Jew. And you have to do this naked, by the way, because you're reborn. So you're spiritually coming out of a spiritual womb in the same state that you would be if you're coming out of a birth canal. That's the rationale."

As for Courtenay's self-concept today, all her identities—black, biracial, and Jewish—act in concert with one another. "At this point in my life, I think of myself as a religious Jew but not a cultural Jew. I don't use Yiddish words, I don't eat bagels, I don't do all the stereotypical things that you think of Jews doing, you know, talk with my hands, that sort of thing."

"Sort of the opposite of your father?" I interjected.

"Exactly," she said. "I think of myself as a black woman who happens to be Jewish," as opposed to the other way around. "Being African American is my foundation, and it's the launching point for everything else. So I primarily see myself as a black woman, and that's never going to change. If I suddenly decide I don't want to be a Jew anymore, I'm still going to be a black woman. And I'm going to have to deal with all the obstacles that are thrown in the path of black women and have been for centuries. But Judaism is something that I took on voluntarily and that I can withdraw from at any time. At this point in my life, I wouldn't. But it's an option."

Yet when faced with the "What are you?" question, Courtenay says her answer varies. It often depends on the race of the questioner. "If anybody asks who is white, I tell them I'm black, because that's all they really want to know," she said. "They see this brownish skin and this hair that's sort of curly and they're thinking, 'You look black,' and I'll just answer the question, 'Yes, I'm black. I have black in me.' That's all they want to know.

"When a black person asks me, 'What are you?' they usually know I'm black. I can count on one hand the number of black people I've met in my life who didn't immediately know I was black. But they see that I'm kind of light-skinned, my hair is sort of straight as black people's hair goes and it's kind of long, and they're trying to figure out what else is in there. And to them, I say I'm bira-cial. That's also sort of a self-preservation thing, because I want them to know right off the bat, 'Look, there's something else in me, so before you go on the whole tirade about Jews trying to take over the world, you need to know this.'"

The issue has come up whenever someone unaware of her family background visits her home and sees the family photos dotting her living room. It seems the Chameleon Effect doesn't apply only to multiracial people; the principle also influences perceptions of our monoracial relatives.

"I have lots of family pictures of my father. And because he was a Jew, he was kind of swarthy," said Courtenay. "I wouldn't call him dark by any stretch of the imagination. But as white people go, he was sort of olive-skinned and had black hair. And I am shocked at the number of people who just assume he's a light-skinned black man. It's not because he looks black, because he doesn't. It's just people's consciousness is so permeated with the idea that everybody has to be uniform that they kind of negate what they're actually seeing and just make that assumption. It's happened so many times with so many people, it just fascinates me. Because my father outside that context is not someone anyone would ever mistake for African American."

In fact, as Courtenay and Ashley were growing up, many people assumed Archie Edelhart wasn't related to his wife and children at all. When the whole family went out to dinner, restaurant hostesses would often ask, "Table for three?"

"My mom would always have to correct them, 'No, table for four,'" said Courtenay. "Obviously, my sister and I went with my mom, but they didn't ever put my father together. It was like, 'Oh,' like they saw my father for the first time. He was kind of blending in with all the white people behind us. Hostesses just never think to put us all together."

"I take it this happened more than once?" I asked.

"Yes!" she said emphatically.

Which is why the racial identity that Courtenay now claims publicly fluctuates based on the situation and on which side of her heritage is most in need of affirmation at any given moment.

"There are some politics to race, and I acknowledge that," she said. "That's why it's so important that we be able to choose. We, as a community, need to be able to say, 'This is what works for me. This is what I'm comfortable with.' I have chosen to identify mostly as black. But there are times when I identify as biracial, and I want the right to do that. And damn anybody who tells me that I can't."

Barbershop in the Hood

"HOW DO YOU TELL A CHILD WITH BLOND HAIR THAT HE'S BLACK?" my mother asked rhetorically.

It was one of our rare conversations about our family and race. We were flipping through the pages of the family photo album and came across some old baby pictures of me. Sure enough, there I was with blond hair.

"But here, my hair looks red," I said, pointing to another photograph taken when I was an infant.

"Well, your hair sort of changed colors over time," my mother responded.

Gee, kind of like my racial identity.

In photograph after photograph, my multiracial heritage leaped out at me. There were pictures of relatives with dark brown skin, followed by pictures of relatives with pale white skin, followed by pictures of relatives with skin of various hues in between.

As it turned out, my parents never did have to tell their blond-haired child he was black. I stopped growing blond hair sometime in elementary school. As an adult, I now see places on my head where no hair grows at all. In the many years between recess and Rogaine, my hair grew darker, slowly evolving toward the deep brown color it is today.

For many African-Americans, hair is a touchy subject. Not because of color, but because of texture. I happened to have issues with both, and I could have used an explanation as to why my hair was neither straight like my white playmates' nor as dark as my other relatives'.

Growing up, my hair was usually cut by my mother. The first professional barbers to cut my hair were white, and quite frankly they didn't always know what they were doing. By the time I actually set foot into a traditional all-black barbershop, I was in my early twenties and had just accepted a reporting position at KGTV in San Diego, California, in the station's minority training program for young journalists.

From the moment I walked into the barbershop, the aroma overwhelmed me. Not the smell of shampoo, or that grotesque odor of a perm in progress. It was the stench of cigarette smoke that greeted me at the door. I'd just walked in to a Barbershop in the Hood, complete with a rendering of an old-fashioned red-and-white-striped barber pole on the sign out front.

If churches represent the cornerstone of social and political life in African-American communities, then I'd say an old-school barbershop ranks a close second. This is not just a place to get a haircut. For black men, especially those old enough to have lived through the civil rights protests of the 1960s, this is a place to hang out, read the newspaper, discuss the problems of the world, and, at this particular shop, smoke. The antismoking fervor that would later clear California workplaces of tobacco had not yet taken root, and nearly every other customer in need of a haircut that day had a cigarette in one hand.

The bars on the shop's windows reminded me that I was in a part of town that's not considered safe after dark. But it was a Saturday morning, and a long line of customers had already started to form. They were seated against the wall, opposite the four barber chairs, where stylists were busy clipping, trimming, and combing. In a back corner, the shop's lone female hairdresser was about to give a young man a shampoo to wash away a gooey mess of chemicals used to straighten his hair.

"Take a number," shouted one of the barbers, pointing to a spot on the wall. I glanced over and saw a stack of small, square pieces of paper hanging by a nail, each with a handwritten number on it. I grabbed the one on top and took a seat to wait my turn. Barbershops in the Hood don't take appointments.

I didn't feel entirely comfortable in that place. With no white people in the neighborhood, let alone in that particular establishment, I was clearly the lightest-skinned person around. Call it insecurity, but I got the feeling some of the people there were looking at me, saying to themselves, "Who is this light-skinned brother? Can't be from around here." But I trusted these barbers with my hair more than I'd ever trusted a white hairstylist in a trendy, upscale salon, in that foreign land of precision cuts and Vidal Sassoon in the more "fashionable" parts of town.

Hair can be a big deal to television newspeople and their bosses. Especially high-profile anchors. But street reporters receive their share of grooming advice, too. I learned this very early in my career.

"You'll need to get that wool sheared," the news director at my previous station, KTVN in Reno, told me rather bluntly just minutes after he'd hired me. I was still in college at the time, having stayed in Pullman after high school to enroll in Washington State University. But I had completed an eight-week internship at the station the previous summer, and the news director had apparently seen enough of my work to think I was ready for full-time employment.

I'd actually had a pretty good head start on a career in broadcast journalism. At age thirteen, I became a volunteer at KWSU-AM, the local public radio station on the Washington State University campus. The station served as a training ground for communications majors, and even though I wasn't in college yet, I was able to learn basic radio production skills right along with the older students. By the time I started college, I was on the radio station's payroll, working there part-time. Television, however, was still new to me, and so were its hair, makeup, and wardrobe requirements.

Before moving to Nevada to start my new job, I had my "wool sheared" by the one white barber in Pullman who had gained my confidence over the years. But I knew I'd have to keep my hair shorter than I was used to in college. After a few weeks on the air, it was time for a trim.

On the recommendation of some of my co-workers in the newsroom, I made an appointment with a white hairdresser in one of those trendy-looking salons I now tend to avoid. He was the husband of a reporter I worked with and cut a number of station employees' hair. But of course, no one at KTVN had the kind of hair I have.

The first time I sat in his chair, he started by picking out my hair, then attempted to trim it using a comb and scissors. He seemed nervous.

"Ouch!" he gasped. He had just nicked the side of his finger with the scissors. A small drop of blood began to ooze out of the tiny wound. He put the comb and scissors down and reached for a Band-Aid.

"So how do they usually cut your hair?" he asked.

Right then, I knew I was in trouble.

"Most of the time, they use those," I said, pointing to the electric clippers I saw hanging up on the wall, its electrical cord draped over a nail.

"Oh, well maybe I should try them," he said, as if he was about to embark on a bold new adventure.

Yikes. I began to wonder what in the world I was going to look like by the time he was finished. I had to go to work that afternoon and appear on the air that night sporting whatever haircut he gave me.

He made a few passes with the clippers. "Hey, this works pretty good!" he said, like he'd just discovered afro sheen or something.

The haircut took an hour. It was the longest haircut appointment I'd ever had.

"You know, I wish I'd had more training in how to cut black hair," he said while brushing off the hairs from my shoulders.

Oh, now you tell me.

OK, so it wasn't the best haircut I've ever had. But it wasn't an entirely bad haircut, either.

I thought about all this as I sat there in San Diego and waited my turn at the Barbershop in the Hood.

"Next!" one of the four haircutters shouted.

My number was up. I climbed into his chair.

He was a big, burly man, well over 250 pounds, with a mustache and goatee. He appeared to be in his early to mid-fifties, making him the oldest of the four barbers working in the shop that day.

"How much you want off?"

"About half," I told him.

"Line around the front?" he asked.

"Huh?" I said, pretending I hadn't heard him. In reality, I didn't know what he meant.

"Do you want a line with the razor around the front?"

"Oh. Yeah, OK, that'd be fine," I said.

He went to work, gracefully handling a pick in one hand and the electric clippers in the other, confident in his craft. Now this is a guy who knows what he's doing, I said to myself.

The remaining customers continued to puff away on their cigarettes as they read the newspaper or flipped through the latest issues of *Ebony* and *Jet* magazines. But at last, I felt I could relax.

As my barber was finishing up, one of the other stylists came around with a broom and began cleaning up all of the hair that had fallen from customers' heads. He swept it up into a small round pile a few feet in front of me. I looked down at the mound of hair and instantly felt my uneasiness return. There, in a sea of jet black hair, I saw a patch of brown. I could tell right away the brown hair was mine. It was similar in texture to all of the other hair on the ground, but the color was clearly different. Does everybody else see what I see? I wondered. It made me uncomfortable.

As strange as it may sound, that pile of hair reflected something about my life, about what it means to be biracial in a black and white world. Seeing my brown locks surrounded by the black hair of the shop's other customers became a metaphor that struck at the core of my experience as a mixed-race person. For the most part, I manage to fit in with black people. Put me in a room full of strangers, and I'll gravitate toward the other black folks who are there faster than I'll strike up a conversation with a group of white people I don't know. And when it's time for a haircut, I know I belong in a barbershop for people with hair like mine. But at the same time, I don't like the feeling that I always stand out in such situations, too. I blend in, but not all the way. Just like that clump of hair on the floor.

Up until that moment, I hadn't really thought of my hair in social or psychological terms. But hair wars are certainly nothing new in black America. At a panel discussion I attended on negotiating multiracial identities in the mid-1990s, one black woman in the audience sought to trivialize the issues facing multiracial people. "This is all just about good hair versus bad hair," she declared. ("Good" hair is a term that has been used to refer to hair that is long, silky, and straight, whereas "bad" hair refers to hair whose texture is more coarse.)

"The politics of hair parallels the politics of skin color," write the authors of *The Color Complex*. "Among Black women, straight hair and European hairstyles not only have been considered more feminine but have sent a message about one's standing in the social hierarchy." The 1960s, the authors note, marked a revolution in attitudes about hair for both black men and women when both sexes felt free to let their hair grow into large afros.[1]

While those days have since passed, "hair remains a politically charged subject," contend Russell, Wilson and Hall. "To some, how an African American chooses to style his or her hair says everything there is to be said about that individual's Black consciousness, socioeconomic class, and probable lifestyle."[2]

Along that line, I often joke that the "comb-over" is one more example of white male privilege. We've all seen those balding white men who try to cover their hair loss by growing out the hair they have left and swishing it over to the other side, or wrapping it all around the head. The technique, I assure you, is only available to men with a particular type of hair and does not work across all ethnic groups. Then again, some would argue it doesn't really work for the white men who try it, either.

In my case, the more hair I lose, the shorter I keep it trimmed. I'm told it looks better that way. But the shorter it is, the more likely people are to look at me and conclude that I am white. It has happened with increasing frequency as my hairline has receded. With a big, full-blown Afro, my hair served as a racial or cultural marker, signaling to the rest of America how I should be classified in our society. Without a prominent "fro" to boldly announce my ethnicity, the racial labeling process becomes more fluid and more subject to varied interpretations.

I still have enough hair to require the services of a barber at least twice a month. I thought I'd found the barbershop of the rainbow generation soon after I moved to Washington, D.C., in 1999. The hair salon was in northwest Washington, a ten-minute walk from the White House. Most of the stylists were white, but two black barbers also had chairs there. An Asian man had a space in another section of the salon for manicures and pedicures.

The place was a little more upscale than I would have liked. And that awful salon smell can overwhelm me if I happen to be getting a haircut at a busy time. But I didn't have to take a number. They take appointments, and a receptionist is there to greet you when you walk in the door.

The shop owner's daughter works at the reception counter part-time. She's hard to peg when it comes to her ethnic identity. She has olive skin and straight, shoulder-length black hair. She speaks English, French, Hebrew, and Spanish. She's a single, multilingual, multicultural, international kind of woman. I struck up a conversation with her in Spanish one day, which drew the attention of her mother, who was between haircutting appointments.

"Eres de Espana?" (Are you from Spain?) the shop owner asked.

"No, Mom, he's American," said her daughter.

"De donde eres?" (Where are you from?) the mother wanted to know.

"Mom, please!" her daughter pleaded. She was clearly looking to put a stop to this ethnic inquisition, perhaps having grown tired of facing the same type of questioning herself. Finally, she'd heard enough.

"Mom, he's from here!" she declared firmly.

No further explanation necessary.

PART 3

THE BACKDROP OF HISTORY

The One-Drop Suggestion

IT IS KNOWN AS THE "ONE-DROP RULE." THOUGH IN THIS DAY AND age, I prefer to think of it as the "one-drop suggestion." But I'm getting ahead of myself.

Throughout American history, determining who is black in the United States has not been as simple as many of us have been led to believe. Africans, Europeans, and Native Americans have been interbreeding, if you will, on the North American continent for centuries, dating back to the 1600s when the first slave ships docked on its shores. Our society, historians like to remind us, has had to deal with mixed-race people in one way or another for quite some time.

So by what criteria, then, is someone black? Is "one drop of black blood" enough? Or does it have more to do with a person's "phenotype," academic lingo for the visible characteristics that point to a person's heritage or genetic makeup? What if different people interpret those visual signs differently? Who makes up these rules, anyway?

Many Americans seem to be under the impression that these are easy questions and that the answers have remained constant over time. They are mistaken.

No legal definition of blackness exists in the U.S. Constitution, and the U.S. Supreme Court has never ruled definitively on what constitutes a black person. The question arose in the Supreme Court's landmark case of *Plessy v. Ferguson* in 1896, some thirty years after the abolition of slavery. A mixed-race man by the name of Homer Plessy had purchased a first-class ticket on the East Louisiana Railroad for travel from New Orleans to Covington, Louisiana. He had done so, it turns out, under the auspices of a group called the Citizens' Committee of African Americans and Creoles, which wanted to test the constitutionality of a state law requiring segregated seating in passenger trains. Plessy boarded the train and proceeded to sit in a railcar reserved for white passengers. The conductor ordered him to move to a coach for colored passengers, and he refused. Plessy was then kicked off the train, arrested by police, and imprisoned. He appealed, claiming his constitutional rights had been violated. The district criminal court judge, John Ferguson, was named as the defendant.[1]

According to legal records, Plessy was actually seven-eighths white and only one-eighth black. In other words, one out of Plessy's eight great-grandparents was black; the rest were white. But as the Court noted, "Plessy declined and refused, either by pleading or otherwise, to admit that he was in any sense or in any proportion a colored man." He maintained "that the mixture of colored blood was not discernible in him; and that he was entitled to every right, privilege, and immunity secured to citizens of the United States of the white race."[2]

The Supreme Court of the United States disagreed. The Louisiana law requiring blacks and whites to travel in separate rail cars was upheld, and the principle of "separate but equal" public accommodations would not be struck down for another fifty-eight years. In its ruling on the Plessy case, the Court also took what legal scholars call "judicial notice" of the widely held belief that partial black ancestry renders a person black.

"The power to assign to a particular coach obviously implies the power to determine to which race the passenger belongs, as well as the power to determine who, under the laws of the particular state, is to be deemed a white, and who a colored, person," wrote Justice Henry Brown for the majority. "It is true that the question of the proportion of colored blood necessary to constitute a colored person, as distinguished from a white person, is one upon which there is a difference of opinion in the different states; some holding that any visible admixture of black blood stamps the person as belonging to the colored race; others, that it depends upon the pre-ponderance of blood; and still others, that the predominance of white blood must only be in the proportion of three-fourths. But these are questions to be determined under the laws of each state, and are not properly put in issue in this case."[3]

Leaving the states to decide who is black produced a system of racial classification in America that is downright dizzying. Professor F. James Davis has traced the evolution of state laws that once gov-erned a person's blackness. By his count, seven states defined a black person as someone with at least one-eighth black ancestry. Virginia had a higher threshold, requiring one-fourth black ancestry until 1910, when the law was changed to reflect the one-eighth black blood criteria. In his book *Who Is Black? One Nation's Definition*, Davis notes that there was also this twist: "Persons in Virginia who are one-fourth or more Indian and less than one-sixteenth African black are defined as Indians while on the reservations but as blacks when they leave."[4]

But wait, there's more.

In Louisiana, the law defined a "Negro" as anyone with "a trace of black ancestry" up until 1970. In that year, the state abolished its one-drop rule and raised the threshold to one-thirty-second black ancestry, meaning someone with just one great-great-grandparent who was black could still be considered black. The law was revised again in 1983, giving parents the right to decide the race of their children at birth, and, writes Davis, "even to change classifications on birth certificates if they can prove the child is white by a preponderance of the evidence."[5]

So let's see if I have this right. Hypothetically, certain mixed-race people in Louisiana could have been legally black under the state's one-drop rule, moved to Virginia where they would have lost their legal status as blacks, unless they were one-sixteenth black and one-fourth or more Native American, in which case they were black— but only when off the reservation.

Davis reports that in South Carolina in the 1800s, a judge declared a person who was known to have one-sixteenth black ancestry officially "white," ruling that his acceptance by whites due to his appearance and reputation was more relevant to determining his racial status than the proportions of white and black blood. Apparently, he was not alone. "In other states in the antebellum South," writes Davis, "there were also occasional court cases in which some persons with one-fourth or less 'Negro blood' were declared legally white."[6]

Is your head spinning yet?

Portland State University black studies professor Darrell Millner tried to put it all in perspective during a 1991 interview for a television documentary I produced on interracial families and multiracial people. "In our history, race was never a biological consideration. It was always a legal, social, and economic consideration," Millner said. "It was in the interest of the country under slavery to have as many people eligible for slavery as possible. And by the legal definition of what a black person was, you therefore maximized who could be eligible for slavery." Obviously, classifying anyone with "a trace of black ancestry" as black cast the widest net.

Although slave owners were first to embrace the one-drop rule, Davis found the concept actually became more widespread after the abolition of slavery. Whites felt they needed a broad standard by which to enforce segregation, distinguish themselves from "coloreds," and maintain white supremacy. The one-drop rule seemed to do the trick. Davis concluded that by 1915, whites in the United States had completely accepted the one-drop rule, and blacks would soon follow.[7]

That explains how my father, born in 1913, was classified as "mulatto" on his birth certificate but "black" on his death certificate. He didn't change. The rules of racial classification did.

The new rules became so ingrained that many Americans, without even realizing it, accepted them as truth. In a way, it's easy to see why. If blacks and whites are forced to attend separate schools, reside in separate neighborhoods, play in separate parks, and socialize in separate clubs, which category do biracial people fall into under that system? The one-drop rule says we belong with the black folks, no matter what our mixture. Therefore, if everyone with "a trace of black ancestry" is subject to the same evils of discrimination, what difference does it make who is one-quarter this or one-half that?

Among social scientists, the practice is known as "hypodescent," in which a child of mixed heritage inherits the status of the parent whose racial group is deemed lower in rank. Davis found that it was this social definition of blackness that generally prevailed in case of doubt. The logic suggests that the white race was to be seen as "pure," and one drop of black blood would taint the bloodline forever.

African-Americans recognized the practical implications of the one-drop rule, accepted the rule as standard operating procedure, and subsequently attempted to turn the reasoning behind it upside down.

Instead of viewing blackness as a "human stain," as novelist Philip Roth put it, why not view it as a source of cultural pride?

"Black is beautiful."

"Say it loud, I'm black and proud."

"Black ain't no color; it's a state of mind."

"The darker the berry, the sweeter the juice."

"Blacks come in all shades."

Once used to promote white superiority, the one-drop rule gained popularity among black folks, as it had the effect of creating more designated black folks. In the struggle for civil rights, as with any political movement, the bigger your numbers, the more power you can potentially wield. It's understandable why my parents, like many racially mixed people, ended up rolling right along with the trend. If oppression is based on "one drop," then it stands to reason that any unifying movement rising up to challenge that oppression would organize around "one drop" as well.

But something happened on my way to black militancy.

The one-drop rule never quite worked the way it was sold to me. If one drop is all it takes to make me black, I began to wonder, then how come some people think I'm white? Even those who recognize that I'm racially mixed have stopped to ponder where to place me in their racial Rolodex.

Under the one-drop philosophy, the racial category to which I am supposed to be assigned is "black." The process should be automatic. Sometimes it is, and sometimes it isn't. But the rule doesn't operate as advertised.

That's why I prefer to think of the one-drop rule as the "one-drop suggestion." It's a more accurate way of expressing how the concept contributes to the formation of racial identities today. It is a tug, a nudge, a bump in the direction of black identity and toward an embrace of black culture.

Biracial people feel that push in various degrees at various times in various situations. For some, it's a light tap. For others, it's a shove. Outcomes vary depending on how we look, where we live, how we interact in the community, the dynamics within our families, and the level of racism we're forced to confront.

Those whose lives are filled with social encounters in which they are viewed as black may point to the one-drop rule as a way of explaining why they have gravitated toward a black identity despite having a white parent in the home. They see the one-drop rule as the historical underpinning that causes them to be perceived a certain way and in many cases causes them to be targets for discrimination. Whether or not the rule makes any sense is beside the point. It reflects their social reality.

For other multiracial people, the one-drop rule strikes them as, well, bogus. They see it as a racist holdover from the days of slavery. It defies logic, ignores the truth of their heritage, and runs counter to their sense of individuality. The concept doesn't resonate with them, and they see no reason to perpetuate such an archaic way of thinking about race and identity.

I see merit in both points of view. I certainly recognize the one-drop rule's place in American history, its impact on members of my family, and the ripple effect on my own sense of my place in society. But it's time to put the one-drop rule in perspective. The rule is not ironclad, and its influence has diminished considerably in the post–civil rights era.

Growing numbers of people are questioning old assumptions about how America defines race, and they're forcing others to do the same. They recognize the legal and social definitions of race that so many Americans take for granted were imposed on us by previous generations—first for the purpose of maintaining racial inequality, then for the purpose of maintaining black solidarity in the face of racial inequality. Maybe it's time to rewrite the rulebook, or at least amend it.

To gain a better understanding of the multiracial experience today, the one-drop rule must be put in check. It would be a mistake to discount the rule altogether; its historical significance cannot be denied. But it does not provide an adequate framework for evaluating the racial identity choices multiracial people are now making. And if individuals are exercising choice, then "one drop" can't be a rule. It is really more of a suggestion.

This change in perspective is necessary so as not to misread what multiracial people are saying if they reject the one-drop doctrine and seek recognition of their mixed-race status. Those who continue to hold firm to the one-drop mindset are likely to misunderstand what's going on. They may wonder whether multiracial people who reject the one-drop rule might also be rejecting their blackness. Are these younger generations of multiracial people—gasp—trying to pass for white?

Hardly.

From what I've seen, something deeper is driving the trend. Many members of interracial families are simply living their lives in ways that are not one-dimensional. Their own personal sense of identity clashes with the one-drop philosophy, and they are insisting on identifying as multiracial to better reflect their multicultural upbringing.

Then there's the loaded term "passing." Even it is subject to a revised interpretation for a new era. The word means different things to different people. Some biracial people, using the term quite broadly, will say that they "pass" for white all the time. They "look white," people perceive them as white, and both white and black folks treat them as white. Those experiences, they say, reinforce the idea that they are not full-fledged members of the black community and contribute to their sense of having a biracial self-concept. They "pass" not because they have taken any steps to convince others they are white or deny the fullness of their heritage; rather, they pass by default.

Others, however, define passing in a narrow, historical context, reserving the term for those who have gone out of their way to hide their black ancestry. Sociologist Reginald Daniel writes, "Passing has meant deliberately shifting one's racial reference group from black to white and should not be confused with situations where racially blended individuals are mistaken for white."[8]

Yet when the term is used casually, it might very well refer to those social situations in which someone is mistaken for white. That is, if people can be "mistaken" for white when a good portion of their heritage *is* white. Some folks have even flipped the term on its end and posed the rhetorical question of whether light-skinned individuals who consider themselves African-American are "passing for black."

In Daniel's definition, the one which seems to be preferred by scholars, passing implies something else entirely and generally carries a more negative connotation. In his book *More Than Black?* Daniel also distinguishes between what he calls "continuous passing" versus "discontinuous passing." Continuous passing, he says, "involves a complete break with the African American community" and is "the most sensational sort of crossing over." Those who engage in continuous passing essentially divorce themselves from their black relatives and overtly reject any connection to their black heritage, sometimes to the point of making racist statements against black people as if to prove their whiteness. "Continuous passing is a gradual process in which emotional ties to African Americans are severed as ties to European Americans are achieved," writes Daniel. "The final break comes when the benefits of becoming white are felt to outweigh the costs of being black."[9]

It turns out that one of my own relatives weighed his options in that regard and made the final break Daniel refers to. Family folklore has it that one of my father's uncles, Charles Lewis, actually changed his name to "Carlos Luis" and passed for Hispanic. I don't know any other details beyond that because "Carlos" was never heard from again.

In contrast, discontinuous passing, Daniel contends, "was a brief trip across the racial divide for an evening in a white restaurant or theater or a more comfortable seat on the train." He reports of some discontinuous passers who held day jobs as whites but then returned to the black community at night, always taking great pains to keep their professional and personal lives separate. Some businesses that catered to whites went so far as to hire "spotters" to detect anyone who might be trying to pass. "These were African Americans whom theater owners hired as racial detectives, in the belief that one African American could always spot another, no matter how phenotypically white that individual might be," writes Daniel.[10] In other words, spotters were people who had finely tuned multiracial radar.

Other discontinuous passers used their looks to advance the cause of racial equality, including Walter White, who served as head of the NAACP from 1931 to 1955. In the 1920s, he traveled throughout the southern United States passing as white to infiltrate white mobs and investigate lynchings. "My skin is white, my eyes are blue, my hair is blond. The traits of my race are nowhere visible upon me," wrote White in his 1948 autobiography, *A Man Called White*.[11]

According to Davis, anthropologists have estimated that White was only one-sixty-fourth black.[12] Yet the civil rights leader considered himself black and viewed passing strictly as a temporary strategy that allowed him to go "undercover" as a white person. "I am not white. There is nothing within my mind and heart which tempts me to think I am," White insisted. "There is no mistake. I am a Negro."[13]

White's identity as a black man solidified on a hot September night in 1906. He was thirteen years old. Race riots had erupted in his hometown of Atlanta, Georgia. An angry white mob had assembled outside his family's house, threatening to burn it down. "It's too nice for a nigger to live in!" one of the rioters shouted.

White's father gave him a gun. "In the eerie light, Father turned his drawn face toward me," he recalled. "In a voice as quiet as though he were asking me to pass him the sugar at the breakfast table, he said, 'Son, don't shoot until the first man puts his foot on the lawn and then—don't you miss!'"

White never pulled the trigger. Instead, neighbors from down the street who had also barricaded themselves indoors opened fire first, and the mob retreated. For White, it was a defining moment. "I was gripped by the knowledge of my identity, and in the depths of my soul I was vaguely aware that I was glad of it," he wrote. "I was glad I was not one of those who hated; I was glad I was not one of those made sick and murderous by pride."[14]

As White's experience illustrates, it is not the one-drop rule itself that causes Americans of mixed racial heritage to identify as black. Rather, it is the resulting life experiences that the one-drop ideology sets in motion that make the difference. On a purely intellectual level, it makes no sense that a person who is sixty-three-sixty-fourths white would consider himself black. After learning of White's upbringing, however, his black identity doesn't sound quite so unreasonable.

I wonder what Homer Plessy would have thought of Walter White and vice versa. Or what both men would think of the growing chorus of mixed-race people opting to identify as multiracial today. Would they see us as crazy, out of touch, or in denial? Or would they view such identity statements as a sign that societal attitudes and individual thought patterns on matters of race have evolved? Although their methods and motivations may have differed, Plessy and White occupy unique places in American history for challenging the racial status quo. In their own way, both men have something valuable to teach us about the wobbly nature of race—and the power of suggestion.

The Power of One Drop

CHARLES BYRD ADMITS HE MAY BE HYPERSENSITIVE TO HYPODESCENT. Simply put, he doesn't like the one-drop notion under any name. He describes it as "odious" and "heinous" and says young biracial people coming of age today cannot fully appreciate the effect "one-drop racism" had on individuals like him.

"They may have read about it, but they've never had to live through it," he says. "In the days of legal segregation in the South, it was in your face every day."

Charles not only frowns on the one-drop rule, he has also come to reject racial labels in general. He maintains that racial identities as we now know them must be jettisoned altogether in favor of what he calls "racelessness." He did not arrive at this position overnight. It is the result of a lifetime of experiences and soul-searching.

As the publisher of a popular Web site devoted to multiracial issues, Charles Byrd is a voice often heard in public debates about the racial identification of mixed-race people. He has been quoted in newspaper articles, has appeared on television shows, and has played the role of agitator on discussion panels. Charles can be very outspoken, and that's putting it mildly. In the course of his advocacy work, he has managed to irritate a good number of people, including fellow biracial people. Even he and I have had our share of disagreements in his online chat rooms.

But when I contacted him to ask for an interview, he responded graciously and invited me to join him and his fiancée at their home in Queens, New York, for dinner. The conversation that unfolded that evening over homemade lasagna and antipasto gave me a better appreciation for his life story and the evolution of his views on multiracial issues.

For starters, Charles is virtually white in appearance. Some might say he *is* white, with his long, straight black hair, light complexion, and European facial features. But he was born to a black mother in 1952 in southern Virginia. He describes his mother as dark-skinned but says other relatives on his mother's side of the family had complexions that were closer in hue to his. His father, who is white, was not a part of his life.

As a child, "I accepted that society called me black," he said. "I wasn't real comfortable with that identification myself. Every morning when you get up and look in the mirror, you see there's this contradiction. And I tried to find some solace in the term 'light-skinned black' and the notion that blacks come in all colors. But there was this contradiction, which I tried to reconcile as best as possible, but it never went away."

He grew up in the town of Abingdon, Virginia, about fifteen miles north of the Tennessee border, where the public schools remained segregated until the mid-1960s. Up until the eighth grade, Charles attended an all-black school and remembers getting picked on by black students.

"In the elementary school, there were a couple of others like me. So we kind of banded together a little bit," he said. "We had the best and the worst of the situation. Sometimes we would wind up being teacher's pets and people would say, well, that's only because of the color of your skin. . . . There was always that glaring difference in skin complexion."

"Were you accepted in the black community?" I asked him.

"We weren't *totally* accepted in the black community, but pretty much so," he said. "No one beat me up. No one chased me around the block or through the neighborhood. People knew my extended family and the black members of my extended family. It wasn't like I was there in a vacuum by myself. So they knew who the other Byrds in town were, especially the darker-complexioned Byrds. I guess it also has to do with the fact that in the quote 'black community,' you do have those instances where you have people like me who appear. Would I have been accepted in the white community in that town if they knew I was part-black? Probably not. Not back in those days."

But the acceptance Charles received in the black community only went so far. He remembers being called a "white nigger," not by white people but by black people. Some of his tormentors were classmates; one was a relative.

"Even my grandfather called me [white nigger] once, my maternal grandfather. He got really upset with me in the house one day. I don't know what the hell I did to encourage that," he said. "I was born out of wedlock. And I think he probably felt offended that his daughter had brought this white kid into his house, and maybe he felt that it offended his sense of blackness."

In 1965, Charles began attending an integrated school for the first time. Already feeling conflicted about maintaining a black identity given the way he looked, integration served to heighten his sense that he was living a contradiction. It was then that the logic behind someone with his appearance being labeled as black began to fall apart.

"The white kids, who didn't know me, would ask me my name and what part of town I was from, and what school I had gone to the previous year. And when I would tell them the name of the school, which was Kings Mountain Elementary School, they would say, 'Now wait a minute, that's a black school. What are you, trying to bullshit me? You couldn't possibly have gone there.' And it would be hard for them to believe me. So after a while I just gave up trying to convince them that I had actually gone to that school," he said.

After one year in Abingdon High School, Charles moved to New York City, where he was exposed to a wider variety of cultures, skin tones, and ethnic groups. His new high school was also integrated, and he found himself with "all these different mixes of people." That environment, he says, further accelerated his rebellion against a black identity. "It's like you're forced to try to prove things to both sides. You're forced to try to prove to whites that you're part-black. You're forced to try to prove to blacks that you're obviously part-white but yet you're down with them. Later on in life, I would meet some blacks who would not believe that I was part-black at all, 'cause I'm so light-skinned. And then I would say to myself, why am I even trying to prove this to you, 'cause it's crazy."

By the age of thirty, Charles saw a need for a forum that would allow members of interracial families to come together and discuss the issues they faced. In the early 1980s, he formed a group in New York City called "Interace," which held gatherings at a local YMCA. He promoted the organization by sending out press releases about its existence, which then led to several media appearances. But the sense of community that Charles had hoped to create didn't materialize, and he left the group within three years.

"I was frustrated over a period of time. I was doing a good job drawing interracial couples who would bring their babies. But the grown adults who were mixed were not coming out and participating," he said. This was a common complaint among biracial adults who had sought out interracial family support groups in the 1980s and 1990s. "I would get letters saying, 'I appreciate what you're doing, but I don't feel it's appropriate at this time,' blah, blah, blah. The couples were willing to come out and share and build that sense of community. But it took a while for some reason for the mixed individuals to want to be public with their mixed-ness.

"And the couples were generally divided as to how to identify their kids. I remember that also," Charles added. "Usually the black parent would want to identify the kid as black, and the white parent would kind of go along with it."

After leaving Interace, Charles began writing a newsletter touching on many of the same issues. The publication, which Charles describes as initially looking like an underground newsletter from the sixties, eventually evolved into *Interracial Voice*. That lasted for two years in print form until he created InterracialVoice.com, which launched in September 1995 and became one of the most comprehensive Web sites on multiracial issues.

Suddenly, the community that Charles had sought to create with Interace materialized online, with mixed-race adults of various combinations posting essays, engaging in dialogue, and writing poetry about their experiences.

"I am still exploring what it means to be both Japanese and Black and still have difficulty trying to express what that means to others," wrote essayist Mitzi Uehara Carter, who identified as "Blackanese." "My body and mentality is not split down the middle where half is black and the other half is Japanese. I have taken the aspects of both worlds to create my own worldview and identity."

"I just discovered this site today, and I plan to keep visiting," another letter-writer posted. "After years of struggling with my identity, I have come to the conclusion that I already know who I am, and that I am not responsible for racially explaining or justifying myself to anyone. The sense of liberation is amazing. I no longer worry about whether my viewpoint is black enough. I'm not afraid that behaving independently will result in accusations of 'trying to act white.' When men on the street tell me that I think I'm too good for a black man, I tell them I'm too good for a sleazy pickup at the bus stop."

Another contributor wrote, "I was so happy to find you on the Internet. I myself have been a target of racism all my life. I am a mixture of American Indian, black, and white. I go by Native American mostly because of my appearance, and the fact that people tend to receive me better than if I said I were black or multiracial. I think this is really sad, but it's true."

"First of all, I am multiracial. Second of all, I am at peace with myself," offered another writer. "You can throw me in any category you want. You can call me black, Asian, white, Hispanic, whatever. I am what I am. I am proud of all my ancestry."

But the online conversations also sparked a number of heated debates. Not being one to shy away from controversy, Charles penned essays calling for a "jihad against race consciousness." He referred to the pressure biracial people feel from the black community to identify as black as "Orwellian mind control," and at one point stated, "I also don't equate mixed-ness with 'minority status' and all the negativity that implies."

Another letter-writer suggested mixed-race people should consciously reject their blackness. "Why reject black and not any other race?" the author asks. "The one-drop rule does not make anyone black; it simply makes black a stigma. And so to reject black is to reject stigma. In rejecting black, one is defending and/or reclaiming one's free will."

So to be an ethnic minority, or to embrace that heritage, is bad, stigmatizing, and negative? some of us wondered. Our detractors often accuse us of wanting to escape being black, and the language used in some of these messages seemed to be playing right into their hands. At least one faction of regular visitors to the Web site became increasingly uncomfortable with some of the posts we were reading.

"What happened to the notion that we are a community of people with individual experiences? Not as popular as wailing about being unfairly tainted with the tar brush, I guess," countered one writer who self-identified as both multiracial and African-American. "Instead of rejecting the concept of race, some folks are content to just reject the concept of black. Not much of a step forward, is it?"

"I know what I am and what I have experienced," added another writer who also has black ancestry. "I have been dismissed by members of all ethnic and racial communities at points in my life, because I 'didn't quite fit,' a common experience for those who cross races, ethnicities, and cultures. I find it ironic that members of this community are also dismissive."

But Charles defended some of the controversial postings. "It's not because we don't want to be black, but we're not black," he insisted over dinner. "If you're part white, how are you black? Then that gets into the definition of blackness. How are you defining blackness? So it's not so much that you don't want to be black, but it is the fact that you're not black to begin with, and you don't want to be claimed against your will by one particular community or the other."

He holds a similar view on the concept of passing. "My philosophy is you can't pass for white unless you're more white than anything else to begin with. So why should we ridicule people for passing for white? It's not that you're passing, that's what you are. You can't successfully pass for white in the company of other, quote 'white' people unless you're probably more that than anything else."

"Unless," I pointed out to him, "you look at it in the context of those people who divorced themselves from their black family members to pass for white, who cut off all contact with their black relatives so they could live this white life."

"And that's not something I would do," he responded, but he added that he would not want to be judgmental of anyone who did. "It's just very hard in society for a near-white person to identify as black and be taken seriously. It really is, man. It's very hard. Blacks don't take you seriously, and whites don't take it seriously."

Now in his fifties, Charles rejects any racial label whatsoever, even "multiracial." Instead he prefers to take a more spiritual view. "I don't identify racially anymore, and I probably haven't in a long time," he said. "Where I am now is almost totally different from where I was in terms of levels of consciousness back in 1980 or '82 when I started my advocacy, or even in 1995 when I put *Interracial Voice* online. I've gone from being a 'light-skinned black' to a 'radical multiracial' to being a human who glimpses his spiritual nature. So I like to think I've grown and matured philosophically and spiritually over the past fifteen or twenty years. Others seeing that say, well, this guy can't decide. He can't figure out what the hell he is. He's flip-flopping all over the place. First he wants this category, next I'm saying do away with categories. But it's just a manifestation of how I think I've grown."

Not everyone grows in the same way. Some grow by developing a strong, unwavering black identity. And it has served them well. But that view won't work for everyone. For others, the "black-only" approach has left a void, a sense that they are being coerced into rewriting their life story to appease those who do not want to accept a more complicated reality.

As Mitzi Uehara Carter put it in her *Interracial Voice* essay, "Our bodies, our presence, our reality is a nuisance to some because we defy a definite and demarcated set of boundaries. We confuse those who are trying to organize ethnic groups by highlighting these boundaries because they don't know how to include us or exclude us."

For his part, Charles insists he has moved beyond that tug-of-war and has embraced a philosophy he has found in ancient religious teachings of the East. "It starts from the premise that you're not your body to begin with. You're the soul that animates the body. You're the eternal spirit that animates the temporary body. These racial and ethnic and even cultural identifications are just temporary identities that will die when the body dies," he said. "Right now, I'm kind of at the level of 'human being,' trying to end the vicious cycle of birth and death here in the material universe and trying to go back home to God." He paused, then added, "But that's a conversation a lot of people are not ready to have."

"I was going to say, that's heavy!" I told him.

With that, he burst into a hearty laugh, the sound of which filled his dining room. We had finished our main course and were ready to move on to dessert.

Root of the Matter

Maria Root and I were sitting in the dining room of her home in Seattle, Washington, on an August afternoon sipping diet cola. "One of the simple things I learned after twenty-five years of being a psychologist is that people aren't real good at putting themselves in other people's shoes," she said.

Amen to that! Those of us who come from interracial families often find ourselves doing battle with armchair shrinks—and occasionally some professional ones, too—over the manner in which we have chosen to express our ethnic identity.

Maria Root is familiar with such conversations. The former University of Washington professor now in private practice has written extensively about the experiences of multiracial people in America and conducted several studies on biracial identity development.

"At a conference of the American Psychological Association, I was chairing some panels on multiracial identity," she said. "People were talking about processes and people with 'confused' identities. And I said, I don't think confusion is an identity. A lot of people talk about that historically, about mixed-race people having confused identities. That is not an identity," she reiterated. "If one is just confused, that's actually a reflection of process. One is stuck."

Maria has devoted a good portion of her professional career to helping members of interracial families get "unstuck" by putting biracial identity and all of its variations in the proper context. Her academic background includes a PhD in clinical psychology and bachelor's degrees in both psychology and sociology, a combination I found intriguing.

"Psychology at the time focused so much on the individual, but the individual existed within systems. Sociology dealt with systems," she explained. "It was kind of my job to put them together."

"To me, that's sort of what the multiracial person has to do," I told her. "You have your individual experience, but also the broader issues of how society perceives you."

"I never thought of it that way, but yeah," she responded. "I don't think individual factors exist alone. They really interact with the systemic factors." When speaking of "systems," Maria is not just referring to society at large and its many subcultures. She sees the family unit as a system, too.

Within those systems, Maria has certainly had her share of practice bridging cultures and reconciling dual identities. She was born in the Philippines to an interracial couple and raised in Los Angeles. "My father's one of those amalgams of Scottish, Irish, German— European white descent." Her mother is Filipino. "And Filipinos are mixed, so it's Malay, Chinese, Spanish, Portuguese," she added.

"I take it that's part of what drove you to this area of study?" I asked her.

"People would assume so. But I don't think it really was that direct," she said, noting that other areas of her work have dealt with trauma, addiction, and minority mental health. "I think I've always just been interested in culture. Even if I hadn't been a mixed-race person but I was living in a Filipino household, I still would have had to go back and forth between the culture out there and the home culture. So culture has always interested me. Race relations always interested me. Identity in general, as a psychologist, had interested me. Even though you think I would have a really pat answer to how I got there, I don't."

While other researchers have examined the multiracial experience by concentrating on stages of racial awareness and development in children and adolescents, Maria's work seems to focus more on outcomes.

"Are there certain key factors that result in someone adopting a biracial identity as an adult?" I asked.

"I think the biggest key factor is historical time period. Truly, if this was 1960, and you were saying, 'I'm biracial,' you'd be a pretty miserable man if you were doing that publicly," Maria answered. "I know some people in 1960 who were doing that, but it was extremely hard and they knew to keep it private. So I think the biggest variable in terms of identifying multiracially is the times we're living in."

Her conclusion is based on countless hours of research involving biracial people across age groups. Her studies have found five different identity strategies common among multiracial Americans of various racial combinations, not just those of black-white mixture: (1) acceptance of the monoracial identity society assigns, (2) adoption of a monoracial identity after working through racial issues, (3) identification with both racial groups, (4) identification as a new racial group, and (5) adoption of a symbolic identity or "multiracial whiteness."

"I don't think any of them are right or wrong," said Maria. "They have their different adaptabilities at different places at different times."

I've tried to spell out each of them below, borrowing portions of text from Maria's published reports interspersed with additional comments and conclusions drawn from our conversation.[1]

Acceptance of the Monoracial Identity Society Assigns

"Biracial people growing up in more racially oppressive settings are less likely to have freedom to choose their racial identity," she writes. Acceptance of the identity society assigns is not necessarily bad. The individual can interpret this positively even though it may stem from an oppressive process in which biracials who are part-white are assigned to their minority race. "You don't even question the identity label because you somehow very early on just accept hypodescent as what it is," Maria explained. In this scenario, the biracial person, while aware of their mixed background, may genuinely feel they belong to the racial group to which they are assigned.

Adoption of a Monoracial Identity after Working through Racial Issues

"In this strategy, the individual *chooses* to identify with a particular racial or ethnic group," writes Maria, noting that this is different from blindly accepting the identity society assigns, because in this case the process is "active" rather than "passive." The biracial person consciously reflects on the matter, and there may be a period of struggle involved. In addition, the group the biracial person chooses may or may not be the identity assumed by family members, assigned by society, or matching their racial features.

Identification with Both Racial Groups

"This may be the most idealistic resolution of biracial status," writes Maria. In effect, the biracial person maintains dual citizenship. "At times, they kind of water one set of roots because it needs it more," she said, but their personality remains similar across groups, and they feel accepted in both groups. When questioned about their background, they may say, "I'm part black and part Japanese," or whatever their particular combination might be.

ROOT OF THE MATTER

Identification as a New Racial Group

"This person feels a strong kinship to other biracial people in a way that they may not feel to any racial group because of the struggle with marginal status," writes Maria, adding, "the individual may move fluidly between racial groups, but view themselves apart from these groups as they have now created a new reference group." Biracial people taking this approach view their multiracial identity in a way that places them in a unique racial category separate from either of their parent groups.

Adoption of a Symbolic Identity or "Multiracial Whiteness"

This process is perhaps the most difficult of the five to explain. The biracial people who fall into this category, when asked how they identify, will say they identify as white but acknowledge a parent or other relative of another race. "It isn't like they are trying to hide anything," said Maria. "They say, 'No, I really like that I'm also African American and that's part of my heritage, but I really identify as a white person.'"

Maria explained this approach by comparing it to white Americans of Swedish ancestry, for example. They may declare their Swedish heritage if asked, "but they don't really know that much about Swedish things. Or they know some, but it's intellectual. And they really appreciate it, they think it's fascinating, they really like that they have this history. They feel proud that that's part of who they are. But it kind of stops there," she says. In other words, they have some awareness of the culture but have not lived it.

A similar phenomenon is apparently now showing up among biracial adults who are white-black, white-Asian, or what have you. They "feel" white. Acknowledging their minority race, while important to them, is largely symbolic. "And the people weren't mixed up on the psychological instruments of adjustment," added Maria, admitting that she herself was surprised to find this identity. "They were well-adjusted; they interviewed as well-adjusted people, which is different from how people would have been ten or fifteen years ago declaring that identity."

In some ways, this identity strategy represents a reversal of the one-drop rule. It is not unusual, for example, for some "black" people to refer to themselves as "multiracial African-American," a quiet nod to their mixed background while their principal identity is black. The symbolic identity concept suggests that the term "multiracial white person" is just as valid, indicating a mixed-race person who's not afraid to say so, but whose principal identity is white.

This fifth identity model could also reflect the intersection of race, culture, and class in the ways people are choosing to define themselves in contemporary American society. "I think sometimes it was also a stand-in for the neighborhoods that they grew up in. They're kind of identifying with a neighborhood racial class structure that their family was a part of, so it all gets mixed in there," said Maria. "Neighborhoods and peers have a lot of influence."

Identities by Age Group

Maria then cross-referenced the results for all five identity strategies by age, leading her to conclude that generation plays an important role in shaping the identities of mixed-race people. "Each generation's identity options differ," she writes. Her research has identified three distinct age groups of biracial adults living in the United States today: (1) those born in the pre–civil rights era, before the late 1960s, (2) those born between the late 1960s and late 1970s, and (3) those born in the post–civil rights era after 1980.

Pre–Civil Rights Era: Born before the Late 1960s

"The first generation could not publicly declare a mixed-race identity without being thought to be confused, disturbed, or self-hating," she writes. "The civil rights movement further required solidarity, and a mixed-race identity was not perceived as being in solidarity with any of the racial pride movements." This first generation, Maria found, was expected to conform to the one-drop rule and as a result tends to identify with a single race. They either accepted the monoracial identity society assigned them or adopted a monoracial identity after working through their racial issues. The other identity strategies do not show up, at least not in significant numbers, among this age group.

Middle Generation: Born between the Late 1960s and Late 1970s

"The middle generation," writes Maria, "grew up during the last phase of major civil rights reform." This group, born between the late sixties and late seventies, was generally discouraged from publicly declaring a multiracial identity. But as the number of interracial families and mixed-race people continued to rise, they could feel the tide starting to shift.

Members of the middle generation followed the first two strategies outlined, either choosing or acquiescing to a monoracial identity. But they also embraced the third option—to identify with multiple racial groups simultaneously. Why pick one race over another? Surely a person can be both. But the idea that multiracial individuals constitute a separate racial group altogether did not catch on with this age group, nor did the concept of multiracial whiteness.

Post–Civil Rights Era: Born after 1980

In contrast, the youngest generation of multiracial adults has had the least exposure to the more overt forms of racism experienced by older Americans. "Until they leave home, many are often not familiar with racism, though this does not necessarily mean they have not been subjected to it. This generation grows up amid many youths with similar multiracial backgrounds and media figures acknowledging their background," Maria writes. "Public declaration of mixed-race identity is not unusual."

With this younger generation of biracials, all five identity strategies are present. Identifying as a new racial group and adopting a symbolic identity show up in this age group, whereas those approaches don't fully register among the others. For the young biracial adult, a wider range of adjustment options has now emerged.

Courtesy: Maria P. P. Root	Accepts Society's Identity	Chooses Monoracial Identity	Multiple Race Identity	New Racial Group	Symbolic Identity
BIRACIAL ADULTS					
Born before late 1960s	Yes	Yes	No	No	No
Born between late 1960s–late 1970s	Yes	Yes	Yes	No	No
Born after 1980	Yes	Yes	Yes	Yes	Yes

To be clear, it is worth emphasizing that the earlier models do not disappear among this age group. They still exist. So it's not as if old-school biracial people all identify *this* way, and young biracial people all identify *that* way. Those born after 1980 may still take on a monoracial identity assigned to them, or make the choice to align themselves with a single race. What's significant is that these are no longer seen as the only viable options. Identifying as biracial has gained greater acceptance—whether that's interpreted as affiliating with more than one racial group, as a separate multiracial group, or taking on a symbolic identity recognizing multiple heritages.

In her own examination of the trend, Kathleen Odell Korgen states in her book, *From Black to Biracial*, that the civil rights movement, the women's movement, the gay and lesbian movement, and the rise of individualism all contributed to the transformation. "Identity-focused politics engulfed U.S. culture. It was out of these movements that today's multiculturalism was born," writes Korgen.[2] "These young adults were the first generation to be taught that diversity is good. Multiculturalism was popular during the majority of their lives. Being unique began to be viewed as a positive rather than a negative trait by society."[3]

The *Christian Science Monitor*, in an article published in August 2000, even suggested that multiculturalism, which it defined as "the acceptance of and celebration of distinct cultural heritages," is giving way to something called transculturalism. Instead of viewing ethnic groups as separate, distinct entities, transculturalism recognizes the "melding, or fusion, of ethnic backgrounds and cultural experiences."[4]

Adds Korgen, "As people sought out and began to embrace their various racial and ethnic roots, it was only natural for many biracial Americans to identify with both sides of their racial heritage."[5]

Of course, these adjustment patterns, while illuminating, are generalities. There are certainly healthy, well-adjusted biracial people who operate outside of the categories for their particular age range as delineated here, and the age ranges themselves are not hard-and-fast boundaries. But in uncovering these trends, the academic literature does provide some much-needed structure for understanding what's going on.

So aside from generation, what determines which of the five strategies a person will use? It's a mixed bag. The research indicates that multiracial people, consciously or not, have managed to gravitate toward whichever identity model seems to work for them. But I wouldn't say the process is an intellectual one, like picking from a menu. It's more like we stumble upon the strategies through our interactions with others, experiment with some of the approaches, and finally land on one that feels right. And then, we don't necessarily stay there.

"I suggest these strategies are not mutually exclusive and may coexist simultaneously, or an individual may move among them," Maria concludes. "Such movement is consistent with a stable, positive sense of identity if the individual does not engage in denial of any part of their heritage."[6]

For the biracial person, these shifts tend to occur without any real awareness of the psychological framework multiracial researchers are now articulating. The process of identity formation is rather haphazard and produces different outcomes in different people, even within the same family. Other studies Maria has undertaken point to this unpredictability. For instance, she found that biracial siblings growing up in the same household often have different identities from one another, even though they were born only a few years apart.

"I think it's actually more the rule than the exception," she said. "People were coming up to me and saying, 'I identify this way, but you should talk to my brother or sister.'"

Her subsequent investigation, known as the Biracial Sibling Project, documented their accounts. "Gender did seem to make a difference in the experience of being a mixed-race person. For example, the female participants experienced an exotification and sexualization not reported by the men," Maria writes.[7] But earlier "gender alignment" theories that biracial boys identify with the race of their father and biracial girls with the race of their mother did not hold up. Too many other factors are involved.

In many cases, variations in how family members processed their racial identity had to do with individual differences in personality, coping skills, and talents between the two siblings. Name-calling and other acts of racial hazing are not experienced uniformly.[8] Biracial siblings, whether same-sex or opposite-sex, internalize these situations differently—as the lives of Ashley and Courtenay Edelhart demonstrate.

In addition, the movement across the five identities Maria describes can either take place gradually over a period of years, or occur almost instantaneously as multiracial people size up a given situation and determine how they want to proceed, as Courtenay Edelhart says she does depending on the race of the person questioning her ethnic background. Such "situational identity" may even have occurred within the context of the research process itself.

"I had a multiracial research interview team. I chose that on purpose," Maria said of her investigation of the five identity strategies. "On some interviews I said, 'If I was an African American researcher asking you this question, what would your answer have been? Would you have been able to give me the same answer?' And they said, 'I don't know, it would depend on how you were in the interview.' I think that's a critical piece as we think about how these identities are still evolving and changing."

Make no mistake, they will continue to change and evolve. It is quite conceivable that a band of multiracial people born tomorrow will grow up with an entirely new way of thinking about race in response to the new social realities of their generation. And they will leave the rest of us wondering what could have happened to produce such a fundamental change in racial attitudes in such a short period of time. At least, let's hope that's what happens.

When Perception Means
Everything and Nothing

I CRINGE WHENEVER I HEAR PEOPLE SAY, "PERCEPTION IS REALITY."

No, it's not, I want to yell. Reality is reality. But perception *is* relevant.

It's a point I find myself making in discussions about what advice we should be giving to young biracial people on dealing with issues surrounding their racial identity. The manner in which these conversations tend to unfold warrants some additional exploration here, as I think it is emblematic of our all-or-nothing way of thinking about race. Typically, participants in the discussion drift into one of two camps. In one camp are those who take the view that perception is everything. It's not about how the individual feels, or the individual's life experiences, or the individual's desire to recognize the full scope of their ancestry. Rather, it is all about how society perceives that person. If society perceives the biracial person as black, then that person *is* black. If society perceives the same individual as white, well, then, that person *is* white. Young biracial people must be prepared to deal with the social realities that result from racial perceptions. Therefore, their identity should follow perception.

Those in the second camp contend that that's all a load of crap. Societal perceptions, they argue, mean nothing. Just because society *perceives* a person in a particular way does not make that person so. Young biracial people should insist on identifying in accordance with the truth of their family background and reject any label society imposes. Who cares what other people think? If society perceives black people as inferior to white people, is that perception one we should encourage young people to embrace as well? Society is wrong, they insist. Perceptions mean squat.

Back and forth the arguments go. One side believes perception doesn't matter at all. The other side believes perception is the only thing that does matter. Neither side is totally right nor totally wrong, but both viewpoints are problematic when taken to the extreme.

There's a huge gray area between these two polar opposites, and that's where I've found most biracial people generally live. Perception is not reality, but it cannot be ignored, either. Our challenge as multiracial people is to figure out where our lives fall within that gray area and strike the right balance between the two approaches, even though they appear to contradict each other.

Oralandar Brand-Williams seems to have mastered the balancing act. But it was a long time coming. She is the light-complexioned daughter of a black woman and a white man. A fellow journalist, Oralandar and I spoke by telephone one evening while she was in between assignments.

As a little girl in the 1960s, Oralandar remembers standing in a neighborhood ice cream shop when a black girl within earshot of her stepped up to place an order. "This girl wanted chocolate and she wanted vanilla," Oralandar recalled. "She told the guy working at the ice cream shop, 'Put my chocolate on top, 'cause I want to show that black is beautiful.' And she turned to me and gave me this smirk. I was only nine years old. I had no clue what she was talking about."

The childhood encounter in the ice cream shop ("We called them confectioneries back then," Oralandar said) would serve as a metaphor for the delicate racial dance she would have to perform at various points in her life. "Put my chocolate on top," the young customer said. For years, that was the message to biracial people. We're supposed to proclaim our blackness and submerge anything else— to, in effect, put black on top.

Born in Greenwood, Mississippi, in 1958, Oralandar didn't need much nudging in that direction. "I knew I was different, but I still thought of myself as a black girl," she said. "I ran into problems with it because people would say, 'How can you be black? You have light skin,' or 'You have straight hair,' or 'You look different.' But that's just a problem that *they* had."

For most of her youth, Oralandar embraced a black identity in large part because of her unique family history. She is the youngest of nine children. Seven of her brothers and sisters are "all-black"—children her mother had with her first husband, who was African American. Only the two youngest, Oralandar and one brother, are biracial.

Her parents, she said, owned a restaurant in Greenwood, which they ran together. Close friends and neighbors in the black part of town where her family lived were aware they were a couple. Otherwise, they kept their relationship largely to themselves. "A lot of people knew because all they had to do was come to the café and see my brother and me, and they could put two and two together—a black woman with very bright, almost white, children," said Oralandar.

But Oralandar never truly got to know her white father. Her parents separated when she was four years old, and her father died before Oralandar's ninth birthday. Her relationships with those family members she did know shaped her identity. "I came from my mom who is black. My sisters and brothers were black. My aunts and uncles were black. You know, all my relatives were black," she said.

"And then I was growing up in the late sixties. I'm watching stuff on TV, people have dogs sicced on them. I think because I grew up at that time, that probably shaped my perspective on myself."

In addition, her mother was heavily involved in the civil rights movement, and the family paid a price because of it. Oralandar described how her mother had been working with the NAACP, the Student Nonviolent Coordinating Committee (SNCC), and the Southern Christian Leadership Conference (SLC) to register black voters in Mississippi. In 1963, "We were literally run out of the South," she said. "I just remember one morning, a lot of hustle and bustle in the house, a lot of activity, people coming in and out, my mother telling people, 'Take what you want.' We were leaving. We were put on a Greyhound bus and brought north. It was because they feared for my mother's life, because she had been very active."

Her father stayed behind in Mississippi while her mother and the rest of the family relocated to Detroit, where Oralandar has lived ever since. All the while, her mother encouraged her never to forget her father's heritage.

"She would always say, 'You are as much white as you are black, and I always want you to remember that. I don't care how society sees you or how they feel about mixed-race people, that is what you are. You are half and half,'" said Oralandar. "But you know, growing up in a mostly black community, you felt that [black] is what you were. And I guess it wasn't until I got in my thirties when I started saying, 'I am biracial.' It was sort of like a declaration, like a coming-out, if you will."

A lot would happen in those intervening thirty years. Growing up in Detroit, Oralandar attended predominantly black schools until 1974, her freshman year of high school. She then transferred into a magnet program, where the student body was mostly white. She lasted three weeks. When a white student she had befriended suddenly wanted nothing to do with her after meeting one of her darker-skinned sisters, Oralandar returned to an all-black school.

"That really hurt me," said Oralandar. "She didn't know I was black or had a black sister. . . . After that, I said, oh, no. I don't want to stay here. I don't want to be a part of this, and left."

At age sixteen, now in a black school again, she attempted to grow an Afro by frizzing and teasing her hair.

"How did that work?" I asked.

"Oh, god. Disaster," said Oralandar.

"What was the motivation for that?"

"I wanted to be like other people," she explained. "I didn't want to be different. But you know what? I was different. I finally had to accept that. I liked different music. I was into Elton John, I was into Alice Cooper. I was into a lot of white rock music. When I was in college, I hid that. I loved Fleetwood Mac. But when my black friends came over, I put on Earth, Wind and Fire, or Stevie Wonder. I was not coming out of that closet."

As our conversation continued, one event in particular that I wanted to discuss with the lifelong Detroit resident concerned a notorious racial hate crime that shocked the city and made headlines around the country. Oralandar, who is now with the *Detroit News*, was working as a news producer at WWJ Radio when it happened.

The victim was a twenty-seven-year-old Asian man by the name of Vincent Chin. There are many lessons that can be drawn from his story. I bring it up here to make a point about the relevancy of racial and ethnic perceptions, the difference between who you are and what someone else thinks you are, and the reconciliation of these dual perceptions.

It all started on the night of June 19, 1982, in a Detroit nightclub called the Fancy Pants. According to newspaper accounts, Vincent Chin and three of his friends had gone to the club to celebrate his upcoming wedding. Ronald Ebens and his stepson Michael Nitz, both white, were also there.

Ebens was a Chrysler worker all too familiar with the ups and downs of the American auto industry. The early 1980s were not good to U.S. automakers, while Japanese-made cars were all the rage among consumers. An anti-Japanese undercurrent was running through much of blue-collar America.

Ebens shouted at Chin, "It's because of you little motherfuckers that we're out of work!" A fight broke out. A bouncer kicked Ebens, Nitz, and Chin out of the Fancy Pants. Outside the club, more words were exchanged. Chin ran away to a nearby McDonald's.

Later, while driving through the neighborhood, Ebens and Nitz spotted Chin near the fast-food restaurant. They pulled over, grabbed a baseball bat from their car, and beat Chin into a coma. He died four days later.[1]

"People likened it to a lynching," recalled Oralandar. Among many African-Americans in Detroit, "it kind of brought back stories that their parents and grandparents had told them," she said.

And it got worse. The two attackers never faced trial for murder. They pleaded guilty to a lesser charge of manslaughter and were sentenced to three years' probation. They served no prison time.

"Oh, people were horrified," said Oralandar. "They just could not believe that somebody could chase another human being down the street with a bat and basically be let off."

The facts of the case suggest the incident represents a prime example of an anti-Japanese hate-crime. Except for one minor detail. Ebens and Nitz had no way of knowing their victim's last name, which in this case would have revealed his ethnicity. Vincent Chin was not Japanese. He was Chinese.

In the great debate that goes on within multiracial circles over whether perception means everything or nothing, I point to the story of Vincent Chin. His attackers perceived him as Japanese. True, he was actually Chinese. But it is also true that he is dead. So how can we say that perception does not matter? On a summer night in Detroit, Michigan, in 1982, it not only mattered, it became a matter of life and death.

Besides, even if Ronald Ebens and Michael Nitz had known their victim was Chinese, would it have made any difference? Would it have prevented the fight? Would they have put down the bat? Or is it more likely they're the type of people who make no such distinctions and lump all Asians together? "Chinese, Japanese, whatever, same thing," I can almost hear them saying.

Multiracial people are subject to the same refrain. "Black, biracial, whatever." "Asian, biracial, whatever." The perpetrators of hate crimes, acts of discrimination, and other racial slights are hardly people to take note of nuances.

But at the same time, the fact that Ebens and Nitz apparently *thought* Vincent Chin was Japanese does not *make* him Japanese. No one would suggest that other Chinese Americans identify as Japanese or check the Japanese box on some government form simply because that's how certain white people see them, or because they're potential targets of anti-Japanese hate crimes. That wouldn't make sense. Yet the "perception means everything" argument says that's exactly what biracial people are supposed to do— surrender a multiracial identity and play along with those who view us otherwise.

Racial and ethnic perceptions have consequences, as the life and death of Vincent Chin illustrates. That's a reality we have to face. But it doesn't mean we have to grant others veto power over how we define ourselves. Again, life in that gray area between perception meaning everything or nothing is a balancing act.

"This is a personal issue, and I've always seen it as that. It's very personal," said Oralandar, referring to matters of race and identity. "There are still people who don't even like to talk about it. There are people who have biracial grandmothers or great-grandmothers. And it was a topic in the family that people were ashamed of."

Oralandar once shied away from talking about her blended heritage herself, fearing that it would appear as though she was trying to distance herself from the black community. Now, however, she says she feels more at ease claiming a biracial identity than ever before, a change she attributes to the rising visibility of interracial families and mixed-race issues.

"I don't like to sound like the tragic mulatto, because that wasn't me at all. But I always felt like I was hiding a part of myself because I didn't want to make other people feel uncomfortable. I didn't want other people to think I was trying to be different when in fact I was different," she said. "As I get older, and I guess our 'movement' is gaining power, I can get comfortable with it. But before, I felt I was setting myself aside. And I didn't feel comfortable with that. I didn't want people to feel like I thought I was better because I was mixed."

Unfortunately, that's still how some folks choose to interpret it.

Black Backlash

THE TERM IS SOMETHING OF A TONGUE-TWISTER: "THE BLACK BACK-lash." Sounds ominous, doesn't it? But I happen to think the label fits. I'm referring to the opposition that exists among many African Americans to the very idea of anyone self-identifying as multiracial.

In the days before multiracial issues had received much public attention, saying "I'm biracial," in my experience, tended to elicit two different types of reactions.

With white people, it was generally, "You're what? Bisexual?"

"No, not bisexual," I'd respond. "Biracial."

"Oh. Well, whatever," they would say, willing to play along even if they didn't completely understand what I was talking about.

The typical reaction from black folks, however, was more along the lines of, "Biracial? Boy, you better check yourself!"

Why the backlash?

"Historically, it was simple," writes University of Wisconsin researcher Michael Thornton. The country had a two-tiered racial system—"whites and blacks, with racially mixed people improved versions of blacks."[1]

And therein lies the problem. Having witnessed America's racial hierarchy in action, many African-Americans have internalized that historical view. Their anger over the unfairness of it then gets projected onto multiracial people, sometimes in the form of open hostility. They assume that biracial people, by virtue of a lighter appearance, have taken on an inner sense of superiority. Rather than seeing the expression of our self-identity as a quest for wholeness, they interpret any acknowledgment of our mixed background as a sign that we have bought into some racial pecking order and are seeking upward mobility within it. And they prefer to hold onto this simplistic, knee-jerk view of the multiracial experience than to undertake a deeper examination of the lives mixed-race people have actually lived.

Never mind that many biracial people grow up feeling ostracized with little or no sense of community in either black or white worlds. Never mind that many of us have never had the sense of superiority they assume we have. We're too convenient a target.

"As a little girl, you have a first impression. And my first impression of the African American experience was that it was going to be painful to me," said Ramona Douglass, an olive-skinned, multiracial woman who has been at the forefront of America's debate over the racial classification of mixed-race people. We sat down for an interview during a conference on multiracial issues in Claremont, California. "I got beat up by blacks," she said. "And I never seemed to pass the African American litmus test. So I have no guilt over embracing my multiraciality from the very beginning."

Ramona's story begins in 1949. That's the year she was born to her Italian American mother and her African American–Scotch Irish–Native American (of Lakota heritage) father. She grew up in New York City. Her family first lived in the Bronx, then moved to Queens.

"You got beat up?" I asked.

"Yes, when I was a little kid. A lot of African American kids at that time who were either considered 'Negro' or 'black'—this was the fifties—viewed me as a 'high-yellow' girl who thought she was too cute to be black. I had Shirley Temple curls, I bounced when I walked, I was too happy.

"I got chased, I got rocks thrown at me by African American kids because their families told them that people who looked like me thought they were better. And they had to bring me down to another level. So I experienced, for me, black terrorism."

"How critical was that in shaping your identity?" I asked.

"It was crystal clear very early I wasn't black. Because if I was, nobody would be doing that to me. So I didn't have any wringing of the hands over whether they would accept me in the black community. It's obvious that I didn't fit," she said, adding that she saw no reason to insist on belonging to a group that didn't want her. "I had sense enough early. I didn't have to be beat up too often to figure out I needed to be looking for friendship elsewhere. . . . I found I had more in common with the Jewish kids I went to school with than I did with the African American kids. There was an acceptance level there."

As Ramona's experience illustrates, the Black Backlash, ironically, ends up producing the very separatism the black community is supposedly trying to prevent. Folks attack us, then have the nerve to act surprised when we elect to kick them to the curb.

It becomes a self-fulfilling prophesy. Black folks rail against biracials for allegedly trying to escape being black. Biracial people get fed up hearing all the nonsense and separate themselves from the black folks espousing such views. That in turn gets misinterpreted as a further rejection of our blackness, producing more criticism that then invites more separation. Around and around the cycle goes.

Courtenay Edelhart experienced the backlash after writing an op-ed piece while working as a newspaper reporter in Los Angeles. Her usual beat was Pasadena city hall. "There was some passing reference to the fact that I was biracial in the column, and I got this really angry phone call from an African American city councilman, basically saying, how dare you call yourself biracial. Get over yourself, you're black. That's what it amounted to. He didn't use those words, but that's basically what he said."

Courtenay's response was firm. "I was like, you know what, my job is to cover the Pasadena City Council, and your job is to serve on the Pasadena City Council. If you want to call me and talk to me about my coverage of politics or an ordinance that's been proposed or anything that has to do with the operation of city government, I will be more than happy to talk to you. But frankly, how I define myself and my family background is none of your goddamn business.

"Well, I didn't curse at him, but that's basically what I said as politely as I could. He hated me for years afterward because as far as he was concerned, I was a horrible sellout Uncle Tom. And you know what? I don't care," she said.

Courtenay went on to describe what she *really* wanted to tell the councilman—and anyone else who shared his views. "You have no idea what I'm about. You don't know what I do in my spare time. You have no idea of the degree of affiliation I have with the black community. How dare you judge me. You don't know me," she said. "So I had the strength at that point in my life to say, you know what, kiss my butt. I'm going to think of myself how I think of myself, and if you don't like it, that's one less person I need in my life."

I understand Courtenay's position. I can't hang out with people who don't respect how I identify. If you've got a problem with interracial couples or multiracial families or biracial people, then you've got a problem with me. If that eliminates certain people who happen to be black from my social circle, so be it.

The Black Backlash can be particularly damaging emotionally, because the lack of validation comes from the very group we have been taught to think of as "our own people." When I experience a racial slight or hear a racial slur directed at me because of my blackness, there are any number of black people I can turn to who sympathize with the predicament. But when the derogatory remark centers around being mixed or having a near-white complexion and comes from African-Americans, where does the biracial person turn?

Professor Thornton suggests living in a society accustomed to pigeonholing people into single racial categories for life further contributes to a negative view of those whose identities are more fluid. Multiracial people, by upending traditional racial borders, have been cast as deviant. "Movement back and forth across color lines is viewed as a pejorative rather than a creative strategy," he writes.[2] Somehow, we've got to correct that thinking.

Having been born in the pre–civil rights era, Ramona is among the generation of multiracial people most likely to follow the one-drop rule. Yet she says she cannot remember a time when she thought of herself as anything other than multiracial. Her upbringing bucked the trend.

"There was no secret; there was no hiding. That conversation was always present. So considering I was born in 1949, it's almost like I was in a time capsule waiting for the '80s to come out of my multiracial closet," she said. "Growing up as Italian American, African American, and mixed-race Native American, I was told very early, 'cause I had a very progressive family, that there are going to be people who are going to identify you based on their own perceptions, based on their own prejudices, and based on their own agendas. But you have the right to choose who you wish to be. Then you've got to read up on who that is, so you can feel grounded.

"So I always had books that dealt with various multiracial or inter-ethnic communities. I had a black cowboy book given to me by my father. I read about the Italian culture that I had. I read about all the multiracial people that were identified as black but were, in reality, multiracial." Ramona went on to name several historical figures, including W. E. B. DuBois, who is said to have had French, Dutch, and African ancestry. "My parents told me the truth about them as opposed to making me believe what school systems or the curriculum was stating."

Rather than attempting to run away from the black community, Ramona's story appears to be that of someone who was pushed away—literally chased away, with rocks. "I didn't experience what I call 'white prejudice' until college," she said. "I had black prejudice first."

After graduating from high school at age sixteen, Ramona enrolled in the Colorado School of Mines in 1966. Sitting in class one day, she asked a white student to pass her a Kleenex, to which he replied, "I don't do favors for niggers."

"I was in a state of shock," said Ramona. "That hostility was new for me. I had never been called that word before."

Later on, she said, "I found people similar to me from the Caribbean. I had friends from the West Indies and St. Thomas, various areas outside of America that did accept me and looked very similar to me. I met a lot of Creole and Cajun people from New Orleans. I looked just like them, and I said, here, this is my community."

But Ramona's "community" was about to grow much larger than she could ever have imagined. By the mid-1980s, more than a dozen different support groups had formed around the country to address issues of interracial families and biracial children. They were similar to Interace, the fledgling organization Charles Byrd had started in New York City but left after a few years when the group failed to attract a significant number of multiracial adults. Ramona, who was living in Chicago at that time, saw a newspaper ad for a local group called the Biracial Family Network. Founded in 1980, the organization held meetings in a church on Chicago's South Side. Ramona discovered the group in 1985.

"The very first day that I went to that organization, I knew at that moment I had arrived home," she said. "I was put on a committee pretty quickly."

Three years later, on November 12, 1988, in Berkeley, California, representatives of the Biracial Family Network joined leaders of similar grassroots organizations around the country to found the Association of MultiEthnic Americans, or AMEA. "We needed to get together because we did not have a national voice," said Ramona. "We were being defined by other communities and by people that really weren't a part of us. Not having our own voice heard was actually a detriment to our children and to ourselves."

At the time, the nation's longest-running interracial family organization was a San Francisco group known as I-Pride, which was founded in 1979. Carlos Fernandez, whose bio describes his mother as a European American and his Mexican father as having "mixed Native American and Spanish ancestry," was I-Pride's president.[3] At AMEA's inaugural meeting, he was elected to lead the new national organization. Ramona was elected vice president. Reginald Daniel, the multiracial researcher from the University of California, Santa Barbara, became secretary. Sara Ross, the leader of a group in Eugene, Oregon, called HONEY, which stood for Honoring Our New Ethnic Youth, was named treasurer.

In all, fourteen community groups were part of AMEA's founding—interracial family organizations from Atlanta, Buffalo, Chicago, Eugene, Houston, Norfolk, Omaha, Pittsburgh, San Diego, San Francisco, Seattle, Washington, D.C., and two groups from the Los Angeles area.[4]

"Just the naming of the organization was a process that was extraordinary," said Ramona. The group debated over whether to call itself the Association of Multi-*Racial* Americans or Multi-*Ethnic* Americans. "We were envisioning twenty and twenty-five years down the line. Would race be the primary concern, or would it be our diverse ethnicities we culturally identified with? We didn't think that race was progressive. We thought that 'MultiEthnic' would actually define a broader spectrum of people and would be more inclusive in the long term."

Either way, the multiracial community was on the verge of finding its national voice, and the conversation was about to take a turn toward the political. The volume of that debate would eventually grow louder. Much louder. As expected, the Black Backlash would quickly follow.

PART 4

EVADING THE BORDER PATROL

Hooking Up

IN THE 1967 MOVIE *GUESS WHO'S COMING TO DINNER*, ACTRESS Isabel Sanford plays Tillie, the black housekeeper to a wealthy white couple portrayed by Spencer Tracy and Katharine Hepburn. Their daughter is engaged to marry a black man, a world-renowned physician played by Sidney Poitier. Watching all the commotion that ensues, Tillie shakes her head. "Civil rights is one thing; this here is somethin' else!"

In one line, Tillie managed to sum up the general undertone that runs through much of America when it comes to interracial marriage. Civil rights, integration, multiculturalism, diversity in the workplace—all that is well and good and right and the way things ought to be. But marriage across racial lines? Well, that's in another category. Yes, attitudes have changed since 1967. But not as much as we like to think they have.

Coincidentally, *Guess Who's Coming to Dinner* was released the same year the U.S. Supreme Court issued its landmark ruling making interracial marriage legal in all fifty states. The case before the Court involved an interracial couple, a white man and a black woman, from Caroline County, Virginia. According to an account of their courtship in *Emerge* magazine, Richard Loving and Mildred Jeter had known one another since childhood. They grew up in the small rural community of Central Point. They eventually dated, and when Mildred became pregnant, she and Richard traveled to Washington, D.C., where they were legally married on June 2, 1958.[1]

At the time, a Virginia law known as the Racial Integrity Act prevented them from getting married in their home state. The law stated, "If any white person intermarry with a colored person, or any colored person intermarry with a white person, he shall be guilty of a felony and shall be punished by confinement in the penitentiary for not less than one nor more than five years."[2]

The law also made it a crime to leave the state for the purpose of getting married only to return as husband and wife, which is exactly what Richard and Mildred did. "Their marriage shall be governed by the same law as if it had been solemnized in this State," the statute read. "The fact of their cohabitation here as man and wife shall be evidence of their marriage."[3]

As *Emerge* reported, five weeks after returning to Virginia, the local sheriff paid a visit to the couple's home in the middle of the night, entered the house through their unlocked door, shone flashlights into their bedroom, and demanded to know why they were in bed together. When the Lovings pointed to their marriage license hanging on the wall, Sheriff R. Garnett Brooks reportedly told them, "That's no good here."[4]

They were promptly arrested and charged with violating Virginia's ban on interracial marriage. On January 6, 1959, the couple pleaded guilty and received their punishment. Rather than send them to jail for a year, the trial judge suspended the sentence on the condition that they move out of the state of Virginia and stay out of Virginia for the next twenty-five years.

In his ruling, Judge Leon Bazile stated, "Almighty God created the races white, black, yellow, Malay, and red, and he placed them on separate continents. And but for the interference with his arrangement there would be no cause for such marriages. The fact that he separated the races shows that he did not intend for the races to mix."[5]

Richard and Mildred Loving packed their bags and relocated to Washington, D.C., while the case made its way through a legal maze of appeals. Finally, on June 12, 1967, the U.S. Supreme Court issued its ruling. All nine justices were in agreement. The state's ban on interracial marriage had to go.

Chief Justice Earl Warren delivered the Court's opinion. "This case presents a constitutional question never addressed by this Court: whether a statutory scheme adopted by the State of Virginia to prevent marriages between persons solely on the basis of racial classifications violates the Equal Protection and Due Process Clauses of the Fourteenth Amendment," the ruling begins. "For reasons which seem to us to reflect the central meaning of those constitutional commands, we conclude that these statutes cannot stand consistently with the Fourteenth Amendment."

The decision goes on to note that the state statute only prohibited interracial marriages when one partner was white. Apparently, black-Asian or black–Native American interracial marriages did not violate the Virginia law, a peculiar twist the Supreme Court interpreted as "designed to maintain White Supremacy."

The Court's ruling concludes with these words: "The Fourteenth Amendment requires that the freedom of choice to marry not be restricted by invidious racial discriminations. Under our Constitution, the freedom to marry, or not marry, a person of another race resides with the individual and cannot be infringed by the State. These convictions must be reversed. It is so ordered."[6]

With those words, the highest court in the land struck down Virginia's ban on interracial marriage and obliterated similar laws still on the books in fifteen other states. In a stroke of poetic justice, the case is officially known as *Loving v. Virginia*.

Sadly, Richard Loving was killed in a car accident in 1975, and Mildred Loving fiercely guards her privacy.[7] But the couple's court victory is obviously a turning point in the history of interracial marriage in the United States.

Inspired by their story, Ken Tanabe created a Web site dedicated to the Loving decision. "I'm part Japanese, part Belgian, which is what got me interested in the entire subject," he explained.

His Web site, LovingDay.org, grew out of a graduate school research project. He stumbled across the case by accident while surfing the Internet. "I was researching something else, not even closely related to interracial marriage," he said. "There it came up in Google, and I was really surprised. I contacted some relatives who were married interracially around the time of the Loving decision and said, 'I can't believe it! Did you know about this?' And they said, 'Of course we knew about it. We evaded this law.' Or, 'We narrowly missed it by a few years when we got married.'"

Ken, whose father is Japanese and whose mother is white, went on to describe how one of his father's cousins married a white man before the Supreme Court ruling. Like the Lovings, they had to travel out of state to do so.

"I just couldn't believe that something so important, something that seems pretty well folded into the civil rights movement, has received such a low amount of press," Ken said of the Loving case. "It's not really in the history books that I read."

Ken's own research on the topic then took on a life of its own. He began looking into the history of interracial marriage in each state. "The laws get fairly complex just because they changed every year," he said. "So what I did was I created a multimedia map. You can click a button, and it will change the year, and then for every year you can see which states had the laws against interracial couples and which states didn't. You can also click on each individual state and you will get an excerpt of that state's law. It's interesting, things that a lot of people have not seen before."

For example, Ken found a California law in place from 1850 to 1948 that declared, "All marriages of white persons with negroes, Mongolians, members of the Malay race, or mulattoes are illegal and void." Maryland law prohibited marriages "between a white person and a person of negro descent, to the third generation, inclusive, or between a white person and a member of the Malay race . . . or between a person of negro descent, to the third generation, inclusive, and a member of the Malay race." Arkansas law stated, "Concubinage between a person of the Caucasian or white race and a person of the negro or black race is hereby made a felony," punishable by up to one year of hard labor.[8]

A native of suburban Washington, D.C., Ken currently resides in New York City and now organizes social get-togethers every June 12 to celebrate the anniversary of the Loving decision. He says eventually he'd like to see similar gatherings take place in communities across the country. "I want this to be something that's really woven into American culture. I want it to be something comparable to Juneteenth," he said, referring to the cultural celebration held in mid-June that some African- Americans consider their true Independence Day. Juneteenth recognizes those slaves who did not receive notice of their freedom until two years after the Emancipation Proclamation.

"If enough people in our country decide to throw a little gathering on this day, before you know it, a lot of people are going to know about it, and a lot more people are going to be thinking about the freedoms that they have," Ken said.

But at the same time, Ken also realizes that overall acceptance of interracial dating and marriage still isn't where many of us would like it to be. "People think of their own personal experiences and say, 'Hey, this is still an issue.' It's not as though everyone is happily living in a utopian society," he said. "People bring home someone of a different race to their parents, and there are problems. I hear about them. People do contact me through the project and tell me stories, some of which are on the Web site."

"I've been with my girlfriend for about ten years. She's black and Cherokee, and I'm Italian," one of the posts on LovingDay.org reads. "We've lived together for a long time. My parents did not accept her at first. Now we can get through a meal with them, but I know that they don't approve. People have treated us strangely at times. One time, we were at an expensive Italian restaurant, and the white waiter thought that it would be appropriate to approach us by saying, 'Hey, wha's goin' awn?' while all of the other customers were greeted cordially."

Another post states, "I was seeing a Mexican guy, and we were not allowed to call each other. My parents would not allow him in the house. My parents are against me dating Hispanics of any kind . . . I have an older sister. Neither of us ever brought home a black guy, so that issue never came up. I would probably get thrown out of my house."

Before Sundee Tucker Frazier's parents married in the mid-1960s, they could have shared a similar story. Sundee's family, which I had pictured as a model interracial household back in Pullman, didn't start out that way. Far from it.

Her mother and father met while in college at Western Washington University in Bellingham, north of Seattle. "My mom's parents were adamantly against it when they heard she was seeing a black man," said Sundee. "My white grandfather came to the campus and confronted my parents and threatened violence against my dad. My mom has told me she had never seen my grandfather that insane. It was just an insane sort of anger that totally shocked her. She had no idea that her parents would respond that violently because they had raised her, of course, to respect all people, and given her this view of all people are equal, but 'just-don't-marry-one' kind of mentality. And here she goes and gets into a relationship with someone of a different racial group and they flip out."

Sundee's parents married anyway. Their campus chaplain performed the ceremony. Only a few close friends were in attendance. After that, "They hid out at my black grandparents'," said Sundee. "Eventually my white grandparents came around. There are a couple things that contributed to that. My birth was one of them."

Sundee was conceived before her parents wed, a fact she didn't realize until she was an adult and "stopped to do the math," she said. Her maternal grandparents had little time to adjust to their new extended family. "I think they realized, if we want to have anything to do with our daughter and our new granddaughter, our first grandchild, we have to come to terms with our son-in-law. We have to accept this marriage," said Sundee. "The pastor of their church really helped them to realize that all people truly are equal in God's eyes, and that they needed to walk their talk as Christians and accept my father."

Sundee says she was unaware of any of this growing up and was stunned when she learned the truth. "I never knew that there were any hostile feelings or tension from my white grandparents about my parents' marriage. I had no clue. When I was twenty years old, my mom sat me down one summer when I came home from college and told me the story," she said. "I never thought to ask about my white grandparents' response to my parents' marriage, 'cause we had always gotten along. When I was with my white grandparents,

I always felt loved and accepted. We celebrated holidays, birthdays together. Even the black and white sides of my family at times would come together for events. So from my perspective, my white grandparents were pretty open-minded people. They were always loving and accepting of me, for sure. It really surprised me to find out that in fact they had been a product of their generation and of their time."

Sundee's black grandparents were more welcoming, allowing her mother and father to move in with them after the wedding. But prior to that, the first time her father introduced his new girlfriend to his parents, heads turned. "When they pulled into the driveway, my grandmother called to my grandfather, 'You won't guess who he brought home.' But my black grandfather was very accepting and kind of assured her it would be all right," said Sundee. "That tends to be more typical. In general, black folks tend to be more embracing of the white person who enters their world than the other way around," she noted.

Sundee's observation is consistent with a 2001 study on interracial relationships conducted by the *Washington Post* and the Kaiser Family Foundation. "Two-thirds of couples in black-white partnerships said at least one set of parents objected to their union at its start," the *Post* reported. "Disapproval is highest in white communities—46 percent of those surveyed say it is better to marry within one's race."

In addition, "86 percent of black respondents said their families would welcome a white person into the fold—31 percentage points higher than the percentage of whites who said they would accept them." The report continues, "About three-quarters of Latino families would warmly accept black people, who ranked somewhat below white people in their eyes. Among Asian families, 77 percent would welcome a new white member and 71 percent a Latino. Black people were somewhat less likely to be accepted, at 66 percent."[9]

Overall, however, researchers concluded that approval of interracial marriage is on the rise and increasing at a rapid pace. More people now say they approve than disapprove, a departure from the attitudes of generations past.

Despite the numbers, I'm still not ready to give the black community a clean pass when it comes to attitudes toward interracial relationships. Granted, the survey found black families were more accepting of interracial unions when compared to white folks. But is that really saying much?

It's been my experience that progressive-thinking white people have been OK with interracial dating for some time. They may not choose to date interracially themselves but have no problem with it if that's what friends or relatives elect to do.

In contrast, I've run into otherwise progressive-thinking black people who not only frown on interracial coupling, they're not afraid to make their objections known right to your face. They embrace liberal politics, support affirmative action, and claim to value diversity. But on interracial romance, they turn sour.

In some cases, their reaction stems from a sense of rejection. Many black women, for example, complain of a lack of available black men to date, while having to live in a culture that reinforces white ideals of beauty. Just look at the vast majority of advertisements for makeup and hair-care products. The media images glorify whiteness in much the same way they glorify youth and thinness. Whether black folks actually buy into those images or not, if black men are crossing racial lines in the dating game, where does that leave black women if no one crosses over to date them?

Looking at data from the 2000 census, it seems the sense of rejection has some foundation. Among the non-Hispanic population, the number of interracially married couples in the United States involving black men and white women was nearly 209,000. That compares with fewer than 79,000 interracial couples consisting of black women and white men.

Meanwhile, there were more than 503,000 marriages of white men to Hispanic women, more than 380,000 marriages between white men and Asian women, and more than 137,000 marriages between white men and Native American women.[10]

The message is hardly a subtle one: when non-Hispanic white men enter into relationships outside of their own racial and ethnic group, they select Latino, Asian, and Native American women in far greater numbers than black women.

Psychologist Maria Root, in her book *Love's Revolution*, suggests sexism also plays a significant role in how the numbers have shaken out. "Male privilege accounts for black men's ability to intermarry much more freely than black women can," she writes. "Men are still in the position of choosing and women in the position of hoping to be chosen."[11]

The civil rights movement may have given men and women greater opportunity to pursue interracial romance, but how often are women the ones doing the pursuing? Not even the strides of the feminist movement have radically altered our notions of gender when it comes to dating. Men approaching women rather than the other way around remains the cultural norm, an arrangement most women don't seem eager to change.

"White men just don't ask me out. So I just really don't have a choice in the matter," said Courtenay Edelhart when I asked her about her preference for black men. "I've had two white boyfriends. One was my first kiss in eighth grade." The other, she says, was a Jewish man she met after her freshman year of college who was fascinated to discover they shared the same faith.

Her sister, Ashley Edelhart Hall, dated a few white men before meeting her husband but found the relationships never worked out.

"They would always end up making some really racist comment, not really thinking it was racist," she said. "Most of the time, they would say they wouldn't normally date a black girl, but they would make the exception for me. Well, what are you going to do when you meet my mom? She's brown. So if you can't really handle black, you're not going to be able to handle me. It's my package. So I just never felt that I could relate to them. How could I ever be serious about a relationship with a person who's making an exception because of the way I look?"

For the biracial person, dating in general raises some interesting questions. For instance, when a friend recommended I check out the online dating site eHarmony.com, I discovered that the questionnaire each applicant is asked to fill out, at that time, did not allow me to select more than one race. Clicking on "black" was instantly canceled out the moment I clicked on "white," and vice versa. I haven't returned to the site since, though I can't say I was all that interested in signing up for the service in the first place. Like many singles, I was mainly curious to see the results of my "personality profile" and what that might tell me about the type of person deemed a suitable match.

As a lifelong bachelor, I have yet to get it right when it comes to relationships and have now grown accustomed to living single. I've gone out with women across the racial spectrum but have never been involved with anyone long term—a fact that I have learned speaks to my issues involving intimacy, commitment, and rejection rather than race. A college professor once told me that in finding a mate, we generally look for someone who either shares certain characteristics in terms of ethnic background, education, religious beliefs, and social class, or someone who has a healthy respect and appreciation for differences in these areas, an awareness of how such differences may play out in our lives, and a sensitivity to our needs.

I've met women who I initially thought fit that bill—some white, some biracial, one who is Japanese—but it's never worked out.

Interestingly, the black women I have gone out with are usually not compatible with me in terms of religion, which we discover very early. I have nothing against anyone who takes their faith seriously, as most members of my extended family do. I just don't share the same sense of conviction, which in a relationship can become a source of tension. Women who are "spiritual but not religious" have potential. But I have a hard time seeing myself with someone whose religious practices loom any larger than that, and most of the black women I meet fall into that category.

Other issues on the dating scene can also arise. As Kathleen Odell Korgen writes in *From Black to Biracial*, "For many biracial Americans, dating is an experience rife with the varied racial opinions of their social network. Instead of being a private relationship between two people, it becomes a public discussion of racial alliance or rejection."12

Sundee had such an experience in college when she became involved with a black student at the University of Southern California. "It definitely created some tension with the other black women on campus. Because at USC, the black community is fairly small, and so everyone kind of knew each other's business. Plus, he was also a football player," she said, which at USC made him well-known on campus. "I heard through him that some of the black sisters were angry at him. They confronted him. You know, 'Why are you dating that light-skinned girl?' Who knows, maybe they thought I was white. I doubt it though, because I was involved with the Black Student Union, and I hung out with black students. So I'm sure they knew I was mixed. But they felt I was too light for him and that he should be with a 'real' sister. That was definitely painful."

In the end, they broke up. "It wasn't about race. It didn't seem like the right fit," said Sundee. "He wanted to get married; I didn't. Spiritually, he was going in a different direction than I was."

Sundee later married Matt Frazier, "a plain ol' white guy from Kentucky," whom she met through her work with the campus ministry. "Quite honestly, I don't know how Matt turned out the way he did in terms of racial openness," she said.

But not all members of his family see things his way. "There was an awkward moment with an uncle who said 'nigger' in my presence, and obviously did not know who I was," recalled Sundee. "I didn't know what to say. I was shocked. And Matt's mom actually spoke up and said, 'That's not right, you shouldn't talk like that.' But I pretty much fled the scene with Matt at that point because it was too awkward for me. I'm not going to stand there and say, 'Hey, you're talking about me.' It was a family reunion event, and there were a lot of people around. But later, Matt told his dad, 'Look, you gotta tell the family.'"

The couple's reaction that day was telling. Even when the in-laws are supportive, the extended family can still make waves. Either the relatives get with the program and at least practice proper racial etiquette, or Matt and Sundee are prepared to walk away.

"My presence in their lives has certainly gotten them to think much more about racial issues," Sundee said of Matt's parents. "I think they're more open than they would have been had they not had a biracial daughter-in-law."

In the final scene of *Guess Who's Coming to Dinner*, Spencer Tracy's character also undergoes a change of heart. He delivers an emotional speech to his daughter and future son-in-law in which he tells them they will encounter many people who will be opposed to their relationship. But he is no longer one of them. He advises them to hold tightly to one another and say to those people, "Screw them!"

The advice is just as appropriate today as it was then. But at the same time, it's also evident that attitudes are changing. Interracial couples now enter a world that is more receptive to their choice of partner than ever before.

One of the messages I found posted to Ken Tanabe's Web site underscores that progress. It comes from a woman in an interracial marriage who had never heard of *Loving v. Virginia* until she stumbled upon LovingDay.org. "I have never realized this before, but I was reading this Web site and found that my biracial son was born on Loving Day 2004," the message reads. "My son is the biggest confirmation of love for me and my husband. Now that I know that his birthday is the same day as the legal decision that allows me to be married to the man I love, it means so much more."

Monoracial People,
Multiracial Families

AT THE END OF THE CIVIL WAR, IT IS SAID, GENERAL WILLIAM Sherman promised newly freed slaves forty acres and a mule as a form of reparations.

It never came to pass.

And yet Irene Johnson ended up with forty acres and a horse.

"I got really lucky," said Irene, laughing at the irony. Irene is a biracial woman who was adopted by a white couple four days after her birth in 1968. She grew up on a forty-acre farm in Conneaut, Ohio, a small town in the northeastern corner of the state near the Pennsylvania border.

"It was so much fun. Obviously we weren't even near the big city. I didn't even know what a big city was. But I appreciate growing up on that farm and just being around nature," she said. "We boarded horses, we had pigs, we had chickens. My dad was a farmer so he was always out on the farm. We had corn, we had tomatoes, and we used to sell all the produce in front of our house. Back then it was an honor system where you could just put the vegetables out there, and people would put the change in and take the food. It was definitely the country."

But as fond as Irene's childhood memories are, her placement with a white adoptive family in a rural white community would have raised the suspicions of the National Association of Black Social Workers. In 1972, the organization produced a policy statement on the importance of "preserving African American families," which it subsequently reinforced in 1994. "Transracial adoption of an African American child should only be considered after documented evidence of unsuccessful same-race placements has been reviewed and supported by appropriate representatives of the African American community," the updated position paper states.[1]

Several decades have now passed since the Supreme Court cleared the way for couples to marry interracially. But adopting children across racial lines remains a dicey subject. Are white parents capable of raising healthy children of color? Irene's answer is a resounding yes.

"Color was never an issue until people on the outside would stare at me and my family, you know, holding hands," she said. "People couldn't figure out which one of my parents messed up, or in their eyes messed up, because you've got this little chocolate child holding these two white people's hands."

Irene's adoptive parents had already raised three biological children by the time she joined the family. Her birth mother, she has since learned, was a fifteen-year-old white girl from a nearby town who had become pregnant by a black boyfriend.

So the fact that her adoption is considered "transracial" speaks volumes about American attitudes toward race. A half-black, half-white child adopted by a black family is considered a same-race placement. The same child placed with a white family is viewed as a transracial adoption.

I met Irene soon after I moved to Washington, D.C., where she now works as a television news photographer. I had no idea she was biracial until she brought it up while the two of us were on our way to cover a story. She has a medium brown complexion and short, wavy black hair. Her family, she says, didn't make a fuss about race.

"My mother was a day care provider. She always took care of kids in our home, so I always had plenty of friends," said Irene. "I always knew I was adopted, so I knew I was different. And that was cool with me."

By Irene's count, the town of Conneaut had only a couple of black families at the time and was void of any semblance of black culture. She grew up listening to country music, was a self-described tomboy, and experienced considerable culture shock when she left home for college and moved into a dormitory at the University of Akron.

"I was overwhelmed," she said. "My suite mates were all from Cleveland. And I guess growing up I just thought all black people lived in Cleveland. So my first year in college, I get the blackest people from Cleveland. I have never been surrounded by so many black people in my life."

Fitting in, she discovered, required making adjustments. "They embraced me, and I kind of got the whole schooling on black folks. I learned a lot," she said. "I found out you don't walk by black folks without speaking to them because they'll think you're stuck-up or you're better than them. You speak to people you don't know. That was my first lesson. I'll never forget, because my first couple weeks on campus, I didn't speak to nobody. And I couldn't figure out why people were like, 'Hey, how you doin'?' I don't know them. But I learned quickly. One of my suite mates took me aside and told me, 'Look, if someone speaks to you, you have to speak back to them because that's what we do. We stick together like that.' And from that point on, I'm like, OK. It wasn't hard at all."

She added, "It was kind of a learning experience for me just to be around the black people, like going to the dances. Old-school music to them was new-school music to me. And that's what I appreciated through the college experience."

Such culture shock, I can imagine, would have sent some students packing. But Irene kept a positive attitude.

"In a way, it might be a shame because maybe I should have known this before I went away to college. Maybe I should have been around my people. But it didn't affect me at all. I don't fault my parents for that. I was loved growing up. That's all that mattered," she said.

If only all adoptions turned out so well.

Michelle Hughes is an adoption attorney and the founder of Bridge Communications, which conducts classes for parents adopting across racial lines. "While there are many transracial adoptees who are biracial whose parents did a wonderful job, there are many whose parents screwed it up royally. And I don't want another generation having to go through that," said Michelle, whose company is based in Chicago. "The ones who screwed them up the most were the ones who took biracial kids and told them they were white."

"There were parents who did that?" I said.

"Oh, yeah, I've met quite a few. I haven't met the parents, I've met the kids," she said.

Michelle, although not adopted, is biracial and has always identified that way. "As I tell people, I came into the world with one white parent and a black parent, and I'm leaving the world with one white parent and a black parent. I'm going to claim them both. And I think that because my parents are married, I probably have a stronger sense of claiming it than some biracial people I know whose parents never married, are divorced, or adopted. The interracial family part was in my face every day in a positive way, and consequently I wish to claim it all."

But Michelle's racial background is largely a secret to potential clients who only know her as a voice over the telephone. When screening prospective adoptive parents, she routinely asks if the couple has a preference for the race of their child. That's when she's told, "We'll take anything but black."

"I'm told that regularly," said Michelle. "Some of those people will take a biracial kid but not a black kid."

"What's up with that?" I asked her.

"For some people, I think they're hoping they can pass that kid off as a white kid. For some people, they think because the kid is half white, 'we'll have some type of identification with him.' I think for people, there's definitely this whole exotic thing going on, and biracial kids are the cutest thing since sliced bread, blah, blah, blah. And then I often hear, 'Well, people in our neighborhood will accept a biracial kid better than they'll accept a black kid,' which— having grown up in a white neighborhood, I don't think it really made a difference whether I was biracial or black.

"I think for the average white American—biracial, black—there is no distinction. But when they start adopting, they start making a distinction," she continued. "They'll take an Asian child, they'll take a biracial child, they'll take a Latino child. A lot of times people will think, if I take this Asian child, they're almost white and they won't have to face any discrimination. So it's always interesting to do panels where people are intending to adopt only from Asia, and you get the adult Asian adoptees out there and they're talking about all their racist experiences. You can sort of see the parents' eyes popping out of their heads. I think there are differences in what the stereotypes are, but still you're going to be a multiracial family."

For Michelle, growing up biracial meant being "black-plus." As she explains it, "You get all the crap of being black, plus all the crap of being biracial." Educating white parents about the realities of interracial families is one of the goals of Michelle's seminars. "We talk about tolerating no racism of any group. We talk about celebrating all cultures. We talk about a loss of privacy," she said. "Whenever you go out as a multiracial family to a restaurant or a mall or church, everyone's going to stare at you and try to figure out, 'how does that family come together?' You can't blend into a crowd. You just can't do it. And I found that to be true as a child, too, even though I'm not adopted. Everybody knew who the heck I was. Part of it was living in a white neighborhood and being the only kid of color besides my siblings. But it was also about my parents being interracially married."

Couples who attend the classes also have homework assignments. Michelle will send them on a scavenger hunt to find such items as black hair-care products or ethnic newspapers and magazines. She asks them to spend time listening to black talk radio and white talk radio and then compare opinions. Another assignment involves putting the couple in a social situation in which 99 percent of the people look like their child.

"The exercise is for them to go and find out what it feels like to be the only one, because often that's what they're about to do with their children," said Michelle.

One in-class assignment, known as the bead exercise, also reinforces the point. "We take beads that represent different races, and then we ask a series of questions," she explained. "The people you work with are mostly what race? The place you worship, the people consist of what race? Your primary doctor is what race? Your best friend is what race?"

Each time, parents place a colored bead corresponding to their answer in a cup. Then they are asked, "The child you're intending to adopt is what race?"

"Often what will happen is people will have eight white beads and one black bead, or eight white beads and one Asian bead. And the black bead or the Asian bead is their kid," said Michelle. "And it's a very visual exercise that allows them to see, 'Oh, my god, my world is really white.' I occasionally get parents who say, 'Wow, my world is pretty diverse, this is pretty cool. I didn't really realize I have as diverse a world as I do.' But most of the time we get parents who have one bead of color in the entire thing."

Despite all that she sees and hears in the course of her work, Michelle is not opposed to transracial adoption. In many communities, same-race adoptions are simply not possible for every child needing a home.

"When it comes to African-American kids, there are not enough black families or white families who want to adopt that healthy black baby. I'm not even talking about crack babies and whatever. I'm talking about healthy black babies. I have never, in the fifteen years I've been practicing, had an adoption agency call me and say, 'Michelle, we have a healthy white baby and we can't find a family for him,'" she said. "If we got into a situation where there are black parents lined up for every one of these black kids, then we can discuss if having black parents is more important than having white parents. But right now, the discussion is whether having parents is more important than having no parents."

Michelle has also seen parents who've adopted transracially and gotten it right. "They made that extra effort to bring diversity into that child's world," she said.

The problem, as I like to say, isn't white parents; it's white parents without a clue.

Barbara Gowan agrees. Now in her forties, she is the biracial daughter of a white woman and a black man who was adopted by a black couple in 1963.

"I used to believe that it's better not to transracially adopt. That used to be my thought, probably because of a lot of the issues that I had about my race and the way people treated me," said Barbara, a school nurse in Springfield, Massachusetts. "I was subjected to a lot of prejudice, probably because I was raised in a predominantly white neighborhood and I wasn't white. I didn't like how that made me feel. So my initial feelings were, they need to stay with their own race."

Her opinion changed, however, when she began doing research for a book she is writing on growing up in adoptive families. "I know one girl who goes to my school who has two white adoptive parents who are wonderful. And they raised a whole bunch of biracial kids and did a great, great job. And I interviewed several transracially adopted biracial adults for my book. And they seem to be happy with how their life was. So now my view has changed. I think it's an OK thing to transracially adopt. However, I think the person doing the transracial adoption really needs to realize that whatever the race of the child they're adopting, it needs to be acknowledged. It needs to be something that they work into their lives."

When she was forty-one, Barbara managed to locate her birth parents and now has a relationship with her biological father, who she says has welcomed her into the family. "I've seen my father probably five or six times. He has a sister who is thirteen years older than me and she's like a sister to me. So I have met some relatives who have kind of filled that void that I was looking for. Even though I thought it would always come from my mother, it ended up coming from my father."

Her biological mother, she says, has indicated she does not want to meet, though the two exchange e-mails. "So I think over the years I've just decided to be grateful for what I have. I don't mean her any harm, and if she doesn't want to meet me, I'm not going to push myself on her. But it did hurt at first because I felt it was because I was black. People can say that's not what it is, but I believe that's what it is," Barbara said. "She told me her husband had black friends but didn't believe in interracial relationships. So I can imagine if that's how he feels, seeing me pop up wouldn't be a pleasant thing for him."

"I never ever cared about meeting my natural parents, because my adoptive parents were my parents," said Irene. "My main thing is I just wanted to see a picture of her, of my mother and father."

As it turned it, she did manage to locate both of her birth parents. Her mother is not interested in meeting, and although she has met her father, she does not have an ongoing relationship with him.

"Do you have any advice for white parents who are adopting black or biracial children today?" I asked Irene.

"My advice has always been to love that child like their own. Never make that child think that he was a mistake. [With] my parents, from day one, I was a Johnson," she said firmly. "It was funny," she added, "I have a black last name."

Children of the Rainbow

THEO HARPER AND BECKY KJELSTROM TOOK A SEAT ON THEIR living room couch, their two children sitting in between them. Bill Livingston, a television news photographer, was in the far corner of the room, making a last-minute adjustment to his lights. Finally, with everything in place, Bill peered into the viewfinder of his camera. "I'm rolling," he said. That was my cue to start the interview.

It was the spring of 1991, and Bill and I were making a documentary on interracial families that would air on KPTV in Portland, Oregon. The Harpers were one of the local families who would be featured in the program. Becky is white. Theo is black.

When Theo and I first discussed participating in the project, he responded with enthusiasm. "But then again, my family tells me I'm the kind of person who could walk into a Klan meeting and say, 'What's happenin', y'all!'" he told me, indicating he would need to consult his wife and children before committing them to an interview. Ultimately, the rest of the family said yes.

The couple's oldest son, Holt, was ten years old at the time. He had a light-to-medium-brown complexion, European facial features, and straight black hair. His younger brother, Tor, was seven years old. He was noticeably lighter in complexion, with more African facial features compared to his brother, and dark brown, curly hair.

The two brothers represent what demographers will occasionally refer to as America's biracial baby boom. In 1970, the U.S. Census Bureau estimated the number of children in interracial families at 460,000. In 1980, the number doubled to 996,000, and by 1990, it had doubled again to more than 1.9 million.[1] In the 2000 census, more than 2.8 million people under the age of 18 were identified as belonging to more than one race.[2]

As the camera rolled, the Harpers told me about their courtship, the reaction of their families when their relationship became serious, and the racism they encountered as an interracial couple. What I didn't know then was how this one family's story would provide such an illustrative case study on the multiracial experience in America. That realization wouldn't hit me for another decade.

Theo and Becky met during their college years in the 1970s when they were both students at the University of Utah. Initially, their decision to marry was a source of tension among both their extended families. But by the time of our interview, they indicated their relatives had since warmed to them as a couple.

The rest of the world, however, still had issues with interracial relationships that the Harpers were forced to confront. Theo described getting pulled over by police in southern Oregon for reasons he believes were related to the fact that he is black and his passenger was a white woman. Becky described the difficulty they had renting an apartment when the two would show up together to meet the landlord.

"Do you see any benefits to being an interracial couple?" I asked them.

"I think one of the benefits to our relationship is you don't close yourself down to your environment," said Theo. "I think there are a lot of things she shows me and I think there are a lot of things that I show her." As an example, the two went on to describe their love of jazz and how each one had exposed the other to jazz artists and styles of music they had not been familiar with before.

Said Becky, "To be honest, being married to a black man and having children now who are part-black has really taught me what racism is all about. You know, for white people, racism is an occasional thing. You may bump into it occasionally, or you may go to a rally occasionally, or you may talk about racism occasionally. But if you're a minority, racism is an every-day, every-second-of-your-life type of thing that you're faced with."

She paused to think about her answer. "That's going to sound like a bummer," she remarked. After all, the question I'd asked had to do with whether there were any pluses to life as an interracial couple. But for Becky, becoming more attuned to racism is exactly that. Having a greater awareness and heightened sensitivity to issues of race, culture, and diversity *is* one of the positive aspects to come from her experience raising an interracial family.

We then started to talk about the children's racial identity. I wanted to know how their two sons would answer if presented with the "What are you?" question.

"I'd probably answer that I'm black," said Holt, the older of the two boys. "But if they were bothering me about it, I'd probably just ignore them."

Tor, however, had a different answer. Like many children I've interviewed, he was somewhat shy about answering questions posed directly to him, unless the questions I asked were then repeated by one of his parents, in which case he would respond to them. Theo, who also seemed curious to hear how his children felt about their racial identity, looked at Tor, who was seated closest to him.

"So what would you say?" Theo asked.

Tor gazed into the eyes of his black father and declared, "I'm white."

"You're white? You think you're white?" asked Theo, sounding somewhat surprised. "You don't think you have black in you?"

"I don't have very much black," said Tor, glancing down at his arm as if to inspect the color of his flesh.

"You're talking about just your skin color," interjected his mother, Becky. "But what about who you are?"

"You know that you're part black and part white, don't you?" asked Theo.

"Yeah," he said. "'Cause my skin looks black and white."

"Your skin looks black and white," Theo repeated, as if to affirm Tor's observation, "like a combination of black and white."

As I watched Tor's interaction with his parents, I could see his thought process at work: if Mommy is considered white, and Daddy is considered black, and my skin color is closer to Mommy's than Daddy's, then I must be white.

His conclusion wasn't all that out of step with how he was sometimes perceived. His parents recounted a trip the family had made to a local Greek festival. Members of Portland's Greek community asked Tor what part of Greece he was from. When Bill Livingston and I were in the process of editing the documentary for broadcast, one of our white co-workers saw the videotape of the two brothers and remarked, "They look Mexican." If Tor was supposed to think of himself as black, that's not the message many of those around him seemed to be sending. Not at that point in his life, anyway.

As the dialogue between Tor and his parents unfolded, Holt sat quietly on the couch. I can't be certain about what he was thinking at that moment. But the expression on his face seemed to say, "I can't believe my brother is saying he's white—and the TV people are here!"

Holt, who is both older and darker in complexion than Tor, showed signs of a higher level of understanding about the social construct of race. His answer—"I'd probably say I'm black, but if they were bothering me about it, I'd probably just ignore them"— also suggests that the motivation of the person asking the question might somehow play a part in how he would respond.

I found myself amazed at how similar these two brothers' thought patterns were to my own childhood logic surrounding race. Both Tor and Holt were repeating the same process I had gone through. For Tor, race was a skin color. Simple as that. For Holt, color was part of the equation, but not the only part.

Neither Theo nor Becky attempted to "correct" either of their children when it came to their racial identity. The conversation that evening was more of an exploration, a discussion aimed at revealing how their children were processing issues about race. I wasn't yet aware of psychologist James Jacobs's work in this area. But it seemed the Harpers, without even knowing it, were following his advice to the letter.

"Children need help from their parents to verbalize racial thoughts and feelings," Jacobs writes. "Supportive interest rather than alarm at the child's ambivalence will facilitate identity development. If the child's racial ambivalence is suppressed, he or she will likely stop actively exploring his or her racial identity and will feel that there is something inherently wrong with or degrading about his or her racial status."[3]

The bottom line: the parents of young biracial children exhibiting signs of what might appear to be "racial confusion" can relax. Those ideas will change over time.

In the years that have passed since I first met the Harper family, I'd often wondered if Holt and Tor's racial identities had changed as they matured. In 2001, I got my answer. That's the year I made a trip back to Portland and arranged to meet with the Harpers once more.

Theo and Becky were celebrating their twenty-fifth year of marriage. Holt was home on vacation from college. Tor was finishing his last year of high school.

"So what's changed?" I asked.

"What hasn't?" Holt responded.

"Well, the children have gotten larger," Theo answered.

That would be an understatement. Holt was now wearing glasses and sporting a mustache and thin beard. Tor had grown huskier and had the body mass of a linebacker. His once short, curly hair had grown out into a full-blown, 1970s-style Afro.

"If somebody asks, 'What are you?' how do you answer that?" I asked them.

"I usually just say everything I can think of at the time—my mom's white, and my dad's black," said Holt. "And if I have the time, I'll say, my dad's black, and there's some South American something in there. And my mom's white, but it's all over the place—English, Swedish, and several other things."

Said Tor, "I'd probably ask the person in return, what's it matter? Are you going to leave now because I'm black?" He pauses. "Or because I'm white? You know, what's it matter to anybody?"

The two brothers had essentially switched positions. Ten years earlier, Holt had been the one who said he would sidestep anyone who was bothering him about race but would otherwise declare a black identity. Tor had declared himself white, saying he "didn't have very much black" in him. A decade later, both had adopted multiracial identities, but Tor was now the one saying he would question the motivation of anyone asking about his background. He had also embraced blackness more fervently than before and, said Theo, had shown greater interest in engaging in the fight against racism.

But none of this came as much of a surprise to their parents. "The kids are exposed to things that a lot of African American children are exposed to because I'm just going to be into those things," said Theo. "And they're exposed to things that children in a middle-class neighborhood in America are exposed to because we live in a middle-class neighborhood in America." Turning to Becky, he added, "And they learn about your family and your heritage because her family is really into genealogy and that sort of thing."

But perhaps the biggest challenge the family had faced since we last spoke had nothing to do with race at all. It was, instead, a matter of life and death.

"A car ran over my head, and whoa!" said Tor jokingly.

But it was no laughing matter.

It had happened eight years earlier, while he was riding his bicycle in their suburban Portland neighborhood. Tor had fallen off the bike and into the path of a car. He was wearing a helmet, which the family credits with saving his life, though the helmet itself was shattered.

Tor remembered little of the accident. As he began to describe what happened, others interrupted to either fill in gaps in the story or correct some of the details he provided. According to the family, when paramedics arrived, they found Tor unconscious and bleeding from the nose. Although the accident occurred just blocks from St. Vincent's Hospital on Portland's west side, Tor was rushed across town to Emmanuel Hospital, one of the area's top centers for pediatric trauma.

"The doctor said he may not live. And I said, 'No, that's not going to happen,'" said Theo. "And we went on from there."

Tor remained in a coma for a month.

Suddenly, any concerns the Harpers had had about the racial issues their children would confront seemed trivial compared with what they now faced. Tor suffered some brain damage in the accident, which has resulted in some minor paralysis to one side of his body—though I wouldn't have noticed had it not been pointed out to me. Physically, his functioning appears normal. Most dramatic, however, is the effect on his short-term memory.

"Some things are just lost totally, like he can never remember them," said Becky. "For example, we'll go to a movie and when we come out of the movie, he'll ask what movie we just saw. But if you tell him what we just saw, then he'll remember it."

According to his parents, medical experts believe his brain is creating the memory but has difficulty retrieving it. As a result, when Tor returned to school, he was placed in special education classes to address what had become a learning disability.

"If you were assigned a chapter in a history book to read," I asked Tor, "would you be able to complete that lesson?"

"Oh, I'd probably have to take notes," Tor answered.

"You live by notes," his brother interjected. "Little pieces of paper all over the house."

Sure enough, before I left their home that night, Tor pointed out various Post-it notes he'd stuck on one cabinet or another to remind him of something. His mother told me that if he were to read a full-length book without taking notes, by chapter three he would have forgotten what he'd read in chapter one.

"What about filling out forms?" I asked, steering the conversation back toward race before the night got away from us. "Like on the census, what did you check?"

"If it's a box to check, I'll pick 'multiracial' if it's there," said Holt.

Although there was no "multiracial" box on the 2000 census, individuals could check more than one racial category, which is what the family says they did.

Said Tor, "I think the best thing for me to do since my head injury is to check 'black,' 'white,' 'Hispanic,' and then put question marks around everything else," he laughed, as if any other heritages he might have are beyond his recollection.

"Do you have any advice for any other interracial families who are raising their children today?" I asked, wrapping up our interview.

"Just ignore people who are treating you badly because you're different from them," Tor offered. "I mean, unless you're going to take them to some multiracial class about how to treat other people, there's not much you can do about it."

Holt suggested that finding the right neighborhood with the right attitude is important. "I think we've also been lucky in growing up in an area that's a lot more open and—not necessarily diverse—but definitely has a good sampling of lots of different nationalities," he said.

"What I see happening is we've kind of found the places where we belong more by our interests than racial orientation at all," said Becky. "The boys were really into sports. Holt's been involved in water polo and swimming, and Tor's been involved in dragon boats with the Special Olympics team. You have to find those places you belong based on your interests more than anything."

Theo nodded in agreement and added, "My thinking is just simply love your kids and enjoy your life. The reality is that there's always going to be someone who doesn't like what you do—no matter who you are, no matter what you do. If you keep living your life by what they think, you're not going to live a very good life. It's important to decide what works for you, where your center is, and work out of that. And I think that's basically what we've done," he said, smiling at his wife of twenty-five years. "Enjoyed life as much as we can."

On Neutral Ground

"SHOULD I WRITE THIS ADDRESS IN PENCIL?" A FRIEND OF MINE asked over the phone.

I had just relocated from Cincinnati, Ohio, to Orlando, Florida, to start my sixth job in a sixth state in eight years. Like many television journalists, I've done my share of moving around in the course of my career, which is not at all unusual for those of us who've chosen this line of work.

"You can write this address in pen," I told my old college classmate. "I'm not moving again anytime soon." Three years after uttering those words, I packed up once more and headed for the nation's capital, where I now work on a freelance basis for a number of news organizations.

I have since come to realize that all the moving and traveling and job-switching I've done has played a role in shaping my views on race, culture, and identity. It is not unlike the experience of "military brats" whose lives are shaped by their family's frequent transfers from place to place, exposing them to a wide array of social customs and practices. The dynamics of race relations differ from city to city and certainly from country to country. The more parts of the world I see, the more I realize how bizarre America's approach to racial classification sounds to people who have grown up outside the United States.

Before I left WKMG-TV in Orlando for Washington, D.C., a television news photographer there had given me the nickname "Mr. Travel."

"How did I earn that?" I asked another co-worker of mine.

"Because you're always going somewhere," he said, as if it should have been obvious to me. And he wasn't talking about my career moves. "You're always planning a trip, or catching a plane, or just flying in from someplace."

It's true my passport has been stamped in a number of ports of call over the years—Japan, Hong Kong, Indonesia, Venezuela, Panama, South Africa, England, Spain, France, Germany—not to mention the frequent-flier miles I rack up for the traveling I do domestically.

But "Mr. Travel"? I just never thought of myself as warranting that label. Wherever I've gone, I seem to run into people who are crisscrossing the planet far more frequently and stopping off in far more places. But I guess in a country where the vast majority of citizens don't even have a passport, the extent of my travel log takes some folks by surprise.

My travel diary cannot compare to that of the Noons family, however. They break all the rules when it comes to race, color, culture, and nationality—and it's because of all the traveling they've done throughout their lives.

Kyra and Bianca Noons were born in Africa in the late 1970s. Their mother is a white Jamaican, and their father is a black Englishman. That is not a misprint. Their Jamaican mother is white, their British father is black, and the girls were born in Africa. To further complicate the story, their parents met in France.

I sat down with Kyra, Bianca, and their father, Tony, in Houston, Texas, where the three now live. They explained their family's history this way: in the early seventies, Tony Noons, who was born in Birmingham, England, had launched an acting career in the United Kingdom and managed to land a role in the musical *Hair*.

"I played the part of Hud. I was in the London show and I was on the national tour in England," said Tony. His career then took him to Paris, where he also enrolled in a language school to learn French. His future wife was a student there as well.

"Valerie walked by and one of the cast members said, 'There's a beautiful girl.' We were introduced and hit it off immediately," said Tony. "And it was the springtime, and you fall in love in Paris in the springtime," he added, with a touch of romance still in his voice.

Tony and Valerie then moved to Kenya, where Tony embarked on his next adventure—leading safari tours. The couple got married shortly thereafter. Their two daughters were born in the capital city of Nairobi—Kyra in 1976, and Bianca in 1978.

"The race thing for me was never a problem," said Tony. "I never allowed that to be a monkey on my back, because that was the problem that people had to deal with. If they have an issue about it, let them deal with it. I've got more important things to do than get into a whole thing about race and this and that. Accept me for who I am. If you have a problem with that, that's your problem, not mine. And that was my attitude."

The family lived in Africa until 1979, then spent seven years in England, where they had two more children, sons Daniel and Luke. From there, they moved to Jamaica and finally moved to the United States in the early 1990s, when Kyra and Bianca were teenagers.

"So we've got all the different cultures in our heritage within us, literally," Kyra said. "And to be honest with you, the only time we got faced with 'What are you?' and had to even think about the whole issue of color or race was in America."

"Because they have to label you somehow," Bianca interjected. "You can't just be 'multiracial.' Come on, now. You're *something*," she said, mocking those who have questioned their ethnicity. "It probably hit me harder moving over here than it did Kyra."

Kyra had moved to the United States first and lived with an aunt until the rest of the family joined her. As a result, the sisters were temporarily assigned to different schools. At about the same time, Tony and Valerie decided to end their marriage.

"When I came over, I was thrown into Westbury High School in Houston," said Bianca. "It was a mainly black school, but not like Jamaican black. I went through culture shock like crazy even though I was coming from Jamaica, where it is mainly black."

"It's all about the people that you're with. If they're accepting and loving of you and who you are, then that side of you or that part of the culture that's within you already will come out," said Kyra. "For us multiracial people, you definitely have to reach a point in your life where you're not trying to be one culture or the other. You just love every aspect that is good of each one that's in you. So I'd have to say you get that from traveling and getting to see other people in action and other cultures."

"A lot comes from the parental position and how they draw from that," said Tony, noting the way in which his attitude on race seems to have rubbed off on his children. "You know who you are as a person, as an individual. You're centered. So from there you can deal with anything that comes about, anything that happens, anything around you, whatever opinions people have, let them come to terms with that. You know who you are."

The approach Tony describes is actually reflected in psychological literature in which researchers distinguish between an individual's "core identity" versus a "role identity." A core identity, writes professor Michael Thornton, "is an essential self, strongly defended and stable." By comparison, a role identity—such as a person's occupation, for example—is subject to change. "The assumption is that racial labels reflect a core identity rather than a role identity," Thornton states. "I choose 'black' from a list because I know that is what society calls me. . . . It may say nothing about my core identity."[1]

While skin color and other physical features may be permanent, racial group membership is up for grabs depending on how a particular society or subculture chooses to define race. I would suggest that for many biracial people, their core identity is tied to their knowledge of their dual heritage, while their role identity may cause them to place more emphasis on one aspect of their background in a particular situation.

My own experience traveling abroad has allowed me to see just how much racial perceptions can shift from culture to culture. As historian F. James Davis has observed, "The same person defined as black in the United States may be considered 'coloured' in Jamaica or Martinique and white in Puerto Rico or the Dominican Republic." That's been my observation in Latin America as well. In Brazil—one country I have yet to visit—the standards change yet again. "The same Brazilian may be referred to by many different Portuguese terms of racial classification, and there is even disagreement about the meaning of the terms of reference," Davis writes. "The implied rule is that a person is classified into one of many possible types on the basis of physical appearance and class standing, not by ancestry. The designation of one's racial identity need not be the same as that of the parents, and siblings are often classified differently from one another."

Even by American standards, neither Kyra nor Bianca "look black." Bianca has a light complexion and sprinkles of blond in her hair. Kyra is slightly darker in complexion and has a darker hair color as well. As a result, people often react with disbelief when they reveal their background.

"I'm talking to a black Jamaican man, and he's asking me where I'm from. And I say Jamaica, and he says, 'You're not from Jamaica. What part of Jamaica?'" said Kyra. "It's not about proving to anybody where you're from. I think a lot of people do that without even realizing it here in this country. They try to put themselves in one category or another. I see some multiracial, mixed black or white people struggling within themselves to say, 'Yo, I'm black,' and they live up to what they think is that culture to make themselves more black, to bring out that side. Or if they want to consider themselves white, you know, they have preconceived ideas of what that culture is, how they act, instead of embracing them all and just being who they are."

Added Bianca, "I thank the Lord that I've been able to travel and experience the outside world from America because it definitely opens your mind. You're not just one track. You see things from a much broader perspective. It's so easy when you haven't traveled— what you know is what you know from where you are and your surroundings. When you're able to travel and experience much more and see poverty and see the rich, too, you just mix it up and love it up. I am blessed."

As the women shared their story, I began to wonder how I would describe their accents. Their father, Tony, as one Houston newspaper put it, sounds like Sir David Frost. But Kyra and Bianca were harder to peg. At times, their voices took on a British accent; at other times, they sounded more Jamaican.

"It can be either/or," Kyra confirmed.

"It switches," added Bianca. "One minute you're this way, one minute you're that. English, Jamaican, just all around. It changes depending on who you're talking to."

"Jamaica was a British commonwealth before it became independent. So it's very close sometimes. For us, anyway," said Kyra.

"How do people react to the accent?" I asked.

"They say, 'Oh, do that again,'" said Bianca.

"Like you're a novelty act?" I said.

"Oh, yeah. God, yeah. It's constant," Bianca answered.

Ironically, Kyra and Bianca have in fact become an act. The two have embarked on a musical career with their father serving as their manager. Their stage name: Neutral Sisters. Audience reaction, they say, has been overwhelmingly positive.

"With Neutral Sisters, they flip the whole thing," said Tony, referring to the way most people connect race and nationality. "They've got them off balance because it's not fitting the norm. You've got this unique situation, and these girls live that."

"How did you come up with the name?" I asked them.

"Well, we're neutral, you know, we're open," said Bianca. "We're a bit of everything. So we just kind of stand neutral."

"And also we want it to be known that we encompass a lot of cultures," said Kyra. "So we're not going to pledge allegiance to one flag. We pledge allegiance to all the flags that are within us."

I had an opportunity to hear the duo perform during my visit to Houston. Like the sisters themselves, their music is hard to pigeonhole but might best be described as up-tempo reggae.

"We don't want our music to be put in a box. If we come with some conscious lyrics or some spiritual connotation, we don't want to be put in the Christian music category or the pop category," said Kyra. "We don't want the box."

"We run from the box," Bianca added.

The title cut on their CD, "Live-N-Direct," serves as an introduction to the pair. As they sing on the refrain, "We are comin' in, live and direct. We are comin' with a different kind of intellect. Just open your mind and comprehend. We're gonna take you on a ride you'll never forget!"

"It seems like your multicultural experience is very much a part of your music," I told them.

"Definitely," said Bianca. "I think that's what's created most of our lyrics, the fact that we've been so open to so many different cultures, races, situations, and been able to develop it into our music and give it to the world."

"We want to bring everybody together. Maybe that's one of my own selfish wants because I'm from everywhere, so I think everybody needs to be mingling," said Kyra. "Everybody's culture is to be embraced. If people can get over the judging a book by its cover and being so shallow to just look at a person and think they know and make all kind of assessments based on what they see before talking to the person, then I think we'd overcome a lot in this society. But that's just not the way it is, is it?"

Not yet. But we're getting there.

PART 5

THE POLITICS OF BEING BIRACIAL

Come to Your Census

IN THE EYES OF THE U.S. CENSUS BUREAU, I AM NOT REALLY "multiracial." No one is. That is a word the agency has gone to great lengths to avoid. And I'm not just talking about the Census Bureau of the past. I'm talking about the Census Bureau of today.

In 2000, more than 6.8 million people checked more than one racial category on the census questionnaire. It was the first time in the history of the national head count that Americans had the option to mark more than one box.[1] I am one of those 6.8 million, having checked both "black" and "white." Common sense says that makes me multiracial. But in pie charts, position papers, and policy statements, the agency refuses to refer to us as America's multiracial population. Instead, we are known as the "two or more races" population.

Still, it's a sign of progress. Prior to 2000, anyone who checked two or more boxes was reassigned to a single racial category based on the whims of the Census Bureau. Those days are now over with respect to the way the Census Bureau tabulates answers from the questionnaire. Other government agencies, however, still engage in the practice when extrapolating census data.

On the surface, it all sounds quite puzzling. But there's a story behind the federal government's avoidance of the term *multiracial* and why some offices are still allowed to reallocate people from the "two or more races" population into a single race.

Like many things in politics, the bureaucratic oddities are the result of a compromise, and this one was years in the making. The short version of the history lesson on how we ended up here begins with the story of an advocacy group known as Project RACE, which stands for Reclassify All Children Equally.

Project RACE was founded in 1990 by Susan Graham, a white woman married to a black man with two biracial children. But Project RACE is markedly different from the other interracial family groups that also formed in the 1980s and '90s. "We're pretty narrowly focused," said Susan when I spoke with her by telephone. "We don't do conventions, and we don't do picnics, and we don't do marches."

Instead, Project RACE lobbies. For years now, its network of volunteers has been lobbying school districts, hospitals, state legislatures, and the federal government to add a multiracial classification to the list of racial categories on official forms. Their efforts have paid off in Florida, Georgia, Illinois, Indiana, Ohio, Maryland, Michigan, and North Carolina, where Susan says various agencies have modified their forms in response to the organization's campaigns.

The initiative all started when Susan received her 1990 census form in the mail. Unable to check just one race for her children, she phoned the Census Bureau and was told that the children take the same race as the mother. "And I said, 'Why arbitrarily the mother? Why not arbitrarily the father?'" Susan recalled. "He said, 'In cases like this, we always know who the mother is; we don't always know who the father is.' I was so outraged by that comment."

At around the same time, Susan says she received a similar form from the Fulton County School District near Atlanta, Georgia, asking her to pick a single race for her son, who had just started kindergarten. School officials, she says, led her to believe the form was optional, but there was a catch. "If a parent doesn't fill it out, the teacher chooses a race for the child based on her 'knowledge and observation of the child,'" Susan said. Her child's teacher decided her son was black. "So we had the same child who was black at school, white on the census, and biracial at home. And I thought, there's something really wrong with this system."

Susan then began trying to change that system on the local and state levels, hoping to build momentum that would work its way up to Congress and the U.S. Census Bureau. Others, including Inter-racialVoice.com publisher Charles Byrd, were focused almost exclusively on the federal level.

On July 20, 1996, Charles led the Multiracial Solidarity March in Washington, D.C., which actually wasn't a march at all, but a rally. Taking his cue from the Million Man March, which had been held the year before, Charles had planned the gathering to call for national recognition of mixed-race people in the form of a multiracial category on the 2000 census, which was then nearly four years away.

The event took place on a hot afternoon on the National Mall, on the west side of the U.S. Capitol. Many of us had made the trip into Washington expecting a crowd of a thousand or more. We ended up with maybe a couple hundred.

"This is a precedent-setting event, and you should be proud that you're a part of it," Charles told the audience from the podium. He then went on the attack, blasting civil rights organizations and others for holding on to the mentality of the one-drop rule. "Identifying all individuals of mixed race as black is nothing more than a lustful embrace of the mythical concept of white racial purity, and proponents of such an ideology are essentially in bed with the slave master."[2]

By the time he was finished, a biracial woman sitting next to me commented, "You know, I don't agree with a whole lot of what he said."

Honestly, I didn't expect that I would. I didn't attend the rally to support Charles Byrd, or to hear the speeches, or even to champion the addition of a multiracial category to the census. I mainly saw it as an opportunity to connect with other mixed-race people whose experiences were similar to mine. Never before had I heard of an event where so many interracial families and multiracial people were expected to gather in one spot at one time. I didn't want to miss it.

By the time of the rally, Ramona Douglass had succeeded Carlos Fernandez as president of the Association of MultiEthnic Americans; she took the reins of the organization in 1994. She had also won a coveted appointment to the federal advisory panel charged with recommending changes to the 2000 census form.

"We had been knocking on that door for six years," recalled Ramona, adding that her appointment wasn't universally supported. "When AMEA got involved with the census advisory committee, there had already been a letter from a number of coalitions stating this was a dangerous decision to even be a part of the conversation. Then once we were part of the conversation, I think there was an expectation that it was going to be one of the parents, one of the monoracial parents that was going to represent the organization"— i.e., somebody like Susan Graham, rather than someone who was mixed-race herself.

Ramona also had a track record of political activism dating back to the 1970s, when she rallied to defend Angela Davis, the black activist and Communist Party member once targeted by the FBI. Ramona's prior involvement in social justice causes, while controversial, did give her some ammunition when critics of the multiracial movement claimed that mixed-race people simply wanted out of the black box.

The fear among traditional civil rights groups, such as the NAACP, was that providing a multiracial category could potentially reduce black political power by effectively lowering the country's official black population. The same scenario could also play out among other communities of color, raising concerns from the National Council of La Raza and the Asian American Legal Defense and Education Fund.[3]

"I was active in the civil rights movement from the early seventies on," said Ramona. "The attempt to say that we weren't sensitive to these issues became ridiculous. And I wouldn't allow them to make that sweeping statement when I had already put my life on the line. I had already put my political position out in the open, which was very far to the left. And I said our organization is far more complex than how you're trying to portray us."

In a further illustration of that complexity, Ramona attended the Multiracial Solidarity March, sharing the stage with Charles Byrd, and was one of the event's featured speakers; nevertheless, the AMEA would later break away from the rally's stated goal, which was the creation of a multiracial category.

In the months that followed, a number of proposals for altering the way the census counted race were discussed. The addition of a multiracial category all by itself was just one of the ideas on the table. Another proposal was to add a multiracial category with sub-identifiers, so that a person would first check "multiracial," then mark any number of boxes listed underneath to indicate a particular combination of races. A third option involved retaining the existing categories but changing the instructions on the form from "check one only" to "check all that apply." And still others wanted to leave everything alone and continue to force multiracial people to pick one, or risk having the Census Bureau decide a single race for them.

Contrary to what Susan Graham had been told over the phone,

before 2000 the Census Bureau did not necessarily assign biracial children to the race of their mother. In a briefing to news reporters in the spring of 2000, census officials said past practices also included assigning a single race based upon the racial categories other households in the same neighborhood reported. Or in the case of someone writing in their race, if they wrote in "black-white," they were classified as black. If they wrote in "white-black," they were classified as white. The Census Bureau took whichever label came first.[4] But all that was about to change.

As the debate over the 2000 census unfolded, AMEA's position shifted. "I always said, multiracial is just one name. It was not the only name that defined us," said Ramona. "We always supported the multiracial category, but in conjunction with the ability to check more than one box. What we discovered through being in Washington is, that was never going to be accepted. There were too many studies that had been done, whether legitimate or not, that stated that would cause too much of a loss, or a state of confusion, for certain communities. It was too much real estate [on the form]. It was too complicated, and they weren't going to do that."

Accepting that political reality, AMEA changed its approach as the options appeared to narrow. "They decided it was either going to be 'check all that apply,' 'check one or more boxes,' or just 'multiracial.' And just 'multiracial' was not any better than 'other' as far as we could see. It was just saying 'other' with another name," said Ramona. "There would be no new data that would come from that. There would be no new data to distinguish who the multiracial community actually was," if all racial combinations were lumped together.

To Charles Byrd, that was exactly the point. "The criticism of the multiracial category was that it wasn't specific enough for the different mixtures. On the other hand, the beauty of it was, it was so vague than anyone could fit into it," he said. "Most people in this country are mixed if they would admit it. Certainly most black people are. Hispanics by definition are mixed; even though they kind of think of themselves as America's brown race, these people are mixed . . . but we've been told from day one that we're part of this group or that group.

"So I always thought that if there was a multiracial or mixed category, a large number of people would go there," he continued. "Eventually, if a majority of people checked multiracial or mixed, what then would be the need of maintaining the categories?" he asked rhetorically. "Maybe I was just being idealistic at that point. But even back then, I saw 'multiracial' as an intermediate step between the society that is obsessed with race to a future society, what I used to call 'racelessness.' I saw that as a conduit between where we are and where we can be. Because I really do think a majority of people could check off multiracial or mixed if they wanted to."

AMEA declared victory when the Office of Management and Budget, which oversees the Census Bureau, announced its final decision in 1997. No multiracial category would appear on the 2000 census at all, but the directions on the form, which also had to be fine-tuned, would read, "Mark one or more races to indicate what this person considers himself/herself to be."

Notice the instructions do not say, "Check all that apply." That's important. The language is very precise, and the verbiage was chosen carefully, asking what the individual "considers" himself or herself to be.

"They were doing research on which terminology or phraseology would be best," said Ramona. "Apparently, the statisticians found there was an impact that was more detrimental to the other racial groups when it said, 'Check all that apply.' Because to them, it meant that you weren't consciously thinking about what do you truly identify with, that you were just putting down whatever might have been in your portfolio, your heritage. And that saying, 'Check one or more' was a way of having you measure what do you truly identify with, what really matters, rather than that whole buffet."

In other words, if you see yourself as biracial, then check the racial categories that contribute to your biracial identity. But if you see yourself as black, then check black alone. Finally, multiracial people had options. We would no longer be told we had to pick just one.

"Honestly, I had a sense of satisfaction when I dropped off that form," said Ken Tanabe, the creator of LovingDay.org, who checked off Japanese and white. "The census is such a boring thing. It's like getting a library card or something, but at the same time, I was truly excited about that."

But Susan Graham wasn't celebrating, and neither was Charles Byrd. Susan doesn't buy Ramona's explanation that a multiracial category with subidentifiers was a lost political cause, since the 2000 census form uses that very approach in measuring other populations. "Under the umbrella of Asian, you have Japanese, Chinese, Korean," Susan noted. "Why should the multiracial community not be able to have that?"

In fact, there are nine subcategories used to measure the Asian population—Asian Indian, Chinese, Filipino, Japanese, Korean, Vietnamese, Native Hawaiian, Guamanian or Chamorro, and Samoan, plus a fill-in-the-blank line for "Other Asian or other Pacific Islander." A person who checks, say, Chinese and Filipino, is counted as Asian, not as someone who checked two "races."

Similarly, a separate question on Hispanic origin first asks respondents, "Is this person Spanish/Hispanic/Latino?" If the answer is yes, three subcategories follow—Mexican/Mexican American/Chicano, Puerto Rican, and Cuban, plus a fill-in-the-blank line for "Other Spanish/Hispanic/Latino."

"When it came down to the wire, even I feel Ramona kind of

capitulated on the issue and gave in more than she should have," said Charles. "Ramona has said that she approaches this from a civil rights standpoint. Yet the civil rights groups were the ones primarily who opposed us from the beginning."

Charles and Susan were disappointed with the new census format largely because of what they suspected would come next— the redistribution of the multiracial population back into single race categories.

The "mark one or more" approach generates sixty-three different racial options after mixing and matching every possible combination. Hispanic origin is a separate question entirely, so each racial combination can also be Hispanic or non-Hispanic, resulting in a total of 126 possibilities. For example, a person can be white and Hispanic, or white and non-Hispanic, or white and black and Hispanic, or white and black and non-Hispanic, or white and black and Native American and non-Hispanic, etc.

When the dust settled, most of the population identifying as multiracial selected only two racial categories. More than 1 million people checked Native American and white. A total of 868,000 people checked Asian and white, while 785,000 checked black and white. More than 2 million people, mostly Hispanics, checked white and "some other race."[5]

The Census Bureau has released the results for all 126 combinations in all their gory detail. But under certain circumstances, other federal agencies are allowed to collapse the census data into single race categories for purposes related to civil rights monitoring and compliance. How do you count multiracial children, multiracial police officers, or multiracial employees when evaluating affirmative action programs, compliance with court desegregation orders, or racial discrimination complaints?

A memorandum dated March 9, 2000, from the Office of

Management and Budget offers these guidelines: "Responses that combine one minority race and white are allocated to the minority race," the memo states. "Responses that include two or more minority races are allocated as follows: If the enforcement action is in response to a complaint, allocate to use the race that the complainant alleges the discrimination was based on. If the enforcement action requires assessing disparate impact or discriminatory patterns, analyze the patterns based on alternative allocations to each of the minority groups."[6]

Simply put, multiracial people whose combination represents two or more minority races can be evaluated either way depending on the situation. But biracial people who are part white are to be reallocated to their minority race, a practice that smacks of the old one-drop rule.

"I knew that's what was going to happen with this," said Charles.

"The multiracial community did itself in," added Susan.

Personally, I think we're still ahead of the game.

The compromise plan actually works for me, at least for the time being. Before the 2000 census, the federal government had no data on multiracial people. Now it does. By collecting, tabulating, and reporting the results of the "two or more races" population, the Census Bureau has a wealth of information on a growing segment of society that it had previously ignored.

Consider the analysis researchers at the Public Policy Institute of California were able to conduct as a result of the new multiracial data. "One striking finding of the study 'California's Multiracial Population' is that multiracial Californians fall somewhere between their single-race counterparts on some measures," says a press release from the institute. "For example, the poverty rate for black/white Californians (16 percent) is about halfway between the relatively low white poverty rate (8 percent) and the relatively high black rate (22 percent)."[7]

Without a way of measuring the multiracial population, such nuances are lost. At the same time, the data allows policy wonks to crunch the numbers in different ways under different scenarios for different applications, so as not to negatively impact civil rights enforcement.

That makes sense to me. There are some areas in which my status as a biracial person is most salient, such as health care.

"There are certain drugs that impact one ethnic or racial group differently than another. But what if you're both? That testing hadn't been done," said Ramona. "And if we didn't exist, why would they be doing a test? I know of an instance where a man was misdiagnosed for four years on a disease that he had because he was racially visibly black, and the disease he had had already been researched as only occurring in people of European descent."

"So if the person is identified as mixed or multiracial from the beginning. . . ."

"It plants the seed for further inquiry," Ramona continued. "Instead of taking the eyeball test, this forces people to look beyond the obvious."

But there are other scenarios in which my status as a black person is most salient. If police departments are racially profiling African-Americans, if I become the target of a hate crime due to my blackness, if an institution is engaged in a pattern of discrimination against black people and I am one of those suffering the consequences, my experiences in those arenas should not be overlooked.

"Those precise categories we were using in the 1960s for civil rights legislation, those categories are not as cleanly bounded now," said Kenneth Prewitt, who headed the Census Bureau at the time of the 2000 head count. "That doesn't mean discrimination has gone away."

Speaking to a group of reporters shortly before stepping down from the agency, he told us, "You cannot measure race precisely. It has to do with emotion, it has to do with identity, it has to do with historical practice, and what you think I am."

That said, the census is the best means we have for providing a statistical snapshot of the country, a demographic picture of the nation. Now that we have a way of counting multiracial people, at last I'm fully a part of that American portrait.

CENSUS 2000 AT A GLANCE

Source: U.S. Census Bureau

Numbers have been rounded

Total number of people checking two or more races:	**6.8 million**
White & "some other race"	2.2 million
White & American Indian–Alaska Native	1.1 million
Asian & White	868,000
Black & White	785,000
Black & American Indian–Alaska Native	182,000
Asian & Native Hawaiian–Pacific Islander	139,000
White & Native Hawaiian–Pacific Islander	113,000
Asian & Black	107,000
Asian & American Indian–Alaska Native	52,000
Black & Native Hawaiian–Pacific Islander	30,000

Number of people who identified as Hispanic or Latino:	**35 million**
Hispanics who checked White	16.9 million
Hispanics who checked "some other race"	14.9 million
Hispanics who checked two or more races	2.2 million
Hispanics who checked Black	710,000
Hispanics who checked American Indian–Alaska Native	407,000
Hispanics who checked Asian	120,000
Hispanics who checked Native Hawaiian–Pacific Islander	45,000

Race Busters, Freedom Fighters, and Multiracial Village People

FOR THE LONGEST TIME, I DIDN'T THINK OF THE GROWTH IN THE number of people publicly proclaiming their multiracial identity as constituting a political movement. But somewhere along the way to Census 2000, we sure began to act like one.

As the controversy over the census garnered more and more attention, I encountered some interesting reactions when I made it known I consider myself biracial. "Oh, you're one of those people," said one Capitol Hill lobbyist familiar with the issue.

But it would be a mistake to think that all biracial people are of the same mind when it comes to formal government recognition of multiple racial heritages. True, a band of activists came together to support a new way of counting race in America that would be more inclusive of multiracial people. But they did so for differing reasons, brought differing perspectives to the cause, and supported differing approaches toward that end. Like any movement, factions developed, and those factions were soon at war with one another.

"It was sad," said Ramona Douglass. "Here we were part of a

community trying to create a sense of belonging, and yet we were calling each other traitors. We were marginalizing ourselves."

"People have said all kinds of things to me, that we're part of a Nazi movement, that I just want my kids to be white and that's why I'm doing this," said Susan Graham. "I've always said that until we can stop counting by race, what I want is for my biracial kids to be counted accurately."

"I did have a different view about what multiracial was all about," said Charles Byrd. "I really don't believe that any group is entitled to a portion of my identity for the purpose of maintaining their artificial head count."

Americans have been debating race and the census for more than two centuries. And it's not over yet. The dialogue that occurred in the years leading up to the 2000 census may very well contain clues to what's ahead in the coming decades as not only the census but public policies overall are reexamined with regard to race.

What I offer here is my own nonscientific, pop-cultural analysis of the factions that emerged and how they ended up at odds with one another. I've resisted attaching any names to the various wings of the movement that I've identified, as the labels and descriptions I've come up with do not capture the complexities of individual positions. They are meant to be taken as generalizations, and I present them only as a guide to sorting through the arguments.

As I see it, the multiracial movement—if we want to call it that—broke down into three basic camps: Race Busters, Freedom Fighters, and Multiracial Village People.

I begin with the Race Busters. They're the ones who are out to destroy contemporary notions of race itself, and they approach this mission with a greater sense of urgency than the others. They are the first to spout scientific research pointing to race as a biologically bogus concept. "Racial" differences, they remind us, represent a small fraction of a person's overall genetic makeup. The sooner we all realize what science has shown, the Race Busters argue, the closer we will be to ridding our society of the evils of racism.

Some Race Busters are also Affirmative Action Busters. They want to end any consideration of race in public policy as it relates to college admissions, hiring decisions, school integration, diversity initiatives, and so on. For the Race Busters, multiracial classification represents a way to muddy the picture, some sort of halfway point toward doing away with the notion of race in the public arena. Their support of a multiracial category was little more than a tactical move toward their longer-term goal.

For the Multiracial Village People, the destruction of race as a social concept, if that were ever to occur, might be a healthy by-product of the movement. But that's not why they're in this fight. The Multiracial Village People view interracial couples, their children, and mixed-race adults as members of a new, separate, expanding community in need of recognition. They view this community as standing apart from other ethnic groups and communities of color, rather than one that encompasses other racial and cultural groups.

If they have children themselves, Multiracial Village People are likely raising them with a strong sense of multiracial identity and may be disappointed if at times their children identify otherwise. They do not see their community reflected in political discourse, represented on race questionnaires, or recognized in society overall. They supported the multiracial category as a way of advancing the interests of their community, with little regard for the implications for any other communities.

Lurking among both the Multiracial Village People and the Race Busters there is a more hard-core group I refer to as the Multiracial Militants. The Multiracial Militants have essentially traded in the one-drop rule for a new doctrine that says if you have one drop of any two or more races, then you must call yourself multiracial. They frown on multiracial celebrities such as Halle Berry, Jasmine Guy, and Lisa Bonet for aligning themselves with black causes and black identity even though they are biracial. Multiracial Militants have a rigid view of multiracial classification and aren't afraid to attack members of interracial families who don't share their opinions.

That brings us to the Freedom Fighters. As the name implies, the goal of the Freedom Fighters is to bring the right of self-identification to multiracial people. In the early days of the census, Americans did not fill out census forms themselves. Enumerators visited homes and recorded the races of those occupying the household as they saw them. Beginning in 1960, however, the census began moving to a system of "self-enumeration," in which individuals decide what race to report, mark the form accordingly, and return it by mail.[1]

That worked as long as the individual selected a single race. Multiracial people, however, had no option to self-identify as multiracial. Until 2000, the Census Bureau still decided for us. So the Freedom Fighters supported a multiracial category to give multiracial people freedom of choice, the same right monoracially identified people had had for decades. For the Freedom Fighters, the argument was straightforward: If your mother is white and your father is black, and you consider yourself black, that's fine. But if you consider yourself biracial, then you ought to be able to indicate that on the census as well.

Fed up with black nationalists, race-based interest groups, and the most militant of the Multiracial Village People trying to dictate how we should identify, the Freedom Fighters are about letting racial identity flow out of our own personal histories, family circumstances, and political points of view, whatever they may be. Many Freedom Fighters might also be termed Freedom Floaters—

they are multiracial people who want the option of identifying differently in different contexts, in which case the "mark one or more" format in lieu of a multiracial category is also acceptable to them.

In short, Freedom Fighters allow for a variety of possibilities in the racial classification game and believe in respecting the choice of the individual. The Multiracial Village People, the militant ones especially, believe racial identity should reflect one's ancestry, irrespective of social interactions and experiences. And Race Busters link racial identity to their political beliefs about what society should do to eliminate race as an issue.

Somewhere in the midst of all the arguing, we seemed to forget why the nation even conducts a census in the first place. That led some folks to conclude we wanted to see a multiracial category for no other reason than our own self-esteem. There's no denying that was part of the picture. After all, isn't that true about other ethnic groups listed on the form? But there are also sound research, education, and public policy considerations that support formal recognition of our population.

The country has been in the business of counting its residents since 1790, as mandated under Article I, Section 2 of the U.S. Constitution. That section states, "The actual enumeration shall be made within three years after the first meeting of the Congress of the United States, and within every subsequent term of ten years," which is why we continue to have a census once a decade. The population count is used to determine how many seats each state is entitled to receive in the House of Representatives and how the congressional districts within each state are drawn.

From the beginning, the census counted race. The Constitution stipulated that census takers were to count "the whole number of free persons" but count slaves as three-fifths of a person for purposes of congressional redistricting. That didn't change until passage of the Thirteenth and Fourteenth Amendments in the 1860s.[2]

According to the Census Bureau's own historians, the first census broke down the population into five categories: free white males over sixteen, free white males under sixteen, free white females, slaves, and other persons. Noting the number of white males by age made it possible to determine how many men were available for military service. It wasn't until 1870 that Native Americans were counted as a separate group, and even then those on reservations were not included in the figures used for congressional apportionment until the 1890 census. Also in 1870, the government began collecting information on the Chinese population, and in 1890 the Japanese population was counted.[3]

The manner in which the country measured the black population changed during this time as well. In *Who Is Black?* professor F. James Davis writes, "Instructions to census enumerators in 1840, 1850, and 1860 provided a 'mulatto' category but did not define the term. In 1870 and 1880, mulattoes were officially defined to include 'quadroons, octoroons, and all persons having any perceptible trace of African blood.'"[4]

The terms "quadroon" and "octoroon" referred to someone with one-fourth black ancestry and one-eighth black ancestry, respectively. Yet apparently they were to be absorbed into the mulatto category, traditionally thought to mean one-half black ancestry. Finally, Davis reports that in 1920, the Census Bureau abandoned the mulatto category, embraced the one-drop rule, and directed that those previously counted as mulatto be counted as black.[5]

The census evolved in other ways, too. Questions now cover topics such as the number of bedrooms in the home, whether the household has indoor plumbing, and how members of the family commute to work. "All of the questions are tied to laws that were passed by Congress," Representative Carolyn Maloney said in an interview on the PBS show *The NewsHour*. "Believe it or not, there are many areas in America where people don't have plumbing. And that's an important question to ask for the environment and for designation of federal funds."[6]

In 2000, Maloney, a New York Democrat, served as the ranking member on the House Subcommittee on the Census and was outspoken on the importance of filling out the survey. "All of our funding formulas are tied to census numbers," she said. "Over two trillion dollars will be allocated in the next ten years based on this data."[7]

That sparked concern that minority groups stood to lose political clout in determining how that money would be allocated if everyone of mixed heritage chose to identify as multiracial. As author Frank Wu noted in his book *Yellow*, the Congressional Black Caucus at one point enlisted radio and television personalities Tavis Smiley and Tom Joyner to spread the word that African-Americans should check the single black box.[8]

Just as advocates for a multiracial category divided into three key factions, opponents of the idea also articulated arguments that fell into predictable patterns. Even though the 2000 census is behind us, their viewpoints still linger. Here again, I've separated the detractors into three groups. I call them the One-Droppers, the Solidarity Seekers, and the Conspiracy Theorists.

The One-Droppers are essentially stuck in a time warp. They are the people who still hold firm to the belief that one drop of black blood makes a person legally, socially, and psychologically black. They reject the concept of identifying as multiracial in any context whatsoever. "Biracial?" they'll say with a scowl. "There is no such thing. One drop of black blood and you're black, case closed. That's the law." Well, even if it's not technically the law—legal definitions of blackness varied by state—the One-Droppers will argue it is a social reality that might as well carry the full weight of the law.

One-Droppers fail to acknowledge the weakening of the one-drop doctrine in the post–civil rights era. There are certainly biracial people today who play along with it. But I would suggest that has more to do with their individual circumstances and past brushes with racism than with an intellectual embrace of the one-drop rule as a rational philosophy. To the One-Droppers, however, the rule is gospel. There is no discussion, no gray area; there are no complexities that demand our attention. The multiracial experience—the reality of our lives as we know it—is just a bunch of hooey.

In contrast, Solidarity Seekers recognize the concept of being biracial but view any proclamation of racial identity through a narrow prism of black political struggle. They're the people who say, "OK, you're biracial. I accept that. I understand you want to honor both your parents." But their statement is then followed by what amounts to a sales pitch: "But in this racist society we live in, it's really important that you do everything you can to help eliminate white racism, and in this case that means identifying with the black side of your heritage, and black alone."

They see the census as a political questionnaire and believe it should be answered in a way that would best support black political power. This places them in direct conflict with the Multiracial Village People, who see the multiracial community as being in need of political recognition and who believe that identifying as multiracial makes just as powerful a political statement.

The Conspiracy Theorists, on the other hand, see a multiracial category as some kind of orchestrated effort to undermine Black America. To the Conspiracy Theorists, the movement is not about freedom of choice. Rather, it's about dividing and conquering. As a headline in a 1995 issue of *Ebony* magazine screamed, "Am I black, white, or in between? Is there a plot to create a 'colored' buffer race in America?" Oh, please.

The Conspiracy Theorists suspect the multiracial movement is a veiled attempt to duplicate South Africa's racial hierarchy, with a separate "coloured" race socially situated between black and white. What do you suppose will happen, they ask rhetorically, if every black person who is mixed with something suddenly declares, "I'm biracial?" Droves of multiracial people presently defined as black will jump at the chance, thereby fractionalizing the black community. Or so they predicted.

But the numbers don't show that's what happened. The number of Americans checking two or more races amounted to 2.4 percent of the population—significant enough for demographers to take notice, but hardly a mass exodus from the black-alone population. Perhaps more significantly, more people indicated they were white–Native American and white-Asian than white-black.[9]

Now that the multiracial movement has been successful in convincing the Office of Management and Budget to find a way to count multiracial people, the argument shifts to what to do with those statistics. As I've said, reallocating the multiracial numbers into single race categories to monitor civil rights compliance seems logical to me. But doing so for any other purpose does not.

Sociologists, demographers, medical researchers, genealogists, marketing companies, venture capitalists, and others turn to census figures when looking for information on societal trends, cultural patterns, and the lifestyles of various population groups. It makes sense for them to have data on the population that identifies as multiracial. Biracial, in this context, is not synonymous with black. Nor is it synonymous with white, Asian, Native American, or any other single race classification.

But as long as the ability to redistribute the multiracial numbers exists, the temptation to do so in all situations may prove too great for those who want to ignore the new racial reality, dismiss the multiracial experience, and hold on to a more one-dimensional view.

"That's the problem with 'check all that apply.' It's so easy to real-locate, it's a no-brainer," said Susan Graham. "I think the whole split in the [multiracial] community was extremely unfortunate. And I don't think there's anybody changing anybody's mind for 2010 or 2020. So there we are."

A Bonding Experience

As THE GREAT CENSUS DEBATE OF THE LATE 1990S ROARED ON, another series of events on the path to multiracial awareness unfolded on the campuses of several liberal arts colleges in the Northeast. Personally, I found the development to be refreshingly nonpolitical in its orientation, although that aspect may have reflected either a lack of political awareness about the census or an indication that dialogue on other issues was simply a higher priority among biracials in their late teens and early twenties.

In search of a safe environment to tell their stories, groups of multiracial students began organizing an annual conference to talk about the mixed-race experience. I got wind of the 1999 conference through the InterracialVoice.com Web site and saw it as another opportunity to advance my own understanding of the topic. Having produced a documentary on the subject while working as a television reporter in Portland, Oregon, I submitted a proposal for a conference workshop in which I would show excerpts from the broadcast and lead a discussion on the issues.

Truth be told, I was really just looking for a way to attend the conference at minimal expense. Like the Multiracial Solidarity March in 1996, the conference sounded like another one of those events that I didn't want to miss.

My plan worked. The conference was set to take place at Wesleyan University in Middletown, Connecticut. My workshop proposal was accepted, and my experience went beyond anything I could have imagined.

Even though I was ten years older than many of the college students in attendance, the sense of connection I felt that weekend seemed to erase any age difference. To walk into a room and find a sea of visibly mixed-race people—folks who looked like me—representing a variety of ethnic combinations and backgrounds was overwhelming.

"These are my people," I remember thinking, and sure enough, we shared many of the same life stories, from the "What are you?" question to pressure to choose sides and declare an allegiance to one race over another. Here, the question wasn't, "What are you?" It was, "What's your mixture?"

By the end of the event, I had received an invitation from Wellesley College in Massachusetts to deliver a similar presentation there. Subsequent invitations from other schools followed, and I became a regular conference attendee for the next several years.

For me, that sense of bonding reached a peak with my third appearance at the annual event in 2001, which was then held at Harvard University. Conference organizers had arranged a group dinner at a Chili's restaurant within walking distance of the Harvard campus, where several dozen of us then proceeded to take over the restaurant's party room.

"Can I ask you guys something?" asked the young waitress serving my table. "So what the hell is this?" she said with a smile.

The waitress had never seen anything quite like it before. We represented the café au lait generation, a wave of caramel-colored people whose ethnic backgrounds she couldn't quite peg. Our group contained a blend of people who looked sort of white, sort of black, sort of Asian, maybe Latino. We were all mixing together, and we all seemed to know each other. There were more than a hundred of us of different shades and hues and races and backgrounds all hanging out together.

We were different, yet at the same time we had something in common. But our waitress couldn't put her finger on what it was. What was the occasion? What brought all these people together?

"We're attending the multiracial conference going on at Harvard," said one of the six people sharing a table with me.

Suddenly a light bulb went on in her head. It all made sense now.

"So you're all multiracial?" the waitress asked, intrigued.

"Yep . . . I'm black and Italian," said one of my dinner companions.

"I'm white and Japanese," said someone else.

And on it went around the table.

"I'm black and white," I told her.

"I'm Chinese and Jewish," said Jen Chau.

Jen, like me, had become a conference regular and was one of the people I looked forward to seeing at each annual gathering. She had been in the audience when I spoke at Wesleyan, and I met her again when I paid a visit to Wellesley College, where she was a student, several weeks later. She is also one of the founders of a Wellesley student group called Fusion, an on-campus organization aimed at addressing the issues of the college's multiracial population.

"It started out as brunch in one of the dining halls on Sundays, and we did that for two years," Jen recalled. "Some of the people felt very strongly that they didn't want to have an organization because that would mean our focus would totally switch to organizing rather then enjoying each other and becoming friends. But as the years went on, we felt we really needed to do it."

FADE

Fusion, she says, was officially founded with half a dozen or so members in 1997, Jen's junior year at Wellesley. "It started off pretty slowly," she said. "But I just remember it being such a huge deal for me, to finally have this group and finally feel like I have a community of my own. I never experienced that before."

Jen was born and raised in New York City. Her mother is Jewish, and her father is Chinese. The story of how they met is "usually not as exciting as people think it's going to be," Jen said. "They were both in school in Boston," her mother at Boston University law school and her father at Northeastern University, when they crossed paths. Simple as that.

"Growing up, how much of an issue was your identity?" I asked.

"It was a large issue, but it was never discussed at home, which made it an even bigger issue," she said. "I was having to deal with these experiences completely on my own. For all intents and purposes, I considered myself a white girl. That's how my parents sort of raised me and my brother, pretty absent of culture. My father didn't want to teach us anything about Chinese tradition, language, anything. Except the food," she laughed. "So we really didn't have any Chinese influence growing up. But I had a lot of experiences that told me I was not this typical American girl that I thought I was. And so that was confusing at times to receive feedback from the outside world that told me I was not like everyone else. And to go home and not really have a space to bring these issues up was just very difficult."

In addition to her public school education, Jen's parents enrolled her and her brother in Hebrew school, which she attended for six years, until the age of twelve. "A lot of my conflict's there, because that was even more of a homogeneous setting than my public schools were. So in a place were everyone has two Jewish parents, or maybe not two Jewish parents but at least two white parents, my brother and

I definitely stood out," Jen said. She recalled other children calling her names like "chicken chow mein" and "Purina dog chow."

"I remember truly hating the fact that my father was Chinese," said Jen, reflecting on the stage of racial ambivalence common among mixed-race young people. "I used to have these dreams where I would be Rachel Silverman or Sarah Werner and had this completely Jewish name and finally felt like I fit in. That kind of harassment was one of the things I had to deal with, and it bothered me because I didn't necessarily feel like I was Chinese.

"I felt the same kind of exclusion from my Chinese family," she continued. "My father has nine younger brothers and sisters and no one married out except for him. So with all these cousins running around, we were the only ones who were different, and we were the only ones who didn't speak Chinese and really felt left out."

Because the issue was so rarely discussed at home, if at all, "I wasn't able to process my experiences in a really healthy way," said Jen. "I didn't try to tackle these issues until I was an adult, and I went to college and actually found other mixed-race people like myself."

It seems many young biracial adults have a similar need to "talk it out," as evidenced by some of the dialogue I've heard at the conferences over the years.

"My dad doesn't have a fetish!" said one student, referring to male fantasies about Asian women. His father is white and his mother is Asian.

"My mom didn't marry my dad because of his penis size!" said another attendee whose mother is white and whose father is black, expressing her frustration with stereotypes about black sexual prowess.

"For the first time in my life, I feel like I belong," one college freshman confided.

In one late-night rap session, Jen called my attention to an artist and philosopher named Adrian Piper, a light-skinned black woman who developed a card to give to any white person who made a racist remark in her presence. Jen expressed a desire to make up similar cards to give to people who ask, "What are you?"

"Dear Friend, I am black," Piper's card begins. "I am sure you did not realize this when you made/laughed at/agreed with that racist remark. In the past, I have attempted to alert white people to my racial identity in advance. Unfortunately, this invariably causes them to react to me as pushy, manipulative, or socially inappropriate." The card concludes, "I regret any discomfort my presence is causing you, just as I am sure you regret the discomfort your racism is causing me."[1]

I decided to run with Jen's idea of making up cards for multiracial people to hand out. The challenge was to come up with the right phrasing to convey an appropriate tone while also getting the message across. Borrowing language from some of the research I had done on multiracial issues, I returned to the conference the following year with a set of wallet-sized cards for just such moments.

"What Am I?" each card reads. "Please do not be offended by this card. It's just that I have been asked about my racial and ethnic background so often, I've grown tired of explaining myself. Such questions make me wonder: Why do you want to know what I am? What drives your curiosity? Does my physical appearance confuse you? Do I challenge what you think you know about the meaning of race? Do my looks, my speech, my name, my demeanor, my mannerisms, my overall presence, have a place in your construction of the world?" The back of the card then states, "I'd like for you to spend some time thinking about these things. In the meantime, if you must have a label to fit me, to classify me, to understand me, then I am," followed by a fill-in-the-blank line.[2] My card concludes, "But I'd prefer to just be Me!"

The instructions were actually quite similar to the approach Jen says she took during moments of racial interrogation. "I had my little angry phase in college," she said. "And then I came to understand that people are curious. Many people don't understand that it gets annoying to have that question thrown at you on a regular basis. I'm definitely more of the mind that it's important to educate rather than just shove people away and have them think badly of you."

Be that as it may, I've become convinced that asking a biracial person about their race is equivalent to asking someone about their religion. It is appropriate only in certain limited situations. Otherwise, it is evidence of the questioner lacking proper social etiquette.

"Usually the 'What are you?' question and all that happens when I'm approached by men," Jen observed. "Men are also the ones who bring up the whole exotic factor."

At Jen's suggestion, I looked up the word *exotic* in *Webster's New World College Dictionary*. Among the definitions are, "Foreign, not native," "Strange or different in a way that is striking or fascinating," and "Strangely beautiful." It should be no wonder, then, why many multiracial people do not find looking "exotic" to be a compliment.

"I think a lot of people are not exposed to mixed people in a large way, so to them we are exotic. But saying that someone is exotic is basically placing them in this 'other' category," Jen explained. "It kind of places you away," thereby reinforcing the racial difference or outsider status just when the biracial person may be looking for a sense of belonging.

Upon graduation from Wellesley, Jen returned to New York City and saw a need for a group similar to Fusion in the broader community. In 2000, she launched Swirl, Inc., which soon spawned chapters in several other cities, including Boston, Philadelphia, and Los Angeles. The groups hold book club meetings, film screenings, discussion sessions, and social dinners.

But there are also signs that Swirl, like other facets of the multiracial community, is widening its mission beyond multiracial awareness to include social justice issues. "So many of our concerns are the exact same concerns as [those of] other communities of color," said Jen. "For some reason, you go to these conferences and everybody wants to figure out what our agenda is, and there's never any answer. Like we're trying to come up with new problems. The problems are the same as other communities are dealing with, civil rights, all of those issues are things that we also have to deal with. But in talking about ourselves as 'mixed race' and this new community, we sometimes forget that those issues still apply to us."

"So as we move into a political sphere," I said to Jen, "are we still going to have a tent that's big enough for people who may not agree with a particular stand politically but still need a place for some emotional healing to occur?"

"It definitely is an issue to have the safe space preserved, but at the same time speak out, and have everybody be comfortable with that," she said. "We want to educate members so they can make decisions accordingly. . . . The reality is, the average member does not know everything that is going on."

Nor does everyone working for the U.S. Census Bureau, as Jen discovered in 2000 when a census taker showed up at her door even though she says she had already mailed in her census form.

"She asked, 'Hispanic or non-Hispanic?' And I said non-Hispanic, and she looked at me and she said, 'Are you sure?' And I think she herself was Latina. And I said yes, I'm sure, I'm not Hispanic. Then she went on to the race question. I said, 'Other Asian' and I asked her to write in the blank, 'biracial.' And she checked it off and then said, 'Biracial? What country is that?'

"That was really kind of scary," Jen laughed. "This person is filling out and taking racial information and doesn't understand the term *biracial*. It was pretty funny."

It's also an indication of how much work there is still left to do.

Ones Who Understand

ON THE FIRST DAY OF KINDERGARTEN, A LITTLE WHITE GIRL WALKED up to Matt Kelley and said, "You're black, and you have purple eyes." At nine years old, he was walking down the street with his older sister when a white kid shouted, "Hello, Chinese people!" As a young adult, he took a job working at a restaurant that employed a number of Latinos and found he was often mistaken for Mexican.

Matt is biracial, or more specifically, hapa—a Hawaiian word meaning "half" that is now commonly used to refer to a biracial person of part Asian ancestry. Matt's mother immigrated to the United States from Korea. His father, as Matt put it, "is a white dude from the Midwest."

"I didn't grow up knowing words like 'biracial,' or 'hapa,' or 'multiracial' existed," he says. Today, it is not unusual for Matt to use those very words in everyday conversation. His career is a direct outgrowth of his experience growing up in an interracial family in the Pacific Northwest. Now in his late twenties, he has channeled his passion for multiracial issues into grassroots organizing. It all started in April 1998, when he posted a message to the InterracialVoice.com

Web site. "A group of multiracial college students from around the country are putting together a magazine dedicated to issues concerning the multiracial experience," the announcement read. "The publication includes political essays, historical analysis, poetry, upcoming events, and other issues pertaining to the multiracial experience. . . . If you have any questions about a possible subscription, would like additional information, or would like to contribute, please e-mail Matthew Kelley."

Matt had no idea where it would ultimately lead.

"I got over 100 responses in one week. People were very excited," said Matt, who at the time was wrapping up his freshman year at Wesleyan University in Middletown, Connecticut.

He moved back home to Seattle that summer, got a job, and nine months later launched *Mavin* magazine. The name has its roots in Yiddish. "It means 'one who understands,'" Matt said. The idea was to offer a publication in which young adults who were either mixed-race or had been adopted across racial lines could tell their own stories. "And it wasn't being told from the perspective of academics or our parents or sociologists or psychologists. It really was about talking about lived experiences," said Matt.

But if you've never seen the magazine on a newsstand near you, it's because from the beginning, *Mavin* has had an infrequent production schedule at best, churning out only one to three issues per year.

"I get a lot of people who are very impressed that a nineteen-year-old started a magazine. I can respect where that comes from. But I also think you can't underestimate the power of naïveté," Matt said. "They say 50 percent of magazines don't make it to issue number three, and that's an overall rate, not talking about ethnic niche magazines. There were some random advertisers, but not enough to support the cost of publication."

While the magazine itself may not have been profitable, what it started continues to pay dividends today. *Mavin* the magazine evolved into the Mavin Foundation, a nonprofit organization shining a spotlight on multiracial issues. The foundation is headquartered in downtown Seattle, and Matt is its founder and CEO. Both the foundation and the magazine originated with similar goals in mind—to build a network, establish resources, and generate awareness of multiracial people and their families.

The resources Mavin is now creating are things Matt and I could have used growing up in the 1970s and '80s in Washington State. Matt was born in Spokane in 1978 and spent the first five years of his life on a farm just outside the city in the small town of Spangle, whose population numbers in the hundreds. "You're probably the only person I've ever talked to who knows where that is," he told me.

I know where Spangle is only because it was a stop on the Greyhound bus route between Spokane and Pullman, a trip I made many times growing up in eastern Washington. As I remember it, the bus driver would turn off the main highway into Spangle, pull up at a drugstore in the center of town, and honk his horn, and if no one came out to catch the bus, he would speed up and continue on down the highway.

Matt's family eventually moved from Spangle across the state to Rollingbay, another small community, located on Bainbridge Island west of Seattle. But it was in the eighth grade, when Matt switched schools, that questions about his identity reached a new level.

"I hadn't really had experiences of what it was like to be the new kid and have to make friends," he said. Having lived in small towns, "where everyone knows who you are already," he wasn't prepared to make the transition to Lakeside School, a private high school just north of downtown Seattle. "Having to explain who I was was a new experience. I just knew I didn't fit in, and I wasn't sure if it was tied to my race, or my class, or where I lived, or my values, or what have you. But I just knew I didn't fit."

Things got better in college. Wesleyan University, it turned out, had a strong contingent of Korean students on campus. As Matt describes it, "There's the Christian Korean group, the smoking-drinking Korean group, the academic Korean group, the Korean American group, the Korean adoptee group. . . ."

And that's not all. Wesleyan also had a multiracial student club, one of the first such groups of its kind in the country.

"I went to one of those first meetings, and it was just this very cathartic, eureka moment of sitting around a table with a dozen other people who all looked very different, who all had very different experiences, but also had a lot of similar overarching experiences, too," Matt said. His involvement with the group sparked his interest in reaching out to others with similar backgrounds. "It was very much this, 'I got to get the word out there and let other people know this network exists, so they don't also grow up feeling isolated.'"

That outreach now occurs through the foundation. When I paid a visit to Mavin's offices in the summer of 2004, I found a small team of workers spread out on the floor stuffing envelopes with invitations for an upcoming fund-raiser. Since its founding on Valentine's Day 2000, the grassroots organization has grown to nine employees. The young staff—no one working there during my visit was over thirty—consists of a few full-time employees, some part-time workers, and several high school and college interns.

The organization sustains itself through grants, individual donations, and product sales. *Mavin* magazine is still in existence as a semi-annual publication, but it's just one of the foundation's projects. Other programs include publication of the *Multiracial Child Resource Book*, which was released in 2003; diversity training and consulting work; a bone marrow project aimed at recruiting more mixed-race donors into the national marrow registry; and a college initiative designed to work with multiracial student groups on campus.

"When we started out, I was very shy and socially awkward. I still have my moments," said Matt. "Our new programs are really focused on interacting with people and creating community."

Meanwhile, the organization also finds itself tackling what seems like an old issue. The battle that erupted over the 2000 census still lingers. While the U.S. Census Bureau allows Americans to "mark one or more" racial categories, other government agencies, social service providers, and educational institutions have yet to change their forms.

"All agencies that receive federal funding are supposed to let people choose more than one, and nearly none of them do," said Mavin's operations manager, Amanda Kay Erekson. She still receives calls from parents of biracial children who say they've been forced to check only one box when enrolling their children in school. "We're trying, one step at a time, to change that," she said.

Like many of the employees who work at Mavin, Amanda identifies as multiracial. She describes her mother as half-Japanese and half-white, and her father as white of German, Norwegian, British, and Scotch Irish heritage.

Actually, "I identify as Japanese American *and* white American *and* multiracial," she said. "White and American are [often] used synonymously. So it's important to distinguish that 'American' does not mean white. My Japanese family has been in this country since 1913. My Japanese family is very much a Japanese American family. So on both sides, it's important for me personally to clarify that," she explained.

In addition to changing forms, the work of the Mavin Foundation is about changing attitudes. "We want to make sure that big companies and government agencies that have diversity programming and training for their employees include multiracial issues. We have found that many of those trainings definitely have a monoracial bias," said Amanda.

"They have activities where they say, 'Separate into people of color and white people.' And there are people who can't go into one of those."

Amanda participated in one of those training exercises while enrolled at Colgate University in Hamilton, New York, in 2001. Like my friend Sundee Tucker Frazier, Amanda found the activity uncomfortable. But unlike Sundee, whose experience in a similar session had taken place almost fifteen years earlier, Amanda had support when she challenged the rules of the exercise.

"I said to the facilitator, who worked on our campus, 'I can't fit into any of these groups.' And he said, 'Oh, you gotta choose one,'" said Amanda. At that point, two other biracial students expressed the same concern. "We started talking and we're like, 'We really can't choose one of these groups.' And he said, 'Oh, you have to, you have to.' Finally, you know, we're holding up the whole process, so finally they said, 'Fine, you three have your own group.'

"So that was the exercise. And it's set up in such a way that mul- tiracial people can't participate fully," Amanda continued. "For us, it ended up being very strengthening because the three of us found each other and related to each other about our experiences, and it worked well for us. But that was no credit to the facilitator or the program. I've heard other people say the same thing. 'Oh, yeah, I was in this diver- sity program, and they made me choose.' I think it happens all the time. I think most diversity programs are very monoracially biased."

Alfredo Padilla came to the Mavin Foundation with a mandate to put some of those diversity programs on notice that they need to catch up with the times. Alfredo heads Mavin's Campus Awareness and Compliance Initiative, also known as CACI. The initiative pro- vides leadership training for multiracial college students, works with student organizations to raise awareness of mixed-race issues, and has launched a campaign calling for the U.S. Department of Edu- cation to enforce the "mark one or more" format on school forms.

"Multiracial issues just aren't on the radar for a lot of people," said Alfredo. Occasionally, some colleges will produce a workshop on mixed-race issues during diversity week, "but there's no real infrastructure or support on campuses to address concerns of multiracial students."

Alfredo was born in Ecuador and has lived in the United States since he was two years old. Raised in the Seattle suburb of Redmond, he attended the University of Washington and checked the box indicating he was Hispanic on his college enrollment form. That put him on a mailing list to receive information about Latino student organizations and other support services available for Latinos on campus. Alfredo is now working to see that multiracial student groups have that same opportunity.

"Not all universities do this, especially smaller universities; they just don't have the resources. But big public and private universities, they have a policy where they contribute resources in order to allow underrepresented communities on their campus to reach out through mailings," he said. "They also subsidize things like ethnic cultural fairs. They usually have specific pots of money that minority student organizations can use. At this point, almost no university extends all of those benefits, all of those subsidies, to multiracial student organizations."

Furthermore, if the university does not have a mechanism for measuring its multiracial population, the institution has no database of multiracial students to begin with, regardless of whether a multiracial student club exists. In addition, how schools collect that data is also suspect if they don't allow for multiple selections when asking students for their race. A stand-alone "multiracial" category does not capture specific mixes on campus. For example, the biracial student who is black and Asian and checks "multiracial" would miss out on any mailings directed to black and Asian students.

"We don't even know if multiracial students at most universities are underrepresented or overrepresented because most universities don't track multiracial students at this point," Alfredo said. "I would argue that the fact that the university doesn't have any support for multiracial students on campus is a strong argument that they should be afforded the opportunity to reach out to their community."

The actual number of schools with established clubs for multiracial students is difficult to track accurately. Some clubs are quite active. Others lie dormant for a period of time until a new crop of student leaders takes charge. As of fall 2005, the Mavin Foundation had developed a list of more than two dozen colleges with active multiracial student organizations, and Alfredo says he has been in contact with several more where students have expressed interest in starting such a club.

Some of those groups have been pretty creative in naming themselves. Brown University has BOMBS, for Brown Organization of Multiracial and Biracial Students. Students at the Claremont Colleges in California started MORE, Multiracial Organization Redefining Ethnicity. Tufts University in Boston has MOST, Multiracial Organization of Students at Tufts. Other student groups include Harvard Hapa, Wellesley College's Fusion, and Wesleyan University's Interracial Students Organization. The list goes on.

"On some campuses, multiracial student organizations are very adept at working with other communities of color and have been very successful doing so and have been embraced and supported by other communities of color," Alfredo said. Other groups, he says, haven't enjoyed such a relationship. "I think that there's a lot of negative racial stereotypes that go with 'mixed.' A lot of those negative racial stereotypes are focused around the idea that mixed people, especially mixed people who are part white, represent a threat to the community, represent a selling-out, and a mistrust and misunderstanding of what their goals are."

"Is there a sense of, why do we need this group?" I asked.

"Stuff like that, yeah," Alfredo responded. "'Why do we need this group?' 'You're white, deal with it.' Or, 'You're Asian, deal with it.'"

Added Amanda, "Whenever you're talking about multiracial issues there are people who say, 'I don't know why we have to talk about all the problems. I grew up in a place where everybody was mixed and we all got along together and we represent the best of the world and someday everyone will be mixed and everyone will be happy.' That's something to consider, but it's not the reality for everyone today."

"There are people out there who see the growth of the multiracial community as an opportunity to stop talking about race entirely, to ignore our historical issues with racism," said Alfredo. "I'm not someone who subscribes to the idea that our goal should be a color-blind society. I subscribe to the idea that our goal should be a society that celebrates diversity. You can't celebrate diversity without acknowledging that diversity exists. So I think it behooves those who are active in the community and who are working on these issues to have a clear goal."

Otherwise, as Matt Kelley has observed, multiracial people may be used to advance a political agenda many of us do not support. "Our experiences, our stories, and our realities are being co-opted," he said. "Sometimes it's in flattering ways, and sometimes it's in scary ways."

In California, for example, anti–affirmative action activist Ward Connerly floated a proposal to add a separate, "multiracial" category to University of California admission forms. The timing of Connerly's proposal raised some questions, in my mind at least, over whether there was an ulterior motive in seeking the change. Then a member of the UC Board of Regents, Connerly recommended the new multiracial category in the fall of 2004, shortly after a California ballot measure he championed known as the Racial Privacy Initiative was defeated. That measure would have stopped state agencies from collecting racial data. Opponents dubbed it the "Racial Ignorance Initiative" and mounted a successful campaign against it.[1]

Unless you were paying close attention, you might have thought Connerly's new proposal to add the multiracial category had broad support among multiracial advocates. After all, it sounds like the kind of thing multiracial people would want to cheer. Connerly himself, while "black" in appearance, has a multiracial background and is married to a white woman.

But in fact, the Mavin Foundation, the Association of Multi-Ethnic Americans, and a Bay Area group known as the Hapa Issues Forum all came out against Connerly's plan. In a joint letter to the Board of Regents, the groups stated, "Mixed-race people by definition represent a diverse cross section of cultural and ethnic heritages, with many multiracial individuals identifying with multiple communities. Limiting their choice to a generic multiracial/multiethnic category ignores this diversity and severely limits the ability of UC to gain a clear and detailed picture of its student population."

As an accompanying news release from the organizations noted, "The UC system currently allows applicants to check one or more racial boxes on undergraduate admissions forms but assigns a single race or ethnic category to applicants who check more than one box when reporting their data to the U.S. Department of Education," a practice the groups also hope to see modified.

Their letter concluded, "We strongly urge you to reject Regent Connerly's proposal for a multiracial/multiethnic category and to support data collection, tabulation, and reporting methods that are compliant with 'mark one or more' federal guidelines."

Ultimately, the Board of Regents voted against Connerly's plan.[2]

Personally, I was glad to see the groups take a strong stand on the issue, particularly Mavin. The organization's growing visibility has signaled that a new set of players—a new generation, in fact—is taking center stage in giving voice to the concerns of multiracial people. Frankly, it's a change I welcome.

"We have had a credibility problem," Matt said, looking at the history of multiracial advocacy. "For instance, I look at who are the primary voices and bodies in the early multiracial movement. They're primarily white parents of black-white biracial kids."

At one point, Matt counted only two out of eight board members of the Association of MultiEthnic Americans who were themselves multiracial. The remaining members of the board of directors were monoracial people in interracial families.

"That made us really susceptible to very legitimate criticism from civil rights groups," he said. "It's like, great, white people are speaking about their nonwhite kids. Granted, [the kids] were both, but society was still seeing them as nonwhite."

Susan Graham of Project RACE defends her participation in the cause. "Moms protect their young," said Susan. "MADD, Mothers Against Drunk Drivers, was started by a mom. Sometimes us moms can get pretty politically savvy and go out and do these things." Of the criticism, she said, "I think that was a way for some of the people who were involved who were multiracial themselves to say, 'We don't want you to do it; we want to do it,'" referring to the advocacy work. "But the fact remains that until Project RACE came along, they weren't doing it. No one was doing it."

Eventually, AMEA would also name a white woman to its top post. Nancy Brown, who is married to a black man and has two biracial daughters, was a founding member of AMEA in 1988. She became the association's president in 2001.

"I think AMEA is at a point now where that's cool," said Matt, who joined the board that same year. More multiracial people have since stepped up to round out the association's leadership, and Matt has become AMEA's vice president, which may make having a white parent as president of the organization a bit more palatable. "When you're talking about what does it mean to be multiethnic or multiracial, I think you need someone who identifies that way," Matt said. "Whether they're a first-generation multiracial person or whether it's further back in their heritage. But if they identify with it, that's critical. And even if they don't identify with it, that's a critical component of the community to acknowledge, too. People who could claim multiracial identity but choose not to."

But respect for the many variations of the multiracial experience hasn't always been evident within interracial circles. "Many times we don't put ourselves and our own stories into a larger context," Matt admitted. "And it comes from a place of feeling isolated for so long. All of a sudden, you're like, damn it, I'm going to talk about *me*, and I'm going to find a place for *me* to fit in."

Referring back to psychologist Maria Root's identity strategies, I asked Matt, "So if I'm one of those biracial people who choose to identify only as black, is there still a place for me in those multiracial student organizations?"

"I would say, some yes and some no," he began. "One thing that's been really important about Alfredo's project is the reaching out to monoracial communities where the message we're sending is, 'We're not a new group, we are all of these groups.' We are a place where people who represent all of these groups can come together and talk about points of convergence.

"This country is having a mixed-race baby boom," Matt continued. "We've got to start talking about it because it impacts everyone, not just our families."

PART 6

BEYOND BLACK AND WHITE

In the Mix

OK, I ADMIT IT. WHEN I TALK ABOUT BIRACIAL IDENTITY, I HAVE A tendency to focus on biracial people of the black-white variety.

Naturally, when I began my exploration of the multiracial experience, I was looking for information to help explain my own journey and connect with people who shared the same background as me. Some would say I am now something of an expert on the subject. I say I am really only an expert on myself.

But the more I came in contact with multiracial people of other combinations over the years, the more I realized how much we seem to have in common. At the same time, I've also learned where our experiences seem to diverge.

Take the one-drop rule, for example. As law professor Deborah Ramirez writes in *The Multiracial Experience,* "The one-drop rule was created to maximize the number of slaves. In contrast, the test used by the Bureau of Indian Affairs for identifying who is Native American, and thus eligible for certain government benefits, is more restrictive. In order to be classified as Native American, an individual must have an Indian 'blood quantum' of at least one-fourth." Individual tribes can also set their own membership qualifications. "Some use blood quantums varying from one-sixteenth to one-half," she writes.[1]

"In my experience, there's a reverse one-drop rule in Asian American communities, where one drop of non-Asian blood makes you not Asian," said Matt Kelley. "I didn't feel pressure growing up to identify with Asian Americans. It wasn't, 'Oh, Matt's a sellout if he doesn't identify with us.' So that pressure isn't there."

He added, "I had grown up thinking I was half-Korean and I was surrounded by a large extended Korean family, all first generation, all Korean-language speakers, which my sister and I basically don't speak, and I mistook their love and intimacy as being the Korean American community." Later, when he went off to college, he says, he realized, "No, Matt, they were accepting of you because you were family, not because they thought you were Korean, because they don't."

Matt's point is underscored by researchers Rebecca Chiyoko King and Kimberly McClain DaCosta in their examination of Hapa Issues Forum (HIF), the California group founded to address concerns of multiracial people with part-Asian heritage.

"HIF seeks inclusion in the Japanese American community and was organized specifically to dialogue with that community," write King and DaCosta. By comparison, "Mixed-race African Americans do not need the rhetoric of inclusion and thus have not organized to dialogue directly with the African American community. For some mixed-race African Americans, inclusion has been forced upon them or is conditional upon acceptance of a black-only identity or a prioritizing of identities."[2]

Through their analysis, they have reached some eye-popping conclusions on the forces that have led to the formation of interracial family support groups. "Hapas, rejected by the Japanese American community, form groups focused on getting that community to include them. Mixed-race African Americans, included in the common understandings of blackness but with an accompanying silencing of other parts of their heritage, form groups focused on validating that experience."[3]

I'd often wondered why several of the national student conferences I'd attended seemed to attract more Asian-white mixes than others and why students of mixed Asian-white ancestry seemed to be the ones organizing most of the events. Some years, I'd even look at the conference schedule and think, where are the workshops on black multiracial issues? Now I'm beginning to see a connection.

"We need to be looking at research that looks at specific mixes, and then starts to look at comparing experiences of different mixes," said psychologist Maria Root. "I do think there is some difference."

The difference, she concludes, boils down to one word: intensity.

"The frequency, the number, the loudness of people in your face," Maria elaborated. "I think it's different in terms of the intensity of the African American community being very concerned about individuals identifying as multiracial. Actually, the Asian American communities have the same concerns, but just aren't vocal in the same way. Some of that's a cultural difference in terms of how things get vocalized, and how things get played out."

Nicki Carrillo can relate.

"I had a very confusing upbringing," Nicki said, attempting to explain her family background. "I'm going to start from the beginning. My mom was married when she was sixteen to a Mexican American guy and had two kids. He passed away in a car accident. A few years later, she met my father, and they never got married. And then she married my stepdad, who is half Filipino."

"And your biological father would be . . . ?"

"Third-generation Japanese. So I didn't know that I was Japanese growing up because they didn't tell me I had a different dad," she said. "I thought I was white and Filipino."

"And how do you identify now?" I asked.

"I just say I'm Japanese and white."

Nicki, who works in the Mavin Foundation's office overseeing the organization's MatchMaker Bone Marrow Project, also grew up in Pullman, Washington. Although she's nine years younger than I am, we had many of the same teachers in the Pullman school system, and we spent the first several minutes of our conversation in the Mavin office swapping stories about life in our small hometown.

"I guess I didn't really fit into one box or one group," she said. "I changed groups of friends constantly, where I was trying to remain friends with everyone."

"You were a floater?" I asked.

"Yes," she confirmed.

Sounds familiar, I thought.

Nicki learned the identity of her biological father at age thirteen and met him for the first time a year later. "I had a rocky relationship with him, and then met the rest of the Japanese American family when I was sixteen, and developed great relationships with them," she said.

But it didn't start out that way. "When I first met my Japanese American family, I compared them to my [mom's] family. It's like night and day—the traditions, the way you're supposed to act, the things you're supposed to do."

"What were some things that turned you off initially?" I asked her.

"Silly things," she said, noting that she was still in her teen years when they were first introduced. "How nobody speaks at the dinner table. You just eat. And then when you're done eating, you're sitting around the dinner table and usually talking about somebody else. My Japanese American family, if they have a problem, they will not go directly to you and tell you that. Everybody will talk about it, and then someone else, who doesn't have the problem with you, will come and tell you. So there isn't a direct conflict. And in my mom's family, if you have a problem, you directly deal with it. You have it out, and five minutes later, it's over."

Nicki says her appreciation for Japanese culture didn't blossom until her college years, when she moved across the state to attend Western Washington University in Bellingham. "My resident advisor was Japanese, and so I started to learn more about Japanese culture and hang around her friends who were people of color and involved in the ethnic student center and very active in the community," she said.

As Nicki's story illustrates, it is quite common for a change in location to trigger a reevaluation on matters of race for members of interracial families. For biracial people who have lived in the same community for most of their lives, the reevaluation may occur when they move away from home to start college. For others, such as Courtenay Edelhart, it happened when her family moved from Chicago to Albuquerque, New Mexico, and then again when she attended Northwestern University. In my case, it occurred when my parents separated and my mother and I moved from suburban Cleveland to Kalamazoo, Michigan.

Another Mavin staff member, Amanda Kay Erekson, embraced her Japanese heritage early but wasn't always as public about it as she is today.

"I was culturally a white person in high school, and I was culturally a person of color in college," said Amanda, who grew up in Eugene, Oregon. But Amanda does not "look" Japanese, a comment she hears frequently given her long auburn hair and European facial features.

"So how did you come to your identity formation?" I asked.

"I don't know exactly what it is," said Amanda. "I'm the oldest of four. And my other siblings, I think, primarily identify as white, even though two of them look much more Asian than I do. And so I'm not sure what in my life or my personality makes it different."

One pivotal moment occurred during her college years while she was on a road trip with a group of three white classmates. One of them began talking about interracial dating.

"Clearly they didn't know me very well, because she basically was saying she would date a black guy, but she wouldn't marry a black guy," said Amanda, who then took the other side in the discussion. "What is the difference? What if you're in love? And she said, 'We wouldn't want half-breeds in our family.'

"That was the first time I ever heard that word for people. So I felt like I had been punched in the stomach. And then I caught my breath and I said, 'Before you say anything else, let me just tell you that my mom is half-Japanese.' And then it got quiet. She still kept her position. She said that it's hard on the children. And I'm like, *I am the children! My mom is one of the children, too! And we're OK!* I couldn't really talk anymore," said Amanda, "and it was pretty much silent for the rest of the trip."

It was not the first time Amanda felt the need to come to the defense of her family, as a college psychology course on racial identity development would remind her. "Our professor asked us all to think about our first memory having to do with race," she said. "My first memory having to do with race was when I was in first grade and my sister was in kindergarten, and she was being made fun of, for looking Asian. And that was the first time where I was sort of like, wow, I'm different from everyone else. And it's not because people saw me as different. It was because they saw my sister as different, and to me, she and I were the same. It was a big deal. To my sister, it wasn't a big deal. She would have people chant 'Chinese, Japanese' to her, probably a lot. But it never happened to me. So the one time when I saw it happening to her, it was very upsetting, and it was something I always remembered."

But there is more to Amanda's embrace of her Japanese heritage than the racist actions of others. She's had a genuine interest in her Asian ancestry since she was very young.

"In elementary school, I did a report about Japan because I wanted to learn about my family's heritage and share that with my class," she said. "In fifth grade, we started hosting students from Japan, and around the same time, my Japanese American grand-mother moved into the town where we lived. So we started getting more Japanese culture, both Japanese and Japanese American culture into our house. And I made really good friends with these students who were visiting from Japan. And again, as long as I could remember, I wanted to learn Japanese, I wanted to go to Japan, and I wanted to learn about my grandmother's experience as a teenager in an internment camp. There's all these things that were just really interesting to me and I always wanted to learn about them, and I felt a connection and a relation to them. I don't think my siblings have had that same desire, I guess."

She added, "I do speak Japanese, but not fluently. I studied all four years of high school and all four years of college and majored in Asian studies. And now I've been to Japan three times, the third time as a semester abroad."

To an outsider, Amanda's identity as "Japanese American *and* white American *and* multiracial" given the way she looks might sound perplexing, an example of someone who took the concept of coloring outside the lines a bit too far. But like all of the multiracial people I've encountered over the course of my work, her identity statement makes perfect sense once the details of her life story are laid out on the table.

A consistent theme runs through the stories I've heard: people do not identify racially based on how they look. They identify based on their life experience. Looks will influence those life experiences, but ultimately it's the experiences themselves and not physical appearance that will decide it, provided of course the individual is being honest with themselves about the life they've lived. That's one thing multiracial mixes of all varieties seem to have in common.

Generation M

HER NAME IS GEETHA LAKSHMINARAYANAN, WHICH IS PRONOUNCED pretty much just like it's spelled. "GEETH-uh Luck-shmee-nar-EYE-an-en," she said.

We met in New York City in April 2005. She was part of the "Generation Mix National Awareness Tour," which I will get to in a moment. First, I had to get my head around her name. It is a reaction Geetha has experienced, by my guess, about a million times.

"I get it all," she said, ranging from "That's the longest last name I've ever seen" to "Where's it from?" and "How long did it take you to learn how to spell it?"

"How long *did* it take you?" I asked.

"I didn't know that it was any different from any other kid's name. So I just learned it like everybody else," she responded.

It was at that point that I started counting. "One, two, three . . ."

"Sixteen," she said, cutting to the chase. Her last name has sixteen letters.

Yep, she had definitely been through that conversation before.

Geetha was part of a group of twentysomethings who were

spending five weeks traveling the country, giving talks, setting up information tables, and speaking to just about anyone to raise the visibility of multiracial people and interracial families. Organized by the Mavin Foundation, the tour schedule called for the group to travel eight thousand miles, making fifteen stops along the way. In each city they visited, the group worked in conjunction with either a community-based organization for interracial families or a multiracial student club from a local college to host a community forum on mixed-race issues.

I met up with the five members of Generation Mix midway through the tour. Their multicolored Winnebago, complete with a "Generation Mix" logo painted on the side, was parked at Riverbank State Park in Manhattan. In front of it were a series of tables with brochures, a book collection, and other material related to the multiracial experience. Perhaps showing my age, the RV reminded me of the bus from *The Partridge Family*, the 1970s television sitcom. In any case, Geetha and I climbed aboard and began our chat.

At twenty-two years old, Geetha is a recent graduate of the University of Michigan in Ann Arbor, which is also the city where she grew up. Her mother is white, and her father is Indian.

"I had a lot of trouble identifying, because my elementary school was not diverse at all," Geetha said of her childhood. "In fifth or sixth grade, a friend and I were counting how many black people there were in the school. I don't know why we decided to do that. But as we were naming them, she said, 'Oh, yeah, and then *you*.' And I didn't really know what to say to that because I didn't feel I was black, because I'm not. But I also didn't feel like I was white. I didn't know there was anything else out there [in terms of] different races. So it took me a while to sort of develop an identity as a person of color and what that meant. Then it took me a while to develop my identity as an Asian American."

Yet from what I've observed, in the United States when a non-Asian says "Asian," they often don't think of people from India as being in that category. Geetha agreed.

"That was a whole other dimension, too," she said. "A lot of the Asian American organizing that goes on at the University of Michigan is Japanese, Chinese, Korean, Vietnamese. There's a strong Indian community, but I felt awkward trying to fit in with them."

Geetha went on to explain how her participation in a mentorship program for Asian American high school students helped reinforce her Asian heritage as she entered college. "That really taught me that there was an Asian American community, that Asian Americans really did have unique issues in terms of race and the history of their immigration," she said.

But at the same time, it also raised more questions about where Geetha felt she belonged. "Do you really fit it?" Geetha said she asked herself. "Could I really understand the experience because my mother's white? Having to 'come out' to people that I had a white mother, they'd say, 'Oh, that makes sense, that's why you're this way.' Or, 'That's why you don't understand this.' So I always felt like I didn't quite fit in that community. I definitely don't fit in the white community in the sense of being white. I have a lot of white friends, and I identify with white culture in the sense that it's sort of American culture, but I'm definitely seen as an 'other.'"

Nevertheless, at one stop on the group's journey, someone brought up the topic of "white privilege" and to what extent Geetha may benefit from having one parent who is white. The concept seems to be garnering more attention in multiracial circles lately and is sometimes referred to as "half-white privilege."

"There's the kind of white privilege you get where somebody sees you and they treat you as being white, and, you know, you have Band-Aids that match your skin. I don't have that kind of white privilege, so I never really thought of myself as getting any white privilege," said Geetha. "But I started to think about the fact that my mom gets all kinds of white privilege, and that definitely gets passed down to me. Everything from situations where it's easier for her to get a job or a loan or something like that, and of course, I received the benefit from that.

"And then other things that are a little more personal," Geetha continued. "A lot of people of color don't hear their own history being taught in classes. But my family history on my mom's side dates back to the Mayflower. So I always felt I was very included in the history books. When we learned about the Pilgrims, I would say, 'Yeah, that's my family right there.'"

"And what did you learn about your father's side?" I asked.

"In my old school, nothing. Absolutely nothing at all," she replied. "Once I started college, I studied American culture and really focused on Asian American studies." But she says there are still gaps in her knowledge of her father's heritage that she would eventually like to fill.

Having lived in Ann Arbor her entire life, Geetha said the Generation Mix tour had been as much an education for her as it had been an occasion to teach. "I think it's been really interesting for me to see what's been going on in other parts of the country," she said. "I think race is perceived differently on the West Coast because there are a lot more Asians, a lot more Latinos. At home, it's more black or white."

In fact, the Census Bureau's own analysis of the nearly seven million people who consider themselves multiracial confirms the geographical differences Geetha noticed. Nationally, 2.4 percent of Americans identified with more than one race. But in California, the number of people marking two or more racial categories represented 4.7 percent of that state's population, the highest in the continental

United States. For the record, Hawaii had the highest percentage overall at 21 percent. In Alaska, the figure was 5.4 percent. By comparison, Alabama, Mississippi, South Carolina, West Virginia, and Maine had the lowest proportion of residents indicating they were multiracial, at 1 percent or less.[1] Those statistics are not a coincidence.

"Whenever you talk about interracial marriage and you have a forum or something, it always goes back to slavery at some point. There's always that legacy," said Aaron Kendeall, another member of Generation Mix. "The Asian Americans don't have any of that stuff to deal with. So it's like a whole different animal."

Aaron's background is black, white, and Native American. His dad is African American and one-quarter Creek. His mom is Irish and German. Raised in Pittsburgh, Aaron has short, dark hair and a light tan complexion.

Twenty-one years old and a student at West Virginia University, one of Aaron's earliest memories involving race happened at age four. While visiting a neighborhood playground, another child asked, "Why is your grandma black?"

Aaron answered as if responding to a riddle. "I said, 'I don't know. Why?' I didn't understand the question," he said. "I just assumed that everyone had different-colored people in their family."

He added, "My cousin is from Florida, and he's really dark. He used to call me 'Light-Bright.' But I think that was another joke thing. We were cool. We hung out all the time."

Others, however, weren't so cool. When Aaron played competitive hockey in high school, white players would, as he says, "drop the N-bomb."

"You get a game suspension for getting in a fight. But if you use a racial slur, you get a ten-game sentence," Aaron explained. "So I would get in fights, and I would get a game [suspension], but the other kid would get ten games."

Still, Aaron says he never wavered from his biracial identity. "I think I just always thought of myself as mixed. Both of my parents raised me. All my family that lives in Pittsburgh is black. But the school I went to was predominantly white. So I was like, between both worlds. It goes back and forth. I just learned I was neither or both."

"Would someone who is darker than you or me have a harder time trying to identify as biracial?" I asked.

"I've noticed that as well, and I'm not sure," Aaron said. "It's so random, being mixed. It's all in the gene pool. My sister's a lot darker than me, but I don't think she identifies as black, either, but as biracial."

"People put these stereotypes on what a mixed person should look like," said twenty-year-old Ashley McDermott, the only other member of the Generation Mix tour with African-American ancestry. "Not everybody's going to turn out to look like that. Me, for instance."

Ashley was raised in Boise, Idaho, by her white mother. Her father is black, but her parents split up when she was just three years old. She has no memory of her mom and dad sharing the same household.

"What I got a lot was people perceiving me as white, because I do have blond hair, and I do have a lighter skin tone," she said.

"Natural blond?" I whispered.

"Yeah," she laughed. "I've never dyed my hair before. That throws people off, too," she said. "My father's really dark, but at the same time I look exactly like him in facial features."

"Did your friends even know?" I asked her.

"Yeah, all my friends knew. I think everybody in my school kind of knew. I'm very proud of that, in fact. I think I just kind of let everybody know," Ashley said. "People would assume that I was adopted when I was with my father. It's harsh because people would also assume that I would be my father's girlfriend, and I'd be twelve years old!"

"How would you know when people were thinking that?"

"People have asked. Distant family members," she said. "When I'd go to reunions with my family, people would be like, 'Oh, is this your girlfriend?' And my dad would say, 'No, this is my daughter.' I'm sure people assume that even now. We went to the grocery store the other day, and we still got looks."

As a result, there were times when Ashley says she made an effort to try to head off any confusion about that when out shopping or waiting in line at a movie theater. "We'd buy our tickets, and I'd say, 'Thanks, Dad.' Or when we're at the store, going clothes shopping for me, I'd say, 'Thanks, Dad,'" making sure anyone nearby would hear her. Now, she said, "I just tell myself I know he's my dad. I don't care what other people think."

Ashley appears to have a similar attitude when it comes to identifying as multiracial. "My mother was really good at letting me decide who I was," she said. "She brought me up with all my cultures, all my heritages."

That wasn't exactly the case in Charles Yesuwan's household. "My family doesn't talk about race at all, actually," he said. Consequently, Charles wasn't fully aware of his ethnic background until he was almost a teenager. His mother is Chinese, and his dad is Thai and Burmese. That combination, he recognizes, may raise a few questions about why he's taking part in a national awareness tour on the mixed-*race* experience, even though he faces similar identity issues.

"I guess to the casual observer, I might just be blanketed as 'Asian American' or just 'Asian,'" he said. "It's been kind of hard to explain, especially to people who aren't Asian, that don't really acknowledge that there are a lot of different cultures and heritages and languages that stem from Asia. As a multiethnic Asian, I consider myself mixed because I am a product of those different cultures and heritages and customs."

Charles hails from Seattle and grew up in a bilingual household. His family spoke both Thai and English. Up until age twelve, he was under the impression his mother was Thai, when in fact her family had immigrated to Thailand from China. He learned the full story when an aunt he had never met before paid a visit to their home.

"The first words that came out of her mouth when she saw me were Chinese words. And I was taken aback," he said. "When I asked my mom about this, she said in a very offhand manner, as if it wasn't a big deal, 'Oh yeah, by the way, I'm Chinese.' And I learned that she knew how to speak Chinese, she knew how to write Chinese, and she never really did any of that in front of us growing up. So that was a big shock for me."

Talking with Charles reminded me of my conversation with Ramona Douglass when she spoke about the naming of AMEA, and whether the group should be called the Association of Multi-*Racial* Americans or the Association of Multi-*Ethnic* Americans. As Charles points out, certain "interethnic" families may experience challenges similar to those that "interracial" families face.

"When a lot of Asian ethnic groups were newly migrated to America, they would not cross ethnic boundaries. If a Japanese person were to marry a Korean person, all hell would break out," he said. Yet for many non-Asians, the lines between the cultures continue to blur.

"I've been finding there's a lot of restaurants popping up, these Asian fusion, pan-Asian restaurants that cater to a wider audience, which is good," said Charles. "But when you look at the menu, and you see chicken teriyaki right next to pad Thai but no discerning, no indication whatsoever where the foods came from, people who aren't necessarily conscious about Asian cultures will probably just say, 'Oh, that's just one race.' I want to educate others that there a lot of cultures behind the term Asian, as with [the term] Latino or Hispanic."

The one member of Generation Mix whom I did not get a chance to meet face to face during their New York City stopover was twenty-three-year-old Jamie Tibbetts, who is Chinese American and white and grew up in the San Francisco Bay Area. A scheduling conflict—more mine than his—prevented us from getting together. But in an online journal the team members kept throughout their trip, Jamie expressed confidence that the tour had made a difference.

"I'm huge on the power of individual interaction and how a simple personal conversation can greatly impact a person and his or her perceptions," he writes. "Or how an article in a paper, or a short segment on a news program can do something similar to open a person's mind and frame of consciousness by exposing them to something they might not ever have heard of before, like a community and culture of mixed-race people. Throughout the tour this is exactly the sort of thing we did."

"The media outlets and things have been huge," said Geetha, who gave several interviews throughout the tour, including one to the *New York Times*.

"I had some preconceived notions about certain areas of the United States, Alabama being one, Texas being another," said Charles. "It's been a welcome surprise for me at least to be wrong with those preconceived notions. I enjoyed talking and sharing with a lot of locals there and just exploring new communities and cultures."

"People who come to the events come for a reason," added Aaron. "It's cool seeing the little kids come by, and the parents and the families. There wasn't stuff like this when I was growing up. So hopefully, their lives will be easier or less confusing."

"This tour made people think about the mixed-race experience in general when they probably never would have thought about it before," writes Ashley in her Generation Mix blog. "I mean, that's how big things are started, right? By the little things that set them off?"

Ashley then closes with a more personal question. It appears directed at her Generation Mix teammates. But I have a feeling she's really talking to the broader multiracial community. "What happens with the five of us in the future?" she asks. "Will things change as far as the multiracial experience goes? What will each of us be doing? Will we still be involved with or be as enthusiastic about the multiracial movement as we are now? Who knows, but I can't wait to see."

My Survival Guide

I HAD JUST CONCLUDED A SPEAKING ENGAGEMENT AT WASHINGTON College in Chestertown, Maryland, when a professor who'd been sitting in the audience approached me. "Can I have a copy of your notes?" she asked.

"A copy of my notes?" I responded. "Well, they really wouldn't make sense to you. They're just a bunch of chicken scratches and a few key phrases to remind me to make certain points."

"Well, what about a copy of your overhead slides?" she asked.

"Oh, I'm really sorry. I wasn't prepared to give out anything like that," I had to tell her.

On the drive back home to the Washington, D.C., area that night, it suddenly hit me. All of the buzzwords and catchphrases and diagrams and literary devices that I'd developed in my effort to explain the multiracial experience to other people were striking a chord. Some of my material was based on academic studies I had read. Some of it I'd just made up, based on my own gut feeling and the experiences I'd had. But from members of interracial families to professors with PhDs, people were telling me that I was on to something.

Just before the 2002 Pan-Collegiate Conference on the Mixed-Race Experience, which was held at Cornell University, I spent the better part of one afternoon cobbling all my material together. I ran off several dozen copies, stuffed them in legal-size envelopes, and passed them out at my conference workshop. I called it the "Mixed Race Survival Guide," and it seemed to go over well. By the end of my seminar, attendees had snatched up all the leftover copies.

I have since refined some of that material, expanded on it in areas where I saw a need, and incorporated other helpful tools into the mix. I now present it here, beginning with "The Bill of Rights for Racially Mixed People," a twelve-point statement developed by psychologist Maria Root out of her research.

Bill of Rights for Racially Mixed People

"I was going around speaking to a lot of student groups, community family groups, and people were telling me things," explained Maria. "With the Bill of Rights, I was really just sitting down trying to summarize what people had told me, and I didn't think anything more of that. But I gave it out to a few people, and I was really surprised. I wasn't surprised that people said, 'Oh, this is my experience.' That was good to hear, that was validation that what everybody has been saying still is true. . . . The surprising piece was how much it really seemed to be needed."

So needed that at one of the first conferences for interracial families, in the early 1990s, "everybody pulled out the Bill of Rights to read it out loud together," Maria said. "It kind of gave me goose bumps."

I, too, found the Bill of Rights incredibly empowering. But as the multiracial movement began to gather political momentum, I decided that in addition to the Bill of Rights, we needed a Declaration of Independence for Multiracial People. What I didn't know then was that Maria was working on her own follow-up to the Bill of Rights.

"I think it is important to have the groups, the organizations, the venues for conversation, the agreement and disagreement-sharing, the variety of experience. People do still need that," she said. "But I think there are some changes in what people are turning to."

"What do you see in terms of changes?" I asked.

"Well, I think a lot of stuff the Bill of Rights was based on—keep in mind I initially wrote it in 1992—but if you look at that, it's a dozen years ago. How we talk about mixed race has changed a bit. The fact that it's represented in the media, that the census changed, there's another generation that's already in their young adult years, actually moving into middle age, where people haven't grown up as isolated," she said.

Bill of Rights for Racially Mixed People
by Maria P. P. Root, PhD

I do not have to justify my existence in this world.

I do not have to keep the races separate within me.

I do not have to justify my ethnic legitimacy.

I am not responsible for people's discomfort with my physical ambiguity.

I have the right to identify myself differently than strangers expect me to identify.

I have the right to identify myself differently than how my parents identify me.

I have the right to identify myself differently than my brothers and sisters.

I have the right to identify myself differently in different situations.

I have the right to create a vocabulary to communicate about being multiracial.

I have the right to change my identity over my lifetime—and more than once.

I have the right to have loyalties and identify with more than one group of people.

I have the right to freely choose whom I befriend and love.

Multiracial Oath of Social Responsibility

That growing awareness is part of what led Maria to develop the Multiracial Oath of Social Responsibility, which she sent to me for feedback while the document was still in its draft form. Subsequent revisions, I noticed, incorporated some of the suggestions I gave her.

"I think a lot of young people are looking for the bridge from their experience to social activism or making a difference in the world," said Maria. "At this point in time, a multiracial person just saying 'I'm multiracial'—it's not the same hard work it was twenty-five or thirty years ago. I think there are enough people to band together that there really is some social activism and some advocacy that can be done. That's part of what's changing," she concluded, noting the work of the Mavin Foundation and the multiracial student groups that have formed on college campuses.

Multiracial Oath of Social Responsibility
by Maria P. P. Root, PhD

I want to make a difference in this world. Therefore:

I strive to improve race relations.

> I know that race and ethnicity are not solely defined by one's genetic heritage;

> I refuse to confine my choices in love or loyalty to a single race;

> I make efforts to increase my knowledge of U.S. racial history;

I know that race and ethnicity can be used as political, economic, and social tools of oppression.

I recognize the people who have made it possible for me to affirm my multiracial identity.

> They are my relatives, friends, and mentors;

> They are people who have crossed color lines to fight discrimination;

> They are people who identified as multiracial before this choice was recognized;
>
> They are people who have exposed and explained the suppression of multiraciality.
>
> I must fight all forms of oppression as the oppression of one is the oppression of all.
>
> I recognize that oppression thrives on fear and ignorance;
>
> I seek to recognize my prejudices and change them;
>
> I know that it is neither helpful nor productive to argue over who is more oppressed;
>
> I recognize that my life interconnects with all other lives.
>
> I will make a difference!

Declaration of Independence for Multiracial People

Like any oath, the Multiracial Oath of Social Responsibility is one individuals can either agree to or not. My Declaration of Independence recognizes that choice. Taken together, I believe the three documents—the Bill of Rights, the Declaration of Independence, and the Multiracial Oath—offer a basic framework for members of interracial families looking for a guide to charting their racial course in post–Census 2000 America.

> ### Declaration of Independence for Multiracial People
> by Elliott Lewis
>
> I am free to identify as multiracial solely as a personal expression of who I am.
>
> My identification as multiracial should not be interpreted as a statement of my political philosophy.
>
> I am free to identify as multiracial and engage in, or remain apart from, social and political movements formed in the name of mixed-race people.
>
> I am free to identify as multiracial and advocate for issues of my own choosing, consistent with my own values.

I am free to identify as multiracial and reject the causes that other multiracial people may embrace.

I am free to identify as multiracial and not take up any political causes at all.

I declare my independence as a multiracial person.

Come to Your Census Form

Not that I want to relive that debate, but I've also concocted a census form of my own. It's known as Elliott's "Come to Your Census" Form. It grew out of my frustration listening to all the cross talk leading up to the 2000 census. Each side in the debate, it seemed to me, was too eager to dismiss the valid points being made by the others. My form asks the race question three different times, in three different ways, so the answers can be evaluated based on their context. I now use the form as a tool in diversity workshops to stimulate discussion on how we see race.

ELLIOTT'S "COME TO YOUR CENSUS" FORM

Section I. Yourself

Fill in the blank with a term of your choosing which best describes your racial identity as you see it, given the totality of your life experience:

_____

Section II. Your Government

For purposes related to the monitoring of civil rights in housing, education, employment, voting rights, law enforcement, and other related services; and for the purpose of evaluating efforts in both the public and private sectors designed to compensate for past racial injustices, promote diversity, and prevent continuing discrimination against historically oppressed populations, please check the category that best describes your racial identity as it is most often perceived by others. The government recognizes that some of the categories listed may not meet any logical or scientific definitions of "race" but asks that you play along anyway using generally held societal views of race at the present time, no matter how screwed up you believe those views may be. After all, this is America.

( ) Black   ( ) White   ( ) Hispanic   ( ) Arab or Middle Eastern
( ) American Indian or Alaska Native   ( ) Asian or Pacific Islander
( ) Universal Person of Color: someone perceived as nonwhite, but who still confuses others by not being easily associated with any other single category.

Section III. Yo Mama

For research purposes in the fields of sociology, anthropology, psychology, genealogy, economics, and medicine, or in other disciplines where contemporary notions of race may be relevant, complete the following: Indicate the racial and/or ethnic breakdown of your parents as best you can and to the extent that you know it. (Example: "$1/2$ black, $1/4$ white, etc.") If you were adopted, please attach a separate sheet explaining your adoptive and biological family situations.

Mother: _____ Father: _____

Six Stages Toward Identity Resolution

Even with the progress we've made in terms of awareness of multiracial issues, I still see a need to develop proper tools for articulating the dynamics of the multiracial experience in everyday, commonsense language—and not just for public relations purposes or so that others can understand where we're coming from. My sense is that young multiracial people especially are in need of some structure for interpreting their experiences that is free of academic jargon and scholarly babble.

My Six Stages toward Identity Resolution addresses some of that, as it captures my own progression in dealing with my identity. It stemmed from a question someone once asked me concerning the process multiracial people go through to arrive at a biracial self-concept. At the time, I said I didn't think there was any mathematical formula to it. It's not like I followed a series of steps, worked my way down to the bottom, and said, "Wow, X equals three." I had no idea how to explain the process, until I came up with the Six Stages.

Six Stages Toward Identity Resolution
by Elliott Lewis

Stage 1: Huh?
   First hints of race-related issues ahead. What's the deal?

Stage 2: Help!
   On race, culture, and identity, these trapdoors keep opening
   up on me!

Stage 3: Oh.
   So that's how this race business works. I guess I'll learn to deal with it.

Stage 4: Hmmm . . .
   Reflection, questioning. I need to make better sense of this madness.

Stage 5: True 'dat!
   OK, now we're getting somewhere. I can definitely relate.

Stage 6: Aha!
   Finally . . . I'm cool with who I am.

Three-Ring Circus of Biracial Identity

Then, in another conversation on being biracial, I found myself reaching for pen and paper to draw what I couldn't quite express in words. I was trying to explain how different people view biracial identity differently. When I was finished, I had three diagrams, each made up of three circles representing white identity, black identity, and biracial identity.

It reminded me of a three-ring circus, which is exactly how I chose to label it—the Three-Ring Circus of Biracial Identity. I've refined the drawings a bit in light of Maria Root's five identity models, but otherwise they are essentially unchanged. Substitute other ethnic groups in place of "black" and "white," and much of the Three-Ring Circus rings true for multiracial people of other combinations.

Three-Ring Circus of Biracial Identity

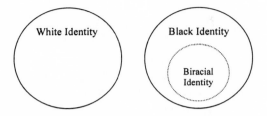

In this model, biracial identity is seen as a type of black identity, or as synonymous with black identity. Someone adopting this view might say, "I'm biracial, but I consider myself black," or "I'm black, although my mom is white."

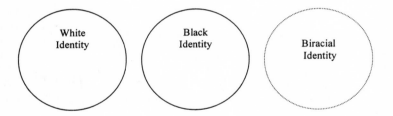

In this model, biracial identity is seen as separate, unique, and distinct from black or white identity. Those who see themselves this way might say, "I'm not white. I'm not black. I'm biracial."

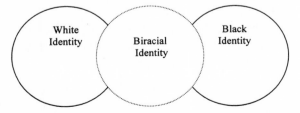

In this model, biracial identity is seen as intersecting, overlapping, and sharing aspects of both heritages. Someone with this view might say, "I am both black *and* white. I'm biracial."

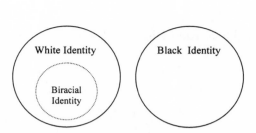

This model represents Maria Root's "Symbolic Identity," a reversal of the one-drop rule in which the biracial person identifies primarily as white while openly acknowledging his or her mixed ancestry.

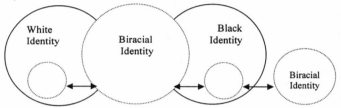

In this model, biracial identity is seen as more fluid, shifting in position to resemble each of the various models depending on the social context.

Seven Habits of Highly Multiracial People

I soon realized I needed a more inclusive way of describing the multiracial experience that would work across different combinations. That's why I made up the Seven Habits of Highly Multiracial People, with apologies to author Stephen Covey, who wrote the best-selling business book *The Seven Habits of Highly Effective People.*

Of course, not all multiracial people live all Seven Habits. Some live six of the seven, or five of the seven. Some might not live any of the seven. That's why I call them the habits of *highly* multiracial people, meaning those whose life experiences reflect their multiracial status in a way that trumps any single race identity hands down.

I've also had people who do not identify as multiracial tell me that many of the Seven Habits apply to them. Some have been adopted across racial lines. Others consider themselves "bicultural" if not biracial. And some have grown up or lived abroad before relocating to the United States. For various reasons, they feel some of the same conflicts over their identity, where they fit in, and how others perceive them. In any event, they find similarities with the struggles of multiracial people.

The Seven Habits of Highly Multiracial People
by Elliott Lewis

1. Undergoes "racial interrogation"

"What are you?" "What is your background?" "Where are you from?" As Highly Multiracial People, we face such questions so often, it feels like an interrogation.

2. Experiences the "chameleon effect" of being multiracial

Shifting, changing, varying public perceptions of our racial identity. We may be seen as African American one minute, Hispanic the next, Filipino an hour later. It's as if we're walking, talking, living, breathing, human inkblot tests for how societies view race.

3. Encounters bewilderment or disbelief when sharing life stories

When Highly Multiracial People try to explain our experiences, we often face a lack of validation. Others will challenge, question, or try to discredit our personal histories and racial experiences, as if these "defining moments" could not have happened.

4. Attacked for a suspected lack of racial group allegiance or authenticity

You don't have to be Highly Multiracial to be familiar with this one. You're "not black enough," or "not Asian enough." You're "running away from your blackness," or otherwise trying to avoid your minority race.

5. Experiences a temporary racial identity crisis

What am I? Where do I fit in? How do I navigate racial issues? The temporary crisis may last anywhere from ten minutes to ten years, or even longer. But the key word is temporary. We go through the crisis on our way toward a resolved identity.

---

6. Develops an interracial, mixed-race, cross-cultural comfort zone

Not surprisingly, Highly Multiracial People feel most at ease in integrated settings, at multicultural events, and at social functions with other interracial families and mixed-race people.

7. Adopts a racial identity acknowledging multiple backgrounds

"I'm multiracial," "I'm biracial," "I'm Hapa" (half-Asian), "I'm Blackanese," "I'm Cablinasian," "I'm black, but my mom is white." Highly Multiracial People find a way to express their mixed heritage.

Game of Life for Highly Multiracial People

"But the habits aren't really habits that multiracial people *do*," said one attendee at the workshop where I first presented the concept. "The seven habits are really more like reactions," she said. They represent things other people do in their interactions with multiracial people.

Her point was well taken, but calling them the "Seven Reactions" would mean losing a clever marketing ploy and making the list less memorable. Nevertheless, it did cause me to rethink the concept. If the Seven Habits are more akin to reactions, then what triggers those reactions? I concluded that they were triggered by events and behaviors of people I call "racial observers." Eventually, I designed a flow chart to spell out that relationship. I call it the Game of Life for Highly Multiracial People.

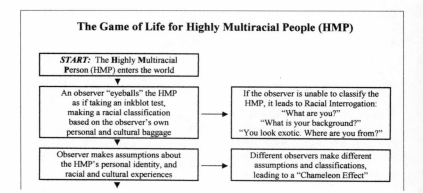

The Game of Life for Highly Multiracial People (HMP)

START: The Highly Multiracial Person (HMP) enters the world
▼
An observer "eyeballs" the HMP as if taking an inkblot test, making a racial classification based on the observer's own personal and cultural baggage → If the observer is unable to classify the HMP, it leads to Racial Interrogation: "What are you?" "What is your background?" "You look exotic. Where are you from?"
▼
Observer makes assumptions about the HMP's personal identity, and racial and cultural experiences → Different observers make different assumptions and classifications, leading to a "Chameleon Effect"
▼

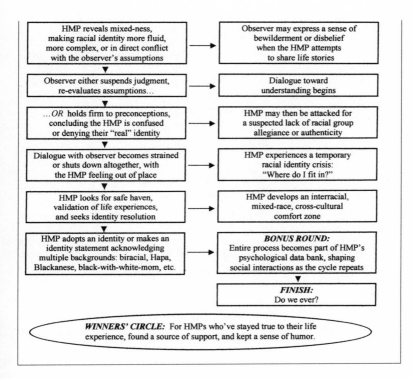

Top Ten Signs You're Living the Multiracial Experience

Finally, the last piece of my survival guide consists of the Top Ten Signs You're Living the Multiracial Experience. I either use it as an icebreaker to start off my speeches or recite it as part of my conclusion to bring my presentations to a close.

Top Ten Signs You're Living the Multiracial Experience

10. At the family picnic, you tried eating chitlins with chopsticks.
9. You prefer the term "melanin-challenged" as opposed to "high yellow."
8. You consider yourself a "person of color" but can't decide what color.
7. You've tried compensating for a near-white appearance by acting "super-ethnic."

---

6. Your "multiracial radar" works better than your "gay-dar."
5. Your family celebrates Rosh Hashanah, Ramadan, Christmas, *and* Kwanzaa.
4. In demographic surveys, when asked for your race, you think it's an essay question.
3. Your idea of a well-balanced meal is sushi, enchiladas, and baklava.
2. When speaking Ebonics, you have a white accent.

And the number-one sign you're living the multiracial experience. . . .

1. You've developed a medical condition that causes your eyes to roll whenever someone asks, "What are you?

I believe that in the end, the multiracial experience is something we should all find a way to smile about.

Where Do We Go from Here?

WHEN I TRAVEL TO SPEAK TO COLLEGES, COMMUNITY GROUPS, OR diversity conferences about the multiracial experience, I am often asked, "Where is this all going?"

"Where is *what* all going?" I usually say.

"You know, the rise in the number of interracial families, the growth in the number of people who see themselves as multiracial. Where is it headed? What's the desired result? Where will we end up?"

Honestly, I have no earthly idea. Neither do most of the people I interviewed for this book. The answers are as diverse as the people responding to the question.

"People have gone different ways," said Susan Graham. "Project RACE has stood very firmly on where we were since our founding fifteen years ago," when it began advocating for a multiracial category.

Though in this case, I'm not so sure staying in the same place is necessarily a good thing. Isn't that how we ended up here in the first place? What used to be standard operating procedure in the way

Americans thought of race and racial identity was an outlook that hadn't kept up with the times. Multiracial people, acting both collectively and individually, set about to update the playbook.

"In every generation, there are issues that become so pressing, it is impossible to stand by and do nothing," said Ramona Douglass. "For my generation, being invisible was no longer acceptable. Being told who we were was no longer acceptable. Today, there's a whole new group of people and a whole new set of issues, and they're going to find their burning agenda and their burning issue, and they'll run with it. And whatever it is, if it speaks to their heart, that's all that matters."

"This huge floating ball of potential could really be moved in any direction," said Matt Kelley, adding that if a multiracial movement continues to exist, he hopes it embraces a progressive agenda. "That's what both excites me and scares me. I don't know where it's going." While others ponder the question, Matt has evidently decided to take his own career in a new direction. As of this writing, he had announced his intention to step down as president of the Mavin Foundation, the organization he founded, in 2006.

Geetha Lakshminarayanan said, "Where it's actually going and where I hope it goes may be different things. I would really like to see a movement that is an anti-racist movement. Why do people organize around race? Because there are still issues of racism. If there weren't, it wouldn't be quite as big of a deal."

But when it comes to racial politics, multiracial people are all over the map.

"I don't think we have a collective sense of what our agenda is. I don't think that we are necessarily in agreement about what we should be moving toward or working on," said Jen Chau. "So I wouldn't be completely comfortable in saying 100 percent, yes, we are a movement."

"During the run-up to the census decision, when the debate was going fast and furious, it dawned on me, hey, this is not the answer anyway," said Charles Byrd. "A multiracial category is not the answer anyway. The answer to this thing is doing away with these stupid boxes altogether. That's the answer."

Actually, I don't think it is. Neither does Jen.

"We need to know the numbers. We need to see how the multiracial population is growing," Jen said. Otherwise, "we're going to have absolutely no information on this community."

I concur. There are three reasons institutions generally inquire about race: to discriminate, to integrate, or to investigate. It's crucial to distinguish between the three.

The collection of racial information for the purpose of enhancing diversity or to investigate allegations of unfair treatment is important. We can argue about how to interpret the data, but we need to have it. Otherwise, in the quest to become "color-blind," society instead becomes "racism-blind," in which case discriminatory practices continue unabated because no information exists to document racial disparities.

I compare it to the collection of crime statistics. No one argues that gathering statistics about crime causes crime. Yet a growing chorus seems to be calling for the government to stop collecting racial information, as if that's what perpetuates racism.

In the case of crime statistics, such research can provide insight into where to assign police officers, where to target crime-prevention efforts, and when to alert the public once serial criminals, crime sprees, or other trends start to emerge. It can also tell us whether our crime-fighting efforts are working. Did that police crackdown, citizen patrol, or neighborhood watch program actually result in less crime, more arrests, and a safer community? We won't know unless we keep crime statistics.

I think of racial statistics the same way. They provide us with valuable demographic information to help track racial progress and identify those sectors of society where more attention is needed. The rise in the number of interracial marriages over the last three decades alone is a sign of considerable social progress that merits additional sociological study. By the same token, analysis of the multiracial population can shed light on new cultural patterns.

But the racial numbers are important for other reasons, too. Are police officers unfairly stopping motorists because of their race? Are financial institutions complying with civil rights laws in their lending practices? How do we know unless we first gather racial information?

As the American Sociological Association stated in a position paper on the subject in 2002, research on race "allows scholars to document how race shapes social ranking, access to resources, and life experiences; and advances understanding of this important dimension of social life, which in turn advances social justice."[1]

The sociologists concluded, "Refusing to acknowledge the fact of racial classification, feelings, and actions, and refusing to measure their consequences, will not eliminate racial inequalities. At best, it will preserve the status quo."[2]

The status quo isn't good enough for Sundee Tucker Frazier. "I don't believe all biracial people are meant to be bridge-makers. I don't think we're the solution to the world's racial problems, and it bugs me when people say that about us. But I believe I've been put in a unique position," she said. "I think people who are white or who are black are able to get into their own world and be comfortable and be fine with segregation. It's like, 'Fine, leave them to themselves; we don't want to interact with them.' I don't think that all biracial people feel this way necessarily, but for myself, I'm not comfortable with that separation.

"I have friends in both worlds. I see things from a different perspective that enables me to see both sides of a situation. I can understand where a black person might be coming from, but I can also understand where a white person might be coming from. And that enables me to be a person to help the two sides understand one another," Sundee continued. "As a biracial person, I cannot settle for there being division between black and white people. I'm highly motivated to see black and white people come together because as long as black and white people remain separated and hostile, I've got to live with that tension."

The good news is that there is less tension now than there used to be. In addition, the multiracial experience, once viewed only at the margins of American life, is slowly inching over to become more mainstream.

"Even though people still love going to certain venues where they can talk about their experience or hear certain things about the mixed-race experience, I just think it's a much more normative experience. Thank goodness," said Maria Root, noting the growth in books, memoirs, psychological studies, and college courses dealing with growing up biracial. For interracial couples raising biracial children today, more resources are now at their fingertips to help their children develop a positive identity.

"I've been so impressed," Maria remarked, "when I've been at some family conferences where parents will say, 'I don't know what it's like to be biracial. I can't guide my child through as though I know the way. But I can provide some foundation. I can get educated. I can provide opportunities for them. But I don't know what it feels like to be a biracial person.'"

Speaking as someone whose mother and father *are* biracial, but identified as black, I would add that even mixed-race parents must understand that their racial realities are not necessarily their children's. Young biracial adults who are now becoming parents themselves should remember that as well. The rules of the game on matters of race are always in flux.

In contrast to how my parents saw themselves in society, I now consider myself "more black than white, but more biracial than anything else." That's about the best way I know how to express it. While some biracial people strive to acknowledge both sides of their heritage with equal weight, in my life the two sides are not equal. In my case, being biracial makes me a "person of color," and it's important for me to express that reality accordingly.

If I add up those moments in my life when I've been called the N-word, when I've been slighted because of my blackness, when I've been seen as different from white folks, my identity leans toward the black side of my heritage. My relationships with black relatives, our family get-togethers over collard greens and corn bread, and my exposure to black cultural institutions and experiences have further reinforced that view. But at the same time, I cannot ignore those moments when I've been viewed as "not black enough," when I've been rejected because of the lightness of my skin, or when I've been considered white, in which case my sense of orientation shifts yet again.

Somewhere along the way, I learned that this shifting was normal for biracial people and would probably go on for the rest of my life. It's sort of like riding in a boat for the first time. It may feel awkward in the beginning, but then you get used to the motion of the water. Some days the seas are rough; most days they're quite calm. Ultimately, I found a community made up of other multiracial people who were sailing the same waters, and the journey somehow became easier.

I cannot pinpoint a moment in time when I finally reconciled the internal conflict. Sometimes I wonder whether that process is ever fully complete. But I do remember the moment when I looked back and realized how far I'd come.

It was a Sunday afternoon in the summer of 2001. A voice mail message left on my cell phone delivered the news that Aaliyah Haughton, a twenty-two-year-old R&B star and up-and-coming actress, had been killed along with eight others in a plane crash in the Bahamas. Michael Fountain, then vice president of news for BET, needed a freelance reporter to fly to the Bahamas to cover the story and asked if I would go.

I landed at Miami International Airport the next morning, where I met up with the rest of my crew. In fact, a whole contingent of media had gathered in the boarding area to catch the next puddle-jumper to a tiny airport on Abaco Island, where Aaliyah's plane had crashed on takeoff the day before.

"Who are you guys with?" asked one of the other journalists waiting for the Continental Express flight. She was an attractive white woman who appeared to be in her late twenties, with straight brown hair pulled back into a ponytail.

"BET," I said.

"Black Entertainment Television?" she asked, looking a bit puzzled.

"Yes. And you?"

"CBS," she said. "I'm working for *The Early Show*. Basically heading down to see if I can book a guest for tomorrow."

We soon boarded the plane, and she took her seat directly behind me.

"So are you an *on-the-air* reporter for BET?" she asked.

"Well, I'm a freelancer, but yes, I'm on-air," I assured her.

Short pause.

"So forgive me for the question," she began. "But are you part black?"

"Yep, that would be correct," I said.

"Hmm . . . you don't really have the features."

By then, the engines on the turboprop had sputtered to life, and we were airborne. As the plane gained altitude over the Atlantic

Ocean, I gazed out the window and thought about the conversation that had just taken place. What struck me the most was how it didn't seem to faze me, which wouldn't have been true a few years earlier. I simply chalked it up to life as a biracial person in America.

For a split second, I was tempted to whip out my "What Am I?" card. But for some reason, I decided not to go there. Not this time. The encounter was a bit awkward, but not as annoying as others I'd experienced.

Scholars Michael Omi and Howard Winant have suggested that we each have our own private compass that we use for navigating race relations. The racial compass is made up of layer upon layer of social assumptions and racial ideas we have internalized over time.[3] It is an important piece of equipment, guiding us through many social situations. But it must be adjusted for the environment and used properly when we make our way through rugged terrain.

Compasses can also grow old. Sometimes they fail altogether, unable to find true north. When that happens, we start to question our own racial orientation and that of others. In reality, what we need is a new racial compass.

In this case, my inquisitor actually "apologized" before posing her question, as if sensing that her compass was faltering. She had entered the Bermuda Triangle of race, color, and identity and wasn't sure how to proceed.

I would suggest that for many biracial people, our racial compasses are more sensitive than others, and they must be calibrated more often for us to navigate effectively. Our challenge is to define our proper alignment with the racial horizon, recognizing that no two individuals will chart the exact same course.

The twin-engine aircraft drifted in and out of the clouds on our way up to cruising altitude. The flight to Abaco Island was scheduled to last about an hour. When we leveled off, the cloud cover blocked out any view of the water below. For the next several minutes, we were flying completely by instruments. I moved away from the window, reclined as far back in my seat as I could—and exhaled.

My compass is set, and I know the way home.

Resources

Organizations

Association of MultiEthnic Americans, Inc. (AMEA)
P.O. Box 341304
Los Angeles, CA 90034-1304
www.ameasite.org

Bridge Communications, Inc.
221 N. LaSalle, Suite 2020
Chicago, IL 60601
312-377-2748
E-mail: bridgecom@core.com
www.bridgecommunications.org

Center for the Study of Biracial Children
2300 S. Kramaria Street
Denver, CO 80222
E-mail: francis@csbc.cncfamily.com
www.csbc.cncfamily.com

Hapa Issues Forum, Inc.
1840 Sutter Street
San Francisco, CA 94115-3220
415-409-4272
E-mail: hif@hapaissuesforum.org
www.hapaissuesforum.org

Mavin Foundation
600 First Avenue, Suite 600
Seattle, WA 98104-2215
206-622-7101
www.mavinfoundation.org

National Adoption Information Clearinghouse
330 C Street SW
Washington, D.C. 20447
888-251-0075
E-mail: naic@caliber.com
http://naic.acf.hhs.gov

National Association for Multicultural Education (NAME)
733 15th Street NW, Suite 430
Washington, D.C. 20005-2112
202-628-6263
www.nameorg.org

National MultiCultural Institute (NMCI)
3000 Connecticut Avenue NW, Suite 438
Washington, D.C. 20008
202-483-0700
E-mail: nmci@nmci.org
www.nmci.org

Pact, An Adoption Alliance
4179 Piedmont Avenue, Suite 330
Oakland, CA 94611
510-243-9460
info@pactadopt.org
www.pactadopt.org

Project RACE (Reclassify All Children Equally)
P.O. Box 2366
Los Banos, CA 93635
E-mail: projrace@aol.com
www.projectrace.com

Swirl, Inc.
244 Fifth Avenue, Suite J230
New York, NY 10001-7604
www.swirlinc.org

U.S. Census Bureau
4700 Silver Hill Road
Washington, D.C. 20233-0001
www.census.gov

Web sites

Eurasiannation.com
Online resource for people of mixed Asian ancestry

InterracialVoice.com
Politically oriented, often controversial site that nevertheless provides a repository of informative news and views on multiracial issues

LovingDay.org
Online resource on *Loving v. Virginia*, a landmark case on interracial marriage

MixedFolks.com
A site celebrating people of multiracial heritage

MixedMediaWatch.com
A blog that monitors representations of interracial couples and multiracial people in popular media

Multiracial.com
Libertarian-oriented, politically controversial site with articles and essays pertaining to the multiracial community

Books

For those wanting to read more about multiracial, multicultural experiences or race relations in general, here are several books I found helpful:

Black, White, Other: Biracial Americans Talk about Race and Identity
by Lise Funderburg
Published in 1994, this book was welcomed by many of us as the book we had been waiting our entire lives for. As part of her work toward a master's degree in journalism, the author interviewed dozens of black-white biracial people and produced a moving collection of stories.

Caucasia
by Danzy Senna
The only fiction book to make my reading list. The novel is set in the 1970s. A black-white interracial couple has two daughters, one of them light-skinned, the other one dark-skinned. The parents split up; the black father takes the darker-skinned daughter with him, while the light-skinned daughter stays with the white mother.

Check All That Apply: Finding Wholeness as a Multiracial Person
by Sundee Tucker Frazier
This book offers readers a Christian perspective on the issues confronting mixed-race people. The author combines her own life story with a faith-based approach to resolving the racial and identity conflicts facing members of interracial families.

The Color of Water: A Black Man's Tribute to His White Mother
by James McBride
The subtitle says it all. The author's mother married a black man and had a huge family, but all the while denied to her children that she was white. Years later, the author persuades his mother to tell her story and reveals the truth.

Crossing the Color Line: Race, Parenting, and Culture
by Maureen Reddy
This book is written by a white woman who married a black man and has a biracial son. Readers follow her on her journey as she discovers the impact of race on her family life. The author is also a college professor, but this book is very well grounded in her real-life experiences.

From Black to Biracial: Transforming Racial Identity Among Americans
by Kathleen Odell Korgen
This book offers an excellent analysis of why some people with known black-white ancestry have a black identity while others consider themselves biracial. The best explanation I've seen yet from an academic on how the underlying racial climate of each generation, along with skin color, social interactions, and personal experiences with racism, all play a role in shaping racial identity.

Half and Half: Writers on Growing Up Biracial and Bicultural
Edited by Claudine Chiawei O'Hearn
This book contains a series of soul-searching essays from a variety of authors of various racial, ethnic, and cultural combinations. One writer discusses being white and Asian, another being Hispanic and Jewish; others write about being black-white, and one about having a mom who is a black American and a dad who is a French-speaking black African.

More Than Black? Multiracial Identity and the New Racial Order
by G. Reginald Daniel
This book offers a historical and research-oriented perspective on racial classification and the development of multiracial identities. An easier read than some of the other academic titles listed here, but still heavy on the sociology.

The Multiracial Child Resource Book
Edited by Maria Root and Matt Kelley
Available through the Mavin Foundation, this book serves as a guide for parents, educators, counselors, social workers, and others on developmental issues of multiracial children and teens.

The Multiracial Experience
Edited by Maria Root
In this follow-up to *Racially Mixed People in America*, a number of contributing authors offer their historical and research-oriented perspectives on the multiracial experience. Like *Racially Mixed People in America*, this book is an academic work full of scholarly jargon.

Of Many Colors: Portraits of Multiracial Families
by Peggy Gillespie and Gigi Kaeser
This is the book version of a photo exhibit that's been touring the country. A variety of families are represented, some black-white, some Asian-white, some biological, some adopted, some gay, some straight, along with a brief synopsis of each.

Racially Mixed People in America
Edited by Maria Root
This is an academic work that provides a scholarly analysis of the experiences and challenges confronting multiracial people. An important text for

researchers and mental health professionals, I found all the insider jargon to be a little much for the average reader.

Showing My Color: Impolite Essays on Race and Identity
by Clarence Page
The author is a Washington, D.C.–based columnist for the *Chicago Tribune*. Readers who enjoy his syndicated newspaper column will enjoy his book. An insightful work on black middle-class identity and black-white race relations in America.

What Are You? Voices of Mixed-Race Young People
by Pearl Fuyo Gaskins
This book is very similar in format to *Black, White, Other*, but aimed at a younger audience. It covers some of the same ground but is a quicker read. The author, who is Asian and white, set out to write the type of book she wished she'd had when she was a teenager. The result is this collection of stories, poems, essays, and commentary covering a variety of ethnic combinations.

When Race Becomes Real
Edited by Bernestine Singley
An examination of black-white race relations seen through the eyes of both black and white writers. The essays offer a down-to-earth, real-world perspective on America's troubles with the color line.

Who Is Black? One Nation's Definition
by F. James Davis
This book focuses on the history of racial classification in the United States and how the legal definition of "black" has changed over time. Davis, a university professor, examines a multitude of state laws, court cases, and social conditions that have influenced how America views race.

Notes

PART 1 / WHO AM I?

Don't Adjust Your Television, I'm Biracial

1. Lawrence Wright, "One Drop of Blood," *The New Yorker,* July 25, 1994, 46–55.
2. Heather Dalmage, "Patrolling Racial Borders: Discrimination Against Mixed Race People," in Maria P. P. Root and Matt Kelley, eds., *The Multiracial Child Resource Book* (Seattle: Mavin Foundation, 2003), 19.

A Mixed and Matched Family

1. Maria P. P. Root, "Experiences and Processes Affecting Racial Identity Development: Preliminary Results from the Biracial Sibling Project," *Cultural Diversity and Mental Health* (Educational Publishing Foundation, Vol. 4, No. 3, 1998), 237–247.
2. James H. Jacobs, "Identity Development in Biracial Children," in Maria P. P. Root, ed., *Racially Mixed People in America* (Newbury Park, CA: Sage Publications, 1992), 203.
3. Ibid.
4. Ibid.

Going West, Growing Up

1. G. Reginald Daniel, *More Than Black?* (Philadelphia: Temple University Press, 2002), 195.

The Wonder Years

1. Karen L. Suyemoto and Juanita M. Dimas, "Identity Development Issues for Multiracial and Multiethnic Youth 15 to 17 Years Old," in Maria P. P. Root and Matt Kelley, eds., *The Multiracial Child Resource Book* (Seattle: Mavin Foundation, 2003), 82.
2. The Associated Press, "Mixed Race Students Report More Troubles," 2003.

3. Ibid.
4. Beverly Daniel Tatum, *Why are All the Black Kids Sitting Together in the Cafeteria?* (New York: Basic Books, 1997), 83.
5. Kathleen Odell Korgen, *From Black to Biracial* (Westport, CT: Praeger Publishers, 1998), 87.
6. Jewell Taylor Gibbs and Alice M. Hines, "Negotiating Ethnic Identity: Issues for Black-White Biracial Adolescents," in Maria P. P. Root, ed., *Racially Mixed People in America* (Newbury Park, CA: Sage Publications, 1992), 224–238.
7. Karen L. Suyemoto and Juanita M. Dimas, "Identity Development Issues for Multiracial and Multiethnic Youth 15 to 17 Years Old," in Maria P. P. Root and Matt Kelley, eds., *The Multiracial Child Resource Book* (Seattle: Mavin Foundation, 2003), 79–81.

The Science and Folly of Race

1. Ellis Cose, *Color-Blind* (New York: HarperCollins, 1997), 11.
2. American Anthropological Association, "American Anthropological Association Statement on Race," 1997.
3. Armand Marie Leroi, "A Family Tree in Every Gene," *The New York Times,* March 14, 2005, A23.
4. American Anthropological Association, "American Anthropological Association Statement on Race," 1998.
5. Sally Lehrman, "The Reality of Race," *ScientificAmerican.com,* January 13, 2003.
6. American Anthropological Association, "American Anthropological Association Statement on Race," 1998.
7. Armand Marie Leroi, "A Family Tree in Every Gene," *The New York Times,* March 14, 2005, A23.
8. National Marrow Donor Program, "Black Patients Need Donors," www.marrow.org.
9. United Press International, "Rod Carew's Daughter Dies of Leukemia," April 17, 1996.
10. Ibid.
11. PBS, "Ask the Experts: What Our Experts Say," www.pbs.org/race.
12. R. C. Lewontin, "Confusions about Human Races," Social Science Research Council, www.raceandgenomics.ssrc.org.

PART 2 / BEIGE LIKE ME
The Bahá'í in Me

1. Sundee Tucker Frazier, *Check All That Apply* (Downers Grove, IL: InterVarsity Press, 2002), 77.
2. Sundee Tucker Frazier, *Check All That Apply* (Downers Grove, IL: InterVarsity Press, 2002), 20–22.
3. Ibid.
4. Ibid.
5. Compiled from www.us.bahai.org; Bahá'í International Community Office of Public Information, "The Bahá'í Faith,"; and Gloria Faizi, *The Bahá'í Faith: An Introduction* (New Delhi, India: Bahá'í Publishing Trust, 1971).

The Chameleon Effect

1. Maegan Carberry, "Multiculti Chic," *Chicago Tribune,* February 16, 2005, 4.
2. Pearl Fuyo Gaskins, *What Are You?* (New York: Henry Holt, 1999), 20.

The Clorox Complex

1. Kathy Russell, Midge Wilson, and Ronald Hall, *The Color Complex* (New York: Anchor Books, 1992), 1.
2. Kathy Russell, Midge Wilson, and Ronald Hall, *The Color Complex* (New York: Anchor Books, 1992), 4.
3. Kathy Russell, Midge Wilson, and Ronald Hall, *The Color Complex* (New York: Anchor Books, 1992), 18.
4. Lawrence Otis Graham, *Our Kind of People* (New York: HarperCollins, 1999), 377.
5. Lawrence Otis Graham, *Our Kind of People* (New York: HarperCollins, 1999), 4.
6. Kathy Russell, Midge Wilson, and Ronald Hall, *The Color Complex* (New York: Anchor Books, 1992), 27.
7. Kathy Russell, Midge Wilson, and Ronald Hall, *The Color Complex* (New York: Anchor Books, 1992), 68.
8. Kathy Russell, Midge Wilson, and Ronald Hall, *The Color Complex* (New York: Anchor Books, 1992), 2.

Barbershop in the Hood

1. Kathy Russell, Midge Wilson, and Ronald Hall, *The Color Complex* (New York: Anchor Books, 1992), 82.
2. Ibid.

PART 3 / THE BACKDROP OF HISTORY
The One-Drop Suggestion

1. *Plessy v. Ferguson,* 163 U.S. 537 (1896)
2. Ibid.
3. Ibid.
4. F. James Davis, *Who is Black?* (University Park, PA: Pennsylvania State University Press, 1991), 9–10.
5. Ibid.
6. F. James Davis, *Who is Black?* (University Park, PA: Pennsylvania State University Press, 1991), 35–36.
7. F. James Davis, *Who is Black?* (University Park, PA: Pennsylvania State University Press, 1991), 77.
8. G. Reginald Daniel, *More Than Black?* (Philadelphia: Temple University Press, 2002), 49–53.
9. Ibid.
10. Ibid.
11. Walter White, *A Man Called White* (Athens, GA: University of Georgia Press, 1995), 3.
12. F. James Davis, *Who is Black?* (University Park, PA: Pennsylvania State University Press, 1991), 7.
13. Walter White, *A Man Called White* (Athens, GA: University of Georgia Press, 1995), 3–4.
14. Walter White, *A Man Called White* (Athens, GA: University of Georgia Press, 1995), 5–12.

Root of the Matter

1. Compiled from Maria P. P. Root, "Experiences and Processes Affecting Racial Identity Development: Preliminary Results from the Biracial Sibling Project," *Cultural Diversity and Mental Health* (Educational Publishing Foundation, Vol. 4, No. 3, 1998), 237–247; Maria P. P. Root, "Resolving 'Other' Status: Identity Development of Biracial Individuals," in H. Brown and M. Root, eds., *Diversity and Complexity in Feminist Therapy* (Hayworth Press, 1990), 185–204; Maria P. P. Root, "Multiracial Families and Children: Implications

for Educational Research and Practice," in James A. Banks and Cherry A. McGee Banks, eds., *Handbook of Research on Multicultural Education* (Jossey-Bass, 2003), 110–124.

2. Kathleen Odell Korgen, *From Black to Biracial* (Westport, CT: Praeger Publishers, 1998), 22.

3. Kathleen Odell Korgen, *From Black to Biracial* (Westport, CT: Praeger Publishers, 1998), 48.

4. Sara Terry, "Mix 'n' Match Society: Going 'Transcultural,'" *The Christian Science Monitor,* August 28, 2000.

5. Kathleen Odell Korgen, *From Black to Biracial* (Westport, CT: Praeger Publishers, 1998), 48.

6. Maria P. P. Root, "Resolving 'Other' Status: Identity Development of Biracial Individuals," in H. Brown and M. Root, eds., *Diversity and Complexity in Feminist Therapy* (Hayworth Press, 1990), 201.

7. Maria P. P. Root, "Experiences and Processes Affecting Racial Identity Development: Preliminary Results from the Biracial Sibling Project," *Cultural Diversity and Mental Health* (Educational Publishing Foundation, Vol. 4, No. 3, 1998), 242.

8. Ibid.

When Perception Means Everything and Nothing

1. Paul Weingarten, "Deadly Encounter," *Chicago Tribune Magazine,* July 31, 1983, 10.

Black Backlash

1. Michael C. Thornton, "Hidden Agendas, Identity Theories, and Multiracial People," in Maria P. P. Root, ed., *The Multiracial Experience* (Thousand Oaks, CA: Sage Publications, 1996), 107–108.

2. Ibid.

3. Maria P. P. Root, ed., *Racially Mixed People in America* (Newbury Park, CA: Sage Publications, 1992), 379.

4. Nancy G. Brown and Ramona Douglass, "Making the Invisible Visible," in Maria P. P. Root, ed., *The Multiracial Experience* (Thousand Oaks, CA: Sage Publications, 1996), 337.

PART 4 / EVADING THE BORDER PATROL
Hooking Up

1. Victoria Valentine, "When Love Was a Crime," in George E. Curry, ed., *The Best of Emerge Magazine* (New York: Ballantine Books, 2003), 17–21.
2. *Loving v. Virginia,* 388 U.S. 1 (1967).
3. Ibid.
4. Victoria Valentine, "When Love Was a Crime," in George E. Curry, ed., *The Best of Emerge Magazine* (New York: Ballantine Books, 2003), 17–21.
5. *Loving v. Virginia,* 388 U.S. 1 (1967).
6. Ibid.
7. Victoria Valentine, "When Love Was a Crime," in George E. Curry, ed., *The Best of Emerge Magazine* (New York: Ballantine Books, 2003), 17–21.
8. Ken Tanabe's LovingDay.org Web site, www.lovingday.org.
9. Darryl Fears and Claudia Deane, "Biracial Couples Report Tolerance, Survey Finds Most Are Accepted by Families," *The Washington Post,* July 5, 2001, A1.
10. U.S. Census Bureau, "Hispanic Origin and Race of Wife and Husband in Married-Couple Households for the United States: 2000," www.census.gov.
11. Maria P. P. Root, *Love's Revolution* (Philadelphia: Temple University Press, 2001), 12.
12. Kathleen Odell Korgen, *From Black to Biracial* (Westport, CT: Praeger Publishers, 1998), 58.

Monoracial People, Multiracial Families
1. National Association of Black Social Workers, "Preserving Families of African Ancestry," www.nabsw.org.

Children of the Rainbow
1. U.S. Census Bureau, "Questions and Answers for Census 2000 Data on Race," March 14, 2001, www.census.gov.
2. Nicolas Jones and Amy Symens Smith, "A Statistical Portrait of Children of Two or More Races in Census 2000," in Maria P. P. Root and Matt Kelley, eds., *The Multiracial Child Resource Book* (Seattle: Mavin Foundation, 2003), 3.
3. James H. Jacobs, "Identity Development in Biracial Children," in

Maria P. P. Root, ed., *Racially Mixed People in America* (Newbury Park, CA: Sage Publications, 1992), 205.

On Neutral Ground
1. Michael C. Thornton, "Hidden Agendas, Identity Theories, and Multiracial People," in Maria P. P. Root, ed., *The Multiracial Experience* (Thousand Oaks, CA: Sage Publications, 1996), 104.
2. F. James Davis, Who is Black? (University Park, PA: Pennsylvania State University Press, 1991), 99–101.

PART 5 / THE POLITICS OF BEING BIRACIAL
Come to Your Census
1. Nicolas Jones and Amy Symens Smith, "The Two or More Races Population," U.S. Census Bureau, November 2001.
2. From a transcript of Charles Byrd's speech posted to www.InterracialVoice.com.
3. Tanya Schevitz, "Multiracial Census Form Poses Dilemma, Organizations Fear Dilution of Numbers," *San Francisco Chronicle,* March 11, 2000, www.sfgate.com.
4. U.S. Census Bureau, "Questions and Answers for Census 2000 Data on Race," March 14, 2001, www.census.gov.
5. U.S. Census Bureau, "Population of Two or More Races, Including All Combinations for the United States: 2000," www.census.gov.
6. Office of Management and Budget, "OMB Bulletin No. 00–02," March 9, 2000, www.whitehouse.gov/omb.
7. Public Policy Institute of California, "Multiracial Californians: A Multifaceted Story," August 13, 2004, www.ppic.org.

Race Busters, Freedom Fighters, and Multiracial Village People
1. U.S. Census Bureau, "Factfinder for the Nation, History and Organization," May 2000, www.census.gov.
2. Commission on the Bicentennial of the United States Constitution, *The Constitution of the United States and The Declaration of Independence* (16th ed.). (Washington, DC: 1992).
3. U.S. Census Bureau, "Factfinder for the Nation, History and Organization," May 2000, www.census.gov.
4. F. James Davis, *Who is Black?* (University Park, PA: Pennsylvania State University Press, 1991), 12.
5. Ibid.

6. From a transcript of a March 30, 2000 interview on *The NewsHour* on PBS, www.pbs.org/newshour.
7. Ibid.
8. Frank Wu, *Yellow* (New York: Basic Books, 2002), 288.
9. U.S. Census Bureau, "Population of Two or More Races, Including All Combinations for the United States: 2000," www.census.gov.

A Bonding Experience
1. Retrieved from www.ku.edu/~sma/printedart/piper1.htm.
2. The "What Am I?" card incorporates language found in Teresa Kay Williams, "Race as Process," in Maria P. P. Root, ed., *The Multiracial Experience* (Thousand Oaks, CA: Sage Publications, 1996), 203.

Ones Who Understand
1. Ian Slattery, "UC Regents Reject Ward Connerly's Multiracial Checkbox," November 18, 2004, www.civilrights.org.
2. Ibid.

In the Mix
1. Deborah A. Ramirez, "Multiracial Identity in a Color-Conscious World," in Maria P. P. Root, ed., *The Multiracial Experience* (Thousand Oaks, CA: Sage Publications, 1996), 56.
2. Rebecca Chiyoko King and Kimberly McClain DaCosta, "Changing Face, Changing Race," in Maria P. P. Root, ed., *The Multiracial Experience* (Thousand Oaks, CA: Sage Publications, 1996), 239.
3. Ibid.

PART 6 / BEYOND BLACK AND WHITE
Generation M
1. Nicolas Jones and Amy Symens Smith, "The Two or More Races Population," U.S. Census Bureau, November 2001.

Where Do We Go From Here?
1. Council of the American Sociological Association, "The Importance of Collecting Data and Doing Social Scientific Research on Race," 2002.
2. Ibid.
3. Teresa Kay Williams, "Race as Process," in Maria P. P. Root, ed., *The Multiracial Experience* (Thousand Oaks, CA: Sage Publications, 1996), 203.